# Contemporary Scottish Fictions

D0889430

For Rebecca and Anicë, with all my love

# Contemporary Scottish Fictions

*Film, Television and the Novel*

Duncan Petrie

Edinburgh University Press

© Duncan Petrie, 2004

Edinburgh University Press Ltd
22 George Square, Edinburgh

Typeset in Ehrhardt
by Norman Tilley Graphics, and
printed and bound in Great Britain
by Antony Rowe Ltd, Chippenham, Wilts

A CIP record for this book is available from
the British Library

ISBN 0 7486 1789 2 (paperback)

The right of Duncan Petrie
to be identified as author of this work
has been asserted in accordance with
the Copyright, Designs and Patents Act 1988.

Published with the support of the Edinburgh
University Scholarly Publishing Initiatives Fund.

# Contents

# Acknowledgements

This project emerged directly out of my previous work on Scottish Cinema, and in particular the book *Screening Scotland*, published by the British Film Institute in 2000. In dealing with recent achievements in the field of film I became increasingly aware of the clear connections with parallel and overlapping developments in other key areas of cultural production which I resolved to examine in more detail. This is the first time in my academic career that I have written about novels and I must acknowledge the support and encouragement of my colleagues in the School of English at Exeter in giving me the courage to venture beyond the more familiar territory of the moving image. I am particularly indebted to the input, advice and support received from Andy Brown, Regenia Gagnier, Helen Hanson, Susan Hayward, Will Higbee, James Lyons, Colin MacCabe, Dan North, Alasdair Paterson, Helen Taylor, Nadine Wills and the staff in Audio Visual and Inter-Library Loan sections of the University of Exeter Library.

I also benefited greatly from various discussions and assistance I received from colleagues and friends in Scotland and elsewhere including Michael Begg, Don Boyd, John Caughie, Eddie Dick, Henry Eagles, Sine Foster, Annie Morgan James, James Mackay, Steve McIntyre, Tony McKibbin, Barbara McKissack, Martin McLoone, Jonny Murray, John Orr and Alan Riach. I owe special gratitude to Susan Hayward and John Orr who took time to read the manuscript, and to Sarah Edwards my editor at EUP.

Finally I would like to thank Rebecca Russell for her characteristic love, support and patience throughout the entire period. This project began just before the birth of our daughter Anicë and consequently life in our household these past two years has been hectic to say the least! I write this a week before leaving Exeter to begin a new job and a new chapter of my life in New Zealand and cannot help but wonder what implications this will have for my obsession with the place I still regard as home.

Duncan Petrie
Exeter, January 2004

# Introduction

*Scotland, National Identity and Cultural Production*

## THE SCOTTISH CULTURAL REVIVAL

The past twenty years have witnessed an unprecedented flourishing of cultural activity and expression in Scotland, embracing a wide range of artistic forms from literature and painting to cinema and theatre. This collective outpouring has been regarded by many critics as compelling evidence of new-found cultural confidence which, in the context of Scotland's increasing unease about its place within the British state, constituted a vibrant and meaningful assertion of national difference. Cairns Craig, for example, argues that 'the 1980s proved to be one of the most productive and creative decades in Scotland this century',[1] while Christopher Harvie declared the period as 'intellectually and culturally comparable not only with the 1920s but with the high years of the Scottish Enlightenment'.[2] In time some commentators were even tempted to conclude that this process of cultural devolution had helped to clear the way for the return of political self-determination and the restoration of the Scottish Parliament in 1999. Tom Devine, for one, suggests that developments in Scotland were comparable to the 'quiet revolution' that occurred in Quebec in the early 1960s in which a cultural awakening similarly 'helped to infuse the crusade for Home Rule with a new impetus and confidence'.[3] An even more relevant comparison could be made with the Irish literary revival of the late nineteenth/early twentieth century, spearheaded by W. B. Yeats, J. M. Synge, Sean O'Casey and James Joyce among others, which in addition to the artistic interrogation and contemplation of Irishness, contributed a potent cultural dimension to political agitation for independence.

This book will explore the Scottish cultural renaissance of the 1980s and 1990s by focussing primarily on the novel, cinema and television drama. These are all narrative-based popular forms that provide the means by which the myths and realities, experiences and dreams of Scotland and its inhabitants have been reflected and asserted, imagined and re-imagined through a process of cultural transmission dating back to the bardic tradition of oral story-telling. Moreover, these are also the forms that have enjoyed the widest and broadest circulation and consumption – both at home and abroad – reinforcing their significance as the primary media through which the cultural transformation of Scotland during the past twenty years has been creatively addressed and conveyed to audiences. Other forms, from painting to music, theatre to poetry, have also been highly significant during the period in question but they lack either the narrative basis or the mass circulation that frame this particular study and give the Scottish revival its all-important visibility. The issue of cultural 'revival' in the context of a sub-national entity located within the British state is also necessarily bound up with the assertion of cultural difference, political self-determination and the creative appropriation of myth and mythologisation – as witnessed in the earlier Scottish renaissance of the inter-war years (a period that also saw the birth of the Scottish National Party) dominated by literary figures such as Edwin Muir, Hugh McDiarmid and Lewis Grassic Gibbon. But unlike Ireland, Scottish identification with and allegiance to the Union remained strong (a factor that is also strongly conveyed via the enthusiastic participation in the British Empire on the part of many Scots), further consolidated by the experience of the Second World War and its aftermath. Indeed, it was to take the discovery of oil in the North Sea, coupled with the first significant electoral gains for the SNP, in the late 1960s for the idea of a devolved or independent Scotland to return to the agenda. Or as Angus Calder puts it, 'the key to Scotland's story in the last third of the twentieth century was a swelling sense of difference from England'.[4] But what was required was some kind of seismic shift in Scottish self-perception towards a confident, viable, distinct and essentially modern national identity. Such a development was to prove initially more attainable in the cultural domain.

But the unprecedented explosion of creativity that marked the 1980s is often seen as a direct response to specific political events, in particular to the disastrous 'double whammy' that had been inflicted upon the Scottish people in 1979. The first blow took the form of the referendum débâcle of 1 March, in which a narrow majority in favour of establishing a devolved Scottish assembly was rendered invalid by a ruling that required 40 per cent of the registered electorate to vote in favour of devolution.[5] While some critics have regarded the result as a collective failure of nerve on the part of the Scottish electorate,[6] others have noted the manner in which this negation of the democratic will, however marginal the result, became transmuted into a straightforward rejection of devolution. This was followed a mere two months later by the triumph of Margaret Thatcher's Conservative Party in the general election, a result emphatically *not* endorsed in Scotland where the

Tories polled less than one-third of the vote. Ironically, the two events were directly linked by a no-confidence motion in James Callaghan's increasingly discredited Labour administration tabled by the Scottish National Party in direct response to the devolution fiasco. The motion was carried by a single vote and so triggered a momentous new chapter in British political history. The in-coming Thatcher Government was driven by a commitment to economic monetarism and deregulation, allowing free rein to enterprise and the operations of the market. This was to be facilitated by a strategy that included major reductions in public spending, the privatisation of public utilities, a reversal of progressive taxation and a curbing of the power of the trade unions. Whatever the benefits afforded to Britain's economic performance, these policies certainly succeeded in creating a more divided and unequal society than at any time since the 1930s. The subsequent deep economic recession hit certain parts of the United Kingdom disproportionately hard, particularly those areas such as Scotland that were structurally over-dependent on the traditional heavy industries of coal, steel, shipbuilding and textiles. Consequently, by 1986 unemployment in Scotland had reached 14 per cent, significantly higher than the UK average of 11.4 per cent.

While the profoundly negative effects of government policy caused a great deal of consternation in various quarters across the UK, in Scotland they contributed to a renewed sense of a distinct national consciousness forged in direct opposition to the very values that underpinned Thatcherism. In marked contrast to trends in England, support for the Conservative Party in Scotland (which had been in slow decline since the mid-1950s) hit an all-time low. In the election landslide of 1983 that effectively endorsed the Thatcherite programme across the United Kingdom as a whole, the Tories could only muster a paltry 28.4 per cent of the Scottish vote compared with 46 per cent in England. This served to underline the growing perception that Scotland was being ruled by an increasingly distant and essentially 'alien' political ideology. As Peter Riddell notes, the Conservative leader stood 'for the values of the English suburban and provincial middle-class and aspiring skilled working class' and consequently her popular appeal was 'very much an English phenomenon' that failed to be replicated in either Scotland or Wales'.[7] William McIlvanney put it somewhat more bluntly in an address to the SNP in 1987:

> We have had bad governments in the past. We have had governments whose awareness of Scotland's problems seemed on a par with their knowledge of the other side of the moon. But we have never, in my lifetime, until now had a government whose basic principles were so utterly against the most essential traditions and aspirations of Scottish life.[8]

The reassertion – and in some cases the revision and modernisation – of these very traditions and aspirations subsequently fell to Scottish writers like McIlvanney who, alongside other members of the artistic and intellectual stratum of Scottish society, began to mount their opposition to the policies and values of the Thatcherite establishment through cultural production.

While the following study will focus on particular creative individuals and their works, it is also important to acknowledge the institutional and collective developments that helped to give much of this activity a sense of coherence and visibility. In the realm of publishing the imagination and courage of small Scottish presses like Canongate and Polygon in their championing of new writers helped to challenge many of the assumptions about the nature, the status and the purpose of indigenous literature.[9] These publishers also helped to reanimate the rich heritage of Scottish writing by republishing neglected or lost classics, which in turn provided contemporary authors with a meaningful and affirmative sense of a vibrant indigenous literary tradition. Moreover, as an offshoot of Edinburgh University Press, Polygon also provided an outlet for various Scottish intellectuals to join the fray, further nurturing and nourishing the cultural revival by providing informed analysis and advocacy of both contemporary and historical achievements.[10] This accompanying intellectual and critical debate was further fostered by literary, cultural and political journals such as *Cencrastus*, *Edinburgh Review*, *Chapman* and *Radical Scotland*.

In the closely related fields of film and television, key institutional developments also occurred. Under pressure from senior management to propagate more diverse strands of 'regional' production, the BBC established a new drama department in Glasgow in 1979. Five years later, the celebrated playwright Bill Bryden was appointed to head up this department and under his inspirational leadership a new high profile era of Scottish television drama was ushered in. Developments in Scottish cinema were somewhat more gradual, although film-makers had received a major boost in the early 1980s through a number of commissions from the newly established Channel Four, aided by the good fortune that the Channel's first Chief Executive, Jeremy Isaacs, was a Glaswegian who appreciated the potential of the Scottish independent sector. The basis for a more stable and consistent nurturing of Scottish film-making was laid in 1982 with the creation of a Scottish Film Production Fund with the rather modest sum of £80,000. But by the mid-1990s resources available to the fund had multiplied almost tenfold due to subventions from various broadcasters including Channel Four, allowing a range of film projects to be supported in the process from features and short dramas to documentaries and animation.[11] The 1990s saw the emergence of other new sources of indigenous finance such as the Glasgow Film Fund, essentially an economic regeneration initiative, and a separate Scottish lottery

fund for film, created in 1995. The latter fund, undoubtedly the most significant new source of finance for film-makers, was initially administered
by the Scottish Arts Council before moving under the umbrella of Scottish
Screen, the new agency established in 1997 to nurture and promote the screen
industries in Scotland.

## NATIONALISM AND CULTURAL IDENTITY

The terrain of nationalism, be it cultural or political, is a contested one that
arouses strong feelings on the part of both advocates and detractors. For many,
particularly those committed to the (increasingly remote and utopian) goals of
international socialism, nationalism continues to be associated with the 'dark
gods' of tribalism and ethnic purity and the atavistic barbarism witnessed
most recently in the Balkans and Rawanda. Yet for other commentators
such as Ernest Gellner and Tom Nairn, nationalism is nothing less than the
inescapable consequence of the uneven process of modernisation, entailing
both positive and negative ramifications. While nationalism may have underpinned fascist movements in the twentieth century, it also provided a focus for
the various liberation struggles against imperialism, particularly in the third
world. Since the first publication in 1977 of his highly influential book, *The
Break-Up of Britain*, Nairn has become one of the pre-eminent intellectual
commentators on nationalism and his own national identity makes him a
particularly significant contributor to the key debates on Scottish nationalism.
Nairn's complex and clear-headed analysis of 'the modern Janus'[12] provides a
means of rebutting the argument that national difference is being gradually
eroded under the homogenising tendencies of global capitalism – indeed, the
process of globalisation in this sense has helped to produce more rather than
fewer nation–states in the world.[13] This idea of nationalism as a necessary
outcome of the process of modernity has also been endorsed by commentators
more directly concerned with the sphere of culture. One of the most significant figures in this respect is Benedict Anderson, whose analysis of nations as
'imagined communities'[14] has proved particularly influential. Anderson identifies the genesis of a modern national consciousness – through which the
nation came to be imagined as both internally limited and sovereign – in the
interaction between the process of capitalism, the development of print tech-
nologies and the existence of human linguistic diversity. This resulted in the
circulation of new 'print languages' via the popular forms of the newspaper
and the novel from the late eighteenth century onwards, which in turn created
new monoglot mass reading publics by encouraging literacy and standardising
language. The particular significance of the novel in this context is acknowledged by Cairns Craig who argues that:

> In the work of the historical novelists of the nineteenth century what was being created was a national imagination: an imagining of the nation as both the fundamental context of individual life and as the real subject of history.[15]

The influence of Anderson's conception of the nation stretches beyond the realm of literary studies, however. Philip Schlesinger locates his ideas within a tradition of 'social communication theory' built on the argument that the essential unity of a people depends on the efficiency of communication among and between individuals and 'that the politically salient container for communicative space is the sovereign nation state'.[16] This neatly lends itself to a consideration of radio and television, which in Britain have explicitly addressed the nation as a community through the concept of 'public service broadcasting'. In this way, Anderson's ideas have also been influential in the conceptualisation and study of 'national' cinemas, which in turn posits the essential dialectic between the national and the international within any contemplation of cultural exchange in the era of mass media. The economic imperative of most film-making entails the need to secure widespread distribution, raising the thorny problem of 'how a national cinema may be taken to affirm a single national self-identity and at the same time be situated in an international system of differences'.[17]

Indeed, the dilemma facing all considerations of national culture is how to construct a meaningful conception of the nation that acknowledges both internal diversity and the complexity of international cross-cultural relations. Paul Willemen frames the question in a useful way, observing that 'the discourses of nationalism and those addressing or comprising national specificity are not identical'.[18] While in a similar vein, John Caughie makes an important distinction between national cinema and television images as on one hand comprising a *representation* of the nation and on the other as *representative* of the nation.[19] While the former process tends to stress ideas of national unity and continuity as providing a distinct brand that can be sold within global image markets, the latter offers diversity, difference and even the possibility of dialogue *within* the audio-visual space of the nation. These key sites of tension – between exclusive and inclusive conceptions of national culture and between the national and international circulation of cultural products – are further indications of the essentially Janus-faced nature of nationalism. But they are also fundamental issues which must be addressed if any account of the national dimension of contemporary cultural production and consumption is to avoid the Scylla of a regressive and essentialist nationalism, and Charybdis defined by the vague contingency of post-national identity politics.

## THE PROBLEM OF SCOTTISH NATIONAL CULTURE

This very problem raised its head in the vigorous intellectual engagement with Scottish national culture that emerged in the aftermath of the events of 1979. In what she termed 'the Scottish predicament', Joy Hendry acknowledged an unfortunate over-emphasis in contemporary writing on national questions. However, this predicament was also nothing less than a direct and necessary response to political failure:

> a pre-occupation which is admittedly inward and introverted; some may say that it is no healthy preoccupation. But until there is a state of Scotland, we have no choice but to be so obsessed. Would it were not so. But we can stop *talking* about the state of Scotland only when we are in a position to *do* something about it.[20]

Hendry's observations were initially made back in 1983 but her concern with a restrictive narrowness in contemporary Scottish culture, preventing Scottish writers and film-makers exploring wider themes and experiences of relevance outside a national frame of reference, has proved tenacious.[21] The persistence of such debates has prompted David McCrone to describe the search for cultural identity as the 'hunting of a Scottish snark', an ill-fated obsession blind to the fact that 'in modern pluralistic societies it is increasingly the case that no singular "national" culture is there to be found'.[22] McCrone's antipathy towards any over-emphasis of ideas of *national* culture in the Scottish case is in part a response to the rather overwrought manner in which indigenous cultural traditions have been identified and analysed. Once again, the ideas of Tom Nairn have been highly influential here, in particular his argument that the Union prompted the emigration *en masse* of the Scottish intelligentsia to London, leaving behind a cultural vacuum that came to be filled with the deformed and regressive sub-national discourses of tartanry and Kailyard. This in turn ensured that Scotland was represented as an essentially backward culture which, if not mourning a lost highland past, was revelling in sentimental and parochial kitsch. Meanwhile 'real' Scottish cultural creativity had been placed in the service of a metropolitan British state, beginning with Enlightenment figures such as David Hume and Adam Smith and continuing throughout the nineteenth and twentieth centuries with the likes of Thomas Carlyle, John Ruskin, William Gladstone, Keir Hardie and John Reith. Nairn's chilling image of tartanry and Kailyard proved very influential in debates during the 1980s, being enthusiastically applied to traditions of visual representation in cinema and television by Colin McArthur, for example, in a tenacious critique of the conspicuous failure on the part of film-makers to critically or constructively engage with the political and social realities of the modern world.[23] It is instructive that both Nairn and McArthur should end up relying heavily on metaphors of psychopathology and an attendant conception of the Scottish national psyche as irredeemably neurotic. The only apparent possibility of curing the patient was for Scottish writers and film-makers to self-consciously throw off their collective tartan security blanket and summon the necessary courage – and the appropriate intellectual resources – to create a more purposeful, self-reflective and progressive cultural engagement with Scotland and the world.

But this analysis of Scottish culture generated a different kind of response from those who challenged the overwhelming negativity and reductionism of the Nairn/McArthur perspective by claiming this was to blind it to the existence of very real Scottish cultural achievements. Such a reassertion of the intrinsic value of indigenous traditions is vigorously advanced by Craig Beveridge and Ronald Turnbull in *The Eclipse of Scottish Culture*. In challenging the metropolitan bias and deeply ingrained inferiorism of many Scottish intellectuals to their own culture, Beveridge and Turnbull focus on the rich progressive legacy of native traditions of philosophy, historiography, anthropology and psychology.[24] While similarly exploding the myth that nineteenth-century Scottish culture represented a vacuum, Cairns Craig goes even further in reclaiming the cultural contributions made by Scots in London as having a relevance for Scottish culture – pointing out that Auden did not cease to be an English poet when he moved to New York. Craig's approach also resists the easy and rather defensive polarity of Scottish versus Anglo-centric/metropolitan culture deployed at times by Beveridge and Turnbull. Rather, he considers the fundamental cultural consequences of the Union on both sides of the border, noting that

> as England was being transformed by the construction of a new British identity which had significant Scottish components ... so Scotland was being transformed by the English elements of the same British identity, and both were resisting uniformity by discovering new ways of relating to their independent pasts.[25]

The key difference between the respective approaches of Nairn and Craig to the concept of the nation and national culture is the move from an essentially linear model based on historical process to a more multi-stranded conception in which spatial relations – the dialectic between core and periphery or that between inside and outside the bounded nation – come to have an importance alongside the temporal relationship between past and present. For Craig, 'culture is a place of dialogue, between self and other, between inner and outer, between past and present, between invented pasts and discovered pasts and value systems past and future'.[26] This also provides a sophisticated answer to 'the predicament' in that while adhering to the nation as the primary unit of cultural identification and expression, Craig's perspective explicitly rejects any restrictive or reactionary conception of national cultures as monolithic, homogenous or sealed constructs. His conception of cultural identity is in part derived from the idea of heteroglossia (those elements within discourse which cannot be reduced to the order of any single, semi-authorised voice or code) introduced by the Soviet cultural theorist Mikhail Bakhtin, who argued that no signifying system was entirely self-enclosed as each utterance in language necessarily draws upon a multitude of meanings, values, social discourses and cultural codes. This in turn allows Craig to recast a more appropriate and productive concept of a Scottish cultural tradition:

> The nature of a national imagination, like a language, is an unending series of interactions between different strands of tradition, between influences from within and without, between the impact of new experiences and the reinterpretation of past experiences: the nation is a series of ongoing debates, founded in institutions and patterns of life, whose elements are continually changing but which constitute, by the nature of the issues which they foreground, and by their reiteration of elements of the past, a dialogue which is unique to that particular place.[27]

A similarly Bakhtinian-influenced perspective is advanced by Angus Calder in his consideration of 'the Carnivalesque activities of the 1980s which Scots improvised to defy the Thatcherite threat to their country'.[28] For Calder, the appeal of the concept of carnival derives from an essential hybridity, incorporating both high and low culture, which also relates – via the tradition of West Indian Carnival – to the concept of mongrelism. These are in turn linked by Calder to the Scottish tradition of communitarianism and to the long and often unacknowledged history of ethnic mixing that has made and remade Scottish culture.[29] This simultaneous endorsement of the nation as the primary site of cultural meaning and identification, alongside the assertion of difference and diversity as the defining features of national culture, provides an ideal framework within which this present study can examine Scottish cultural expression in the 1980s and 1990s. It also suggests that Hendry's 'predicament' is something of a straw man. For if to contemplate the specificity of the national involves an apprehension of this complex multitude of interactions – from within and without, past and present – then individual writers or film-makers who appear fixated on the condition of Scotland should be judged by the breadth and sophistication of their engagement and not prejudged on the grounds that such a fixation is necessarily narrow and limited *per se*.

## LIMITING THE FIELD

The main reasons behind the decision to limit this study to the forms of the novel, cinema and television drama have already been stated. Despite their obvious differences, there are also significant points of contact between all three. For example, film and television draw heavily on the novel as source material for adaptation, while novelists (and dramatists) have in turn written scripts for film and television, some of which are original works. At the same time, at the institutional level the worlds of film and television are now so intertwined that any separation becomes increasingly artificial. Almost every film produced for a theatrical release in the United Kingdom is financed in part by television and will subsequently be viewed by considerably more people on the small screen – initially via DVD and video prior to broadcast – than in the cinema. Moreover many directors, producers, writers, technicians and actors regularly work across the divide and consequently Scottish film and television are often discussed within the same frame of reference.[30] However, in contrast, studies of Scottish literature and film have tended to be kept resolutely apart and in that respect this book is treading new ground.

Recent developments in Scottish literature have been insightfully explored in detail by a number of critics, constituting a significant field of scholarly activity. Douglas Gifford, for example, has very usefully mapped the field of twentieth-century Scottish literature in terms of three conceptually distinct, if overlapping 'waves'. The first of these comprises the inter-war renaissance obsessed with a mythopoeic vision of a golden past as a means of spiritual and cultural regeneration. The second wave comprised a post-war reaction which gave rise to a hard-edged tradition of urban social realism that went out of its way to repudiate any whiff of romanticism or mythology through the advocacy of sceptical materialism. While the third wave, which coincided with the cultural fermentation of the 1980s, constituted a dialectical synthesis of aspects of the previous two traditions that significantly reintroduced elements of magic and myth. This synthesis served to generate works of fiction that explicitly embraced cultural and aesthetic diversity and plurality while resol-utely holding on to a sense of national specificity. As Gifford argues:

> Scottish literature of the eighties was marked by its commitment
> to radical new ground breaking; to re-assessing its older texts, to
> re-examining the place of women in town and country, to exploring
> ways of using a recognizably Scottish perspective in viewing the world
> outside, to simultaneously re-asserting the validity of Scottish fictional
> and literary tradition as source material for contemporary creativity.[31]

This in turn complements and reinforces Cairns Craig's resurrection of a meaningful sense of tradition in the Scottish novel derived in part from a productive engagement with the ideas of the Scottish philosopher Alasdair McIntyre, in conjunction with insights derived from Bakhtin. The former providing a defence of tradition as a dynamic and constantly evolving frame-work of thought rather than backward-looking or necessarily retrospective, with the latter informing Craig's assertion of the multi-stranded and diverse nature of traditions themselves.

Craig's insightful analysis of Scottish cultural history has inspired my own attempts to map the history of Scottish cinema and to reassess the traditions of cinematic representation of Scotland within a more inclusive and positive framework, articulated most fully in the book *Screening Scotland.* This study was also inevitably conceived as a response to the 'tartanry/Kailyard' analysis of Scottish cinema offered by Colin McArthur and his colleagues in *Scotch Reels*, by focussing on the various ways in which ex-ternally constructed images of Scotland have functioned as a vehicle for the dreams and fantasies of metropolitan culture. At the same time these aesthetic and generic traditions – including the Island Film, the Jacobite Romance and the Urban Industrial narrative – also served to articulate key sites of tension and struggle around class and gender as well as nationality, and around identity formation in relation to economic production and consumption, all of which remain of fundamental relevance to Scotland. Finally, *Screening Scotland* also set out to argue for the emergence of a process of devolution within British cinema that was leading to the emergence of a distinct, if still necessarily tentative and fragile, Scottish national cinema. This has been subsequently endorsed by Martin McLoone who applies the devolutionary process to the entire 'Celtic fringe' of British cinema to include Wales and Northern Ireland alongside Scotland:

> The tendency in recent films emanating from the Celtic periphery
> is to attempt to move cinematic representation beyond the dominant
> imagery and traditional iconography that have defined it. The
> re-imagining that is taking place in Scotland, Wales and Northern
> Ireland involves a reworking of national or regional tropes and
> stereotypes. If many of these are the inventions of the metropolitan
> centre, nevertheless their reinterpretation impacts on a concept of
> Britishness which is already under pressure.[32]

The following study is divided into two distinct Parts. Part I focuses on those developments in the novel, cinema and television drama that most directly engage with the processes and effects of social and political change and their consequences for questions of culture and identity. Beginning with a con-sideration of the overtly proletarian, masculine and urban associations of

Scottish culture epitomised by Clydesideism, this Part of the book proceeds to examine alternative kinds of response to a changing world, embracing in the process alternative meditations on masculinity and class as essential components of national identity, the recognition and examination of female subjectivity and experience as a challenge to the overtly male-centred version of Scottishness, and the new forms of social and cultural identities consolidated in the increasingly post-industrial circumstances of the 1990s. Part II will explore certain significant thematic and generic trends in Scottish cultural production which in turn relate back to deeper traditions and obsessions. These include contemporary expressions of distinctly Scottish articulations of the Gothic and detective fiction, both of which derive much of their character from the heritage of secular Calvinism in Scotland. Equally significant are the figure of the child or orphan within biographical and autobiographical fictions, and the theme of travel as a means of identifying and probing the complex issues of history and geography respectively: on one hand, the historical relationship between the present and past and, on the other, between the kind of national and the international dimension at the heart of conceptions of nationalism.

## NOTES

1. Cairns Craig, from his Series Preface to the *Determinations* series of monographs published by Polygon.
2. Christopher Harvie, *Scotland and Nationalism: Scottish Society and Politics, 1707 to the Present*, third edition (London: Routledge, 1998), p. 200.
3. T. M. Devine, *The Scottish Nation* (London: Penguin, 2000), p. 609.
4. Angus Calder, *Scotlands of the Mind* (Edinburgh: Luath Press, 2002), p. xi.
5. The referendum result was 51.6 per cent to 48.4 per cent in favour of a Scottish assembly. However, the low turn-out of 63.8 per cent meant that this less than one-third of the electorate voted yes, well short of the 40 per cent requirement.
6. Lamented by William McIlvanney in his poem 'After: March 1979 – The Cowardly Lion', in *Surviving the Shipwreck* (Edinburgh: Mainstream, 1991).
7. Peter Riddell, *The Thatcher Decade* (Oxford: Basil Blackwell, 1989), p. 3.
8. William McIlvanney, 'Stands Scotland Where it Did?', in *Surviving the Shipwreck*, p. 245.
9. Scottish writing also found supporters in the London publishing world, most notably Robin Robertson who at Secker & Warburg and subsequently Jonathan Cape helped to promote the careers of James Kelman, Irvine Welsh, Janice Galloway, A. L. Kennedy, Duncan McLean and Alan Warner.
10. The most significant of these include Cairns Craig, Tom Nairn, Christopher Harvie, Tom Devine, David McCrone, Colin McArthur, Murray Pittock, Craig Beveridge, Ronald Turnbull and Robert Crawford.
11. See Duncan Petrie, *Screening Scotland* (London: BFI, 2000), Chapter 8, and Ian Lockerbie, 'Pictures in a Small Country: The Scottish Film Production Fund', in Eddie Dick (ed.), *From Limelight to Satellite: A Scottish Film Book* (London: BFI/SFC, 1990).

12. Tom Nairn, *The Break Up of Britain*, second edition (London: Verso, 1981), p. 349.

13. In 1901 there were officially 41 sovereign nation–states in the world, by 2002 this had increased to 193. The United Nations was formed in 1945 with 51 members, it presently has 191.

14. See Benedict Anderson, *Imagined Communities* (London: Verso, 1983).

15. Cairns Craig, *The Modern Scottish Novel* (Edinburgh: Edinburgh University Press, 1999), p. 9.

16. Philip Schlesinger, 'The Sociological Scope of National Cinema', in Mette Hjort and Scott Mackenzie (eds), *Cinema and Nation* (London: Routledge, 2000), p. 24.

17. Ibid. p. 26.

18. Paul Willemen, 'The National', in *Looks and Frictions: Essays in Cultural Studies and Film Theory* (London: BFI, 1994), p. 210.

19. John Caughie, *Television Drama: Realism, Modernism and British Culture* (Oxford: Oxford University Press, 2000), p. 202.

20. Joy Hendry, 'Editorial', *Chapman*, Nos 35/36, July 1983, p. 1.

21. See, for example, Eleanor Bell, 'Who Sings for Scotland?: Reflections from Inside a Predicament', *Cencrastus*, No. 63, 1998.

22. David McCrone, *Understanding Scotland*, second edition (London: Routledge, 2001), p. 145.

23. See, for example, Colin McArthur (ed.), *Scotch Reels: Scotland in Cinema and Television* (London: BFI, 1982) which subjects the representation of Scotland in film and television to a rigorous analysis of this order.

24. See C. Beveridge and R. Turnbull, *The Eclipse of Scottish Culture*, and C. Beveridge and R. Turnbull, *Scotland After Enlightenment* (Edinburgh: Polygon, 1997).

25. Cairns Craig, *The Modern Scottish Novel*, p. 30.

26. Cairns Craig, *Out of History: Narrative Paradigms in Scottish and British Culture* (Edinburgh: Polygon, 1996), p. 117.

27. Cairns Craig, *The Modern Scottish Novel*, p. 31.

28. Angus Calder, *Revolving Culture: Notes from the Scottish Republic* (London: I. B. Tauris, 1993), p. 11.

29. Calder cites Celtic, Norse, Anglo-Saxon, French, Dutch, Irish, Jewish, Italian and Asian influences in this rich cultural pot-pourri.

30. See Colin McArthur (ed.), *Scotch Reels*; Eddie Dick (ed.), *From Limelight to Satellite*; David Bruce, *Scotland the Movie* (Edinburgh: Polygon/SFC, 1996) and Duncan Petrie, *Screening Scotland*.

31. Douglas Gifford, 'Imagining Scotlands: The Return to Mythology in Modern Scottish Fiction', in Susanne Hagemann (ed.), *Studies in Scottish Fiction: 1945 to the Present* (Frankfurt: Lang, 1996), pp. 36–7.

32. Martin McLoone, 'Internal Decolonisation? British Cinema in the Celtic Fringe', in Robert Murphy (ed.), *The British Cinema Book*, second edition (London: BFI, 2001), p. 190.

# Part I

# Politics and Aesthetics

# CHAPTER I

# Down among the Big Boys

## INTRODUCTION

The intellectual engagement with Scottish culture sparked by the events of 1979 led some critics to attack the deficient ways in which Scotland had not only been represented by others but, more seriously, had (mis)represented itself. Such debates became fixated on the pernicious effects of the pervasive discourses of tartanry and Kailyard, mythic structures that were funda-mentally regressive, elegiac and symptomatic of a national inferiority complex. The reinvigorated engagement with questions of culture, politics and nationalism gave substance to an alternative discourse which, unlike tartanry and Kailyard, projected a Scotland that was urban, industrial and working class in character and consequently closer to the real-life experiences of the majority of Scots. Labelled 'Clydesideism' – in recognition of its em-blematic association with the heavily populated, industrialised and proletarian West of Scotland[1] – this initially seemed to offer a more progressive cultural frame of reference through which a viable Scottish identity could be reimagined. As John Caughie anticipated in 1982, such a break with the discourses of tartanry and Kailyard would facilitate an active engagement with alternative versions of history:

> the traditions, for example, of the literature and theatre based in
> working class experience which, since the twenties, have seemed to
> offer the only real and consistent basis for a Scottish national culture;
> and the histories of resistance and struggle exemplified by Red
> Clydeside, the Crofters' Wars or the Lanarkshire weavers.[2]

Moreover, this new emphasis chimed with the kinds of political and cultural polarisation wrought by Thatcherism, in particular the re-emphasis on the existing association in Scotland between national identity and class consciousness as a means of asserting a sense of both opposition and difference. As David McCrone observes, 'Scotland's relationship with England has taken on "class" connotations to the extent that class and nationality are often insinuated.'[3] Unsurprisingly, this has had a profound influence on Scottish cultural production, as is clearly demonstrated by the emphasis in twentieth-century Scottish literature on the lives and experiences of ordinary working people in both urban and rural contexts. Moreover, the hierarchical distinction between 'the novel' and 'the working-class novel' in England is inverted in the case of Scottish fiction, precisely because of the Anglicisation of the Scottish middle and educated classes. Or as Cairns Craig puts it:

> the expression of Scottishness has come to depend on the classes which
> are least touched by English values: lower class and working class
> culture has thus come to be the repository of all that has been elided by
> the Scottish bourgeoisie's mimicry of English values.[4]

The tragic irony here is that by the early 1980s the culture and tradition of Scottish working-class political radicalism were in the process of being systematically undermined by the very political and economic forces it might have been mobilised against. As we have seen, one of the major consequences of the deep economic recession that marked the early years of Thatcherism was the dramatic demise of the traditional heavy industries of coal, steel, shipbuilding and textiles; destroying jobs, livelihoods and (ultimately) communities in the process. At the same time, the Thatcher Government proceeded to systematically undermine the power of the trade unions to oppose their economic and industrial policies. Consequently, almost as soon as it had emerged as a meaningful idea, Clydesideism had already been rendered 'mythic' in its association with the loss of a particular kind of 'authentic' Scottish community and way of life, and consequently became no less elegiac or nostalgic than tartanry or Kailyard.

As a potentially progressive discourse, Clydesideism was also compromised by its overtly masculine associations with hard physical labour and boisterous leisure pursuits such as football, gambling, excessive drinking and violence. Not only does this severely limit its applicability as a projection of an inclusive national culture, it is also woefully out of step with the historical realities of Scottish political radicalism – ignoring, for example, the significant female participation in the political struggles that gave meaning to the idea of Red Clydeside. Moreover, the discourse fails to grasp the social and political implications of mass unemployment and related changes in the economy and in labour markets. Caughie, this time writing in 1990, notes:

As 'real' productive labour (the culturally inscribed 'masculine' domain'), disappears into consumption (the 'feminine' domain), the myth becomes more desperate; and when masculinity can no longer define itself in 'hard work' it increasingly identifies itself with the 'hard man' for whom anguish, cynicism and violence are the only ways to recover the lost dignity of labour.[5]

While Scottish proletarianism can justifiably be posited as a progressive cultural response to the dominant values and class power of the British establishment, the elision of class and nation also tends to generate a rather crude and reductive opposition between a Scottish identity that is essentially proletarian, communitarian, demotic, gregarious and virile and an English-ness characterised as bourgeois, self-interested, stuffy, repressed and effete. Consequently, this kind of discourse necessarily privileges an overtly mascu-line and heterosexual concept of native virtue, in line with other projections of proletarian and socialist culture, which is itself regressive and pernicious. In this context the figure of Margaret Thatcher, as a particular and somewhat unusual embodiment of metropolitan hegemony, becomes even more sym-bolically charged. The dominant image is of Thatcher as a castrating virago, ruthlessly lording it over her cabinet of sycophantic public schoolboys and systematically trampling underfoot all who dared to oppose her. In the Scottish context, the figure of the right-wing, patrician 'Iron Lady' is doubly threatening precisely because she was both female and tough – the contempt which oozes from William McIlvanney's description of 'the woman in Downing Street' as 'a cultural vandal' threatening the very essence of Scottish cultural identity in her wilful destruction of 'hard-earned traditions'[6] speaks volumes. Consequently, the struggle against Thatcherism mobilised certain forces that served to construct yet another regressive, pathological and self-defeating image of a Scotland out of kilter with the forces of history. Ian Spring even regards the proletarian 'hard man' figure as 'a particularly potent form of inferiorist discourse'[7] in which any sense of heroic victory is illusory and meaningless – 'enacted on a stage that is only a netherland of the real world, condemned by oppression to remain apart from it'. The triumph of the proletarian hard man over adversity is consequently rendered no more liberating than the victory of a Roman slave in gladiatorial combat.

## DOWN AMONG THE BIG BOYS

Yet this is too simplistic a response to the range of creative responses that have been subsumed under the category Clydesideism. And just as it has been possible to identify countervailing traditions to tartanry and Kailyard, so I will now turn my attention to some of the key cultural works of the 1980s that would appear to be central to the Clydeside discourse, in order to provide a more complex and nuanced assessment of this particular vision of working-class Scottish culture. I am interested in particular in the contribution of a trio of creative individuals who all had established their reputations as chroniclers of Scottish working-class experience and struggle prior to the advent of Thatcherism. This influential group comprises the novelist William McIlvanney, the television dramatist Peter McDougall and the writer/director/producer Bill Bryden who, despite beginning his career in the theatre, has worked with equal success in film and television. While various aspects of their respective education and formation as creative artists differ considerably, all three were brought up in West Coast towns closely associated with traditional heavy industries – McIlvanney in Kilmarnock, the heart of the Ayrshire coal fields; McDougall and Bryden in the shipbuilding port of Greenock. Interestingly, all three have often mistakenly been categorised as 'Glaswegian' writers, but while the city of Glasgow certainly plays an important role in the work of each man, equally significant are the people, the physical environment and the histories of their own home towns (albeit in the case of McIlvanney, Kilmarnock becomes the fictionalised town of Graithnock). This has facilitated a first-hand insight into and understanding of the localised social consequences of the decline of the traditional heavy industries on provincial towns that conspicuously lack the kind of alternative opportunities more readily available in larger cities. But it also creates an important tension, most notable in the novels of McIlvanney, between Glasgow and its hinterland, reinforcing the 'outsider' status of some of his characters who have been drawn to the city.

McIlvanney had published his first two novels, *Remedy is None* (1966) and *A Gift from Nessus* (1968) while working as a teacher, but it was the 1975 Whitbread-winning *Docherty* that secured his reputation as a writer. Set in the first quarter of the twentieth century, the novel charts the life of an Ayrshire coal miner and his relationship to both family and community, celebrating in the process the virtues of socialism and masculinity, against a backdrop of economic exploitation, poverty and the carnage of the First World War. Hailed as a classic expression of Scottish identity as essentially and unashamedly proletarian, *Docherty* was also a reaction by McIlvanney to the profound social limitations of the bourgeois fiction he had encountered at university. His response was to focus on the lives and experiences of those excluded from the cannon: 'I wanted to write a book that would create a kind of literary genealogy for the people I came from, the people whose memorials were parish registers.'[8] After the literary success of *Docherty*, McIlvanney unexpectedly turned his attention to the more popular and accessible genre of crime fiction with the novels *Laidlaw* (1977) and *The Papers of Tony Veitch*

(1983), both featuring the exploits of hard-bitten Glasgow detective Jack Laidlaw. But the advent of Thatcherism prompted a return to more overtly political and socially motivated impetus, which is evident in both McIlvanney's journalism and his creative writing. The latter includes his 1985 novel *The Big Man*, the tale of an unemployed Ayrshire miner who is lured into the illegal world of bare-knuckle boxing by a ruthless Glasgow gangster, and the 1989 collection of interconnected short stories, *Walking Wounded*, described by the author as a novel without a central character, or 'a kind of people's novel'.[9] Both books engage directly with the impact of government policy on ordinary working people, returning to and updating in the process the concerns with working-class struggle and solidarity that had characterised *Docherty*. *The Big Man* also reflects McIlvanney's on-going dialogue with the substance of working-class masculinity, and in particular the existential struggle of men to live 'authentic' and meaningful lives whatever economic and social adversities they may face. In the 1990s McIlvanney published two further novels: *Strange Loyalties* (1991), the third and final contribution to the 'Laidlaw' series, and *The Kiln* (1996), a portrait of the life of a dissenchanted and introspective writer who also happens to be the grandson of the eponymous hero of the original *Docherty*.

Unlike the university-educated McIlvanney, Peter McDougall left school at 15 and toiled in the shipyards in his native Greenock before moving to London in the mid-1960s, where he initially worked as a painter and decorator. McDougall started writing in the early 1970s with encouragement from the playwright and actor Colin Welland, establishing himself with a number of successful television plays for the BBC. *Just Your Luck* (1972) and *Just Another Saturday* (1975) explored themes of sectarian bigotry, the betrayal of youthful idealism and, in the case of the latter work, the culture of machismo and violence that prevents many 'hard men' from growing up. This preoccupation became more central in the subsequent high-profile television films *Just a Boy's Game* (1979) and *A Sense of Freedom* (1980), the latter adapted from the autobiography of convicted murderer Jimmy Boyle, and came to be regarded as a defining characteristic of McDougall's *œuvre*. But at the same time the dramas also deal perceptively with male friendships, which are often depicted as an extension of the code of the playground. *The Elephant's Graveyard* (1976) is particularly interesting in this respect, being the tale of two unemployed men who wander the hills above Greenock rather than facing up to the necessity of finding work. Significantly, the two dramas that constitute McDougall's own direct response to the impact of Thatcherism – *Shoot for the Sun* (1987), dealing with the devastating problem of heroin addiction in Edinburgh, and *Down Where the Buffalo Go* (1988), concerned with family breakdown against a backdrop of rising unemployment – are similarly structured around a central male friendship. And while both replay many familiar McDougall concerns, the problems of the wider social world come to intrude more than ever before on the lives of his protagonists.

Both McIlvanney and McDougall were writers explicitly championed by Bill Bryden during his tenure as head of drama at BBC Scotland from 1984 to 1993. Bryden came to prominence with the stage plays, *Willie Rough* (1972) and *Benny Lynch* (1975), both subsequently adapted for television, which mark out an interest in Scottish working-class experience with important connections to McIlvanney and McDougall. Loosely based on the experiences of Bryden's grandfather, a riveter and shop steward in a Greenock shipyard during the First World War, *Willie Rough* has much in common with *Docherty* in its concern with the weighty issues of social inequality, trade unionism, religious bigotry and militaristic jingoism. While *Benny Lynch* represents an important contemplation of the 'hard man' figure, charting the tragic rise and fall of the boy from the Gorbals who became flyweight boxing champion of the world in 1935, only to die of drink in poverty eleven years later at the age of 33. Bryden's interest in the relationship between the reality and the myth of a figure like Lynch led him write a screenplay about the legendary western outlaw Jesse James, which became the basis for the 1980 Hollywood film *The Long Riders*, directed by Walter Hill. The influence of the Western can also be identified in Bryden's subsequent television films of the 1980s, *Ill Fares the Land* (1983), a dramatisation of the famous 'death' of the community of St Kilda, and *The Holy City* (1986), a modern-day telling of Christ's Passion which combines aspects of *Shane* and *The Magnificent Seven*.

The raw immediacy of McDougall's dramas have also drawn comparison with the genre. Ian Spring has described *Just a Boy's Game* as 'transparently motivated by the cowboy or western film',[10] while Jeremy Isaacs, producer of *A Sense of Freedom*, has commented that McDougall's major achievement as a dramatist has been his importing of the Western into British film-making 'using the violence that exists in the underworld of Glasgow'.[11] Like *Benny Lynch*, McDougall's hard men represent a particularly Scottish version of the tough, cynical gunslinger, whose reputation and status depend entirely on the ability to fight. But whereas Bryden's touchstone is the classical tradition of John Ford, characterised by a poetic engagement with human conflict and morality, McDougall's transposition of the Wild West to the streets and bars of Greenock and Glasgow owes much more to the brutal and morally ambivalent variant of the genre associated with Clint Eastwood, Sam Peckinpah and screenwriter Alan Sharp – another son of Greenock who after a brief career as a novelist and television dramatist made his name in Hollywood in the early 1970s.

As creative individuals inspired by the lives and struggles of ordinary people, McIlvanney, McDougall and Bryden all confront the problem of how to represent working-class experience in terms that will be understandable and recognisable to the very members of society that their work claims to represent. This has been posed in quite specific ways in relation to McIlvanney and the formal properties of the novel. Several critics have identified an important disjuncture between the language of McIlvanney's narrative voice and the dialogue spoken by his characters – which Cairns Craig refers to as 'the mutilating dialectic of English-writing author and Scots-speaking character'.[12] In the case of a novel like *Docherty*, McIlvanney is faced with the problem of how to convey thought processes and feelings of characters that are, by implication, too complex to be rendered in dialect. This necessitates for Craig the use of 'a language so erudite and literary that they can only be read ... as a *translation* from one language system to another'.[13] However, on the other hand, Gavin Wallace regards the 'constant war between an at times baroquely over-sophisticated literary English narrative voice and an equally sophisticated urban Scots dialogue' in McIlvanney's fiction as creating

> not the contradiction or weakness that some critics have suggested, but an attempted reconciliation between two antithetical sets of cultural values – standard English uniformity as opposed to individual Scottish community – forced into an eloquence in which they articulate *for each other*.[14]

Whatever the respective merits, this kind of argument over cultural contestation and the uses of language became central to debates at the heart of the creative reinvigoration of Scottish identity during the 1980s, a reminder of the important cultural issues at stake.

The aesthetics of television drama are very different to those of the novel and Peter McDougall's adherence to a particular variant of realism presents less of an immediate problem in this respect. As I have argued elsewhere,[15] his work has benefited a great deal from the aesthetic possibilities afforded by shooting and editing on film rather than video, allowing the film-makers to escape the confines of the studio and get out onto the streets. This not only facilitated a greater 'realism' in terms of having characters located in real environments, it also brought television drama into a closer alignment with the aesthetics of cinema and away from the conventions of the theatre. Consequently, elements such as composition, lighting and editing came to have as important a role as action, situation and dialogue. And while the writer has retained a major creative role in the process, television drama is still a highly collaborative process involving the contribution of a variety of creative individuals. This necessarily involves some transformation of the writer's original concepts, and consequently distinct directorial styles can be identified across McDougall's body of work: from the immediacy, fluidity and pace of the films directed by John Mackenzie such as *Just Another Saturday*, *The Elephant's Graveyard*, *Just a Boy's Game* and *A Sense of Freedom*, through the slower, more austere and distanced aesthetic deployed by Ian Knox in *Down Where the Buffalo Go* and *Shoot for the Sun*, to the lighter and more comic tone of Charlie Gormley in *Down Among the Big Boys* (1993).

When compared to the formal properties of the novel, the aesthetics of television drama inevitably place a greater emphasis on the exterior world of characters and their physical environment than the interrogation of internal thoughts and feelings. While this may avoid any tension between different registers or uses of language, nevertheless the often impassive blank demeanour and emotional inarticulacy of McDougall's protagonists render the understanding of motivation very difficult for an audience. This retardation of meaningful communication is often further constrained by the codes that operate in the overtly masculine space of the workplace and the pub – environments more conducive to enigmatic wisecracks and humorous banter than the open and overt articulation of complex feelings. The space where the McDougall protagonist is least at ease is in the feminsed domestic arena, an environment that features significantly in only one of his dramas, *Just Your Luck*, which is also his only work to be shot as a conventional studio-bound theatrical play. It is also significant that McDougall's most intimate drama, *The Elephant's Graveyard*, is a dialogue-driven two-hander that explicitly distances the characters from the social constraints and codes of the urban world, providing instead a 'neutral' space where reflective discourse on the male working-class predicament becomes possible.

By combining the roles of writer and director, Bill Bryden has exercised a greater degree of creative control over his cinema and television projects than McDougall. He is also less bound by the dictates of realism, preferring to construct narratives that relate to contemporary social issues in an oblique manner through the use of allegory and metaphor. Bryden is also more aesthetically eclectic, blending different styles and influences in the construction of his fictions. In addition to the Fordian motifs of the struggle of man against the environment, nature against 'civilisation', tradition against modernity, *Ill Fares the Land* also evokes the contemplative visual poetry of Bill Douglas, while the opening sequence featuring aerial footage of the St Kilda Islands accompanied by an informative voice-over clearly draws upon the techniques of the Griersonian documentary. The inspiration for *The Holy City*, on the other hand, came directly from the theatre. Adapted in part from W. L. Lorrimer's New Testament in Scots, the drama is a reworking of the life and death of Christ set in present-day Glasgow and featuring David Hayman as the enigmatic stranger who preaches redemption, hope and of a better world to come in unapologetically socialist and nationalist terms.[16] Bryden had become increasingly concerned with what he regarded as 'a terrible loss of faith – in leaders, unions, family, political parties',[17] and this had inspired his inventively staged productions of the three medieval 'Mystery Plays' with the Cottesloe company at the National Theatre in London. Conceived as a recreation of populist street theatre in which the actors and audiences mingled, bringing Christianity down to earth in the process, the 'Mystery Plays' set the tone for *The Holy City* which, despite the naturalistic utilisation of familiar Glasgow city-centre locations, relies heavily on theatrical technique. This is most apparent in the narrative commentaries provided by Hughie, the wisecracking pub sceptic, and Inspector McBain, the self-doubting policeman responsible for arresting the new messiah.

## FROM BIG MEN TO BIG BOYS: MCILVANNEY, MCDOUGALL AND THE STRUGGLE FOR MEANING

The discourse of 'Clydesideism' embodies a complex relationship between individual and collective experience in which the idea of a shared working-class consciousness, rooted in political struggle and a culture defined by hard physical work and boisterous leisure activities, sits alongside a concern with the individual subject who is representative yet somehow still unique and distinctive. This tension assumes different forms in the work of the creative individuals under consideration here. For example, the exceptional qualities of the individual in McIlvanney's fiction is immediately conveyed by his frequent use of eponymous titles: *Docherty*, *Laidlaw*, *The Big Man*. And despite the unequivocally communitarian standpoint and socialist sympathies of these novels, the definitive characteristic of working-class life lies not in Marxist revolutionary action, but rather in rebelliousness. As McIlvanney himself puts it:

> Rebellion is made by individuals, revolution is made by committees. The loneliness of a rebel establishes kinship. The kinship of revolutionaries creates loneliness. One proclaims individuals, the other denies them. Whoever proclaims individuality establishes a fraternity with our own. Whoever denies individuality through a cause leaves us alone with ours.[18]

This antipathy towards the programmatic and totalising aspects of Marxism also attests to the existentialist philosophy that lies at the heart of his view of humanity's *raison d'être*. While acknowledging the need to improve 'the shared conditions in which we live', for McIlvanney, the essential purpose of such action is to provide the conditions under which the individual can 'inhabit more fully the necessary and unalterable terms of (his or her) existence'.[19] This philosophical influence on McIlvanney's fiction has also intensified over time – indeed, Beth Dickson suggests that one of the key shifts from *Docherty* to *The Big Man* is precisely the move away from a socialist agenda to a more fundamental concern with the existential struggle of the individual. This also reflects the gradual erosion of class consciousness and social fragmentation that intensified under Thatcherism, the consequences of which McIlvanney has described as 'the perceived shipwreck of social idealism – the loss of belief in our ability to reconstruct society towards a more justly shared community of living'.[20]

The influential significance of existentialist philosophy in Scottish writing – which in addition to McIlvanney can be found in the work of, among others, Alexander Trocchi, Alan Sharp, James Kelman and Alan Warner – is insightfully discussed by Cairns Craig in terms of its dialectical relationship to Calvinism. In addition to being perhaps the dominant influence on the Scottish mindset, Calvinism's dependency on determinism and totality provides important points of conenctions with the conception of Marxism that McIlvanney scorns. As Craig suggests:

> if Calvinism throws into relief the issue of human choice by denying its significance in a world of predestination, existentialism's insistence on human choice throws equally into relief the predetermined patterns of life of those who refuse the challenge of authentic choice.[21]

It is this very challenge of 'authentic choice' that is the central focus of *The Big Man*. In deliberately stark contrast to Tam Docherty, Dan Scoular struggles under the burden of his reputation as a local hero to the villagers of Thornbank. Regarded as a man whose legendary toughness is matched only by his honour, Dan is depicted as a flawed and self-doubting individual, a hard man increasingly unable to cope with unemployment, poverty and a marriage rapidly unravelling in an atmosphere of spite and hostility. Dan's fight is primarily an internal struggle for meaning and it is significant that the novel makes no reference to the 1984/85 miner's strike – unlike David Leland's (1990) film adaptation with its opening images of picket line violence and Dan's return home after a short prison sentence for assaulting a policeman. The incentive for agreeing to take part in an illegal bare-knuckle fight is primarily economic, yet in the process Dan is not only forced to confront the viciousness, inhumanity and exploitativeness of the criminal underworld, but he also discovers a new self-awareness that gives him back the self-respect and motivation to live his life meaningfully.

This awakening involves a series of painful confrontations that allow Dan to recognise the misconceptions and obstacles hampering his progress as a human being. At the heart of this process is a deconstruction of the code of machismo that has traditionally defined the Scottish hard man, leading Carol

Craig to suggest that *The Big Man* represents a key turning point in McIlvanney's fiction at which the 'monument' erected to the kind of masculinity epitomised by his previous heroes like Tam Docherty is shown to be built on sand.[22] The first moment of self-revelation comes when Dan witnesses proof of his wife Betty's affair with Gordon Struthers, a rumour that had been eagerly reported to him by one of the Thornbank villagers who hold Dan in awe as the virtuous embodiment of traditional working-class masculinity. But far from administering the expected violent chastisement to his wife and her lover, Dan is rendered incapable of such action. Rather, his thoughts turn to the futility and hypocrisy of violent retribution, his own failings as a husband, and of his mother's revelation of the suffering she had endured in her life with his father – a man hitherto associated with the virtues of toughness and, significantly, the one and only person to ever beat Dan in a fight:

> Stripped of who he thought he was, of Wullie Mairshall's moth-eaten robes of manhood, he felt the chillness of honesty. He had balanced in himself two forces: a rage that could have demolished the furnishings of the pub and anybody who got in his way, especially Betty, and a certainty of how useless doing that would be. He knew simultaneously his strength and its pointlessness.[23]

This transformation of consciousness is reinforced during the fight with Cutty Dawson, a contest which Dan wins by finding within himself a ruthless will to win:

> Trying to focus on the fragmentary images of Cutty that felt as if they were coming at him from every angle, Dan seemed to himself to be fighting all those working class hard men who had formed the pantheon of his youth, men who in thinking they defied the injustice of their lives had been acquiescing in it because they compounded the injustice by unloading their weakness on to someone else, making him carry it. Dan's past self was among them. So was his father …[24]

Such understanding paradoxically gives Dan the resources to beat Cutty by battering him blind – the only thing in his life that will give him the courage and strength to cope with this devastating insight is his wife and children, and the only way he will regain them is to win the fight. But Dan must also be reconciled with Cutty – which he does by visiting his injured opponent in hospital and giving him a share of the prize money he has taken from the gangster Matt Mason – before he can return to the care and love of his family with a clear conscience.

On the surface, Peter McDougall's television plays share with McIlvanney's novels a socially inclusive concern with the 'real' lived experience of 'ordinary' working-class people and a similar focus on the trials and tribulations of masculinity. But unlike McIlvanney's self-reflective and often exceptional heroes, McDougall's protagonists are more limited as social actors, young men trapped in a kind of 'eternal adolescence'.²⁵ McDougall's vision of working-class experience is also more pessimistic than McIlvanney's, the struggle for meaningful choice and fulfilment eclipsed by a concern with the kind of self-defeating and essentially meaningless dead ends people find themselves in. McDougall's protagonists are also more ambiguous in their personal qualities, being irrepressible, humorous and tough, but also caustic, cruel and emotionally inarticulate. Again, in contrast with McIlvanney, the family is frequently depicted not as a source of comfort and strength but rather as a deeply flawed institution populated by impotent fathers, smothering mothers and bitter wives. The world of work is equally devoid of virtue and meaning, and it is significant that in McDougall's dramas written before the recession of the early 1980s, employment is treated with a great deal of ambivalence – in both *The Elephant's Graveyard* and *Just a Boy's Game*, the central characters skive off from work with the same casual contempt they might previously have truanted from school. This catalogue of restricted opportunity invariably forces McDougall's young male protagonists to seek their excitement and camaraderie from friends who are equally unequipped for the rigours, complexities and responsibilities of adult life, preferring instead to get drunk, solicit the favours of 'easy women', and prove their hardness in the 'mean streets' and pubs of Greenock or Glasgow.

By the the mid-1980s McDougall had begun to directly respond to certain aspects of Thatcher's Britain, although, like McIlvanney, his interest is primarily in the consequences policies have on people's lives rather than in any direct political critique or analysis. Consequently *Shoot for the Sun* confronts unflinchingly the human cost of heroin addiction in terms of the misery, degradation and utter hopelessness that had become a way of life for many in the new 'underclass' created by the government's economic pro-gramme. The drama also acknowledges the particular gravity of this problem in Edinburgh – where the historic and picturesque city-centre served to conceal some of the most deprived housing estates in Europe and human misery more readily associated with Glasgow. The two small-time pushers at the centre of *Shoot for the Sun*, Geordie and Dinny (played by Jimmy Nail and Brian Cox respectively), also represent a new kind of self-serving Thatcherite entrepreneur, ruthlessly exploiting a captive market while conveniently ignor-ing the devastating effects their trade is having on a community in which even schoolchildren have become ensnared in the local 'market'. But they too fall foul of the law of the market when their activities are effectively 'terminated' by a bigger and more ruthless supplier.

McDougall's subsequent drama, *Down Where the Buffalo Go*, marked a return to his home town of Greenock, now gripped in the depths of economic recession. But while the film is obliquely concerned with the effects of unemployment on the cohesion of community and family life, it is emotional rather than material poverty that is the major focus of this complex and multi-stranded work. Once again it revolves around a central male friendship, this time between Willie (Andrew Byatt), a mild-mannered shipyard worker on the verge of joining his father on the dole, and his lugubrious brother-in-law Carl (Harvey Keitel), an American serviceman based at the nearby nuclear submarine base, who has chosen to make his home in Scotland. The men are linked through shared emotional turmoil and familial disintegration. Willie is acrimoniously separated from his wife and access to his kids is severely restricted, while Carl's marriage to Willie's sister Rachel is on the verge of collapse, a situation similarly complicated by the involvement of a child. Willie's predicament is exacerbated by economic misfortune, redundancy robs him of the resources to purchase the carpet that will allow him to see his children. Carl's problem, on the other hand, is rooted in his chronic inability to either communicate or to act to change his life in a positive, meaningful way. While Dan Scoular in *The Big Man* resolves his conflict through action, Carl ossifies through inaction, and despite sentimental reminiscences of 'home' that he conveys to his daughter, he considers the 'American dream' is a lie and ignores his wife's desire to emigrate. This passivity annoys even Willie and at one point he poignantly remarks to his brother-in-law – 'sometimes I think you came here to die!' The emotional bleakness of the drama is visually enhanced by the drab, grey vistas of Greenock, Dunoon and the surrounding landscapes of the Clyde estuary in winter.

Carl's emotional disintegration is also powerfully conveyed in the raw performance and impassive expressions of Keitel, using his hard muscular body to exacerbate his sense of powerlessness in the scene where having been deserted by his wife and daughter, he strips naked and lies down on the living room carpet like a mortally wounded animal. The only thing that preserves any semblance of redemptive hope for Carl are children, both his own daughter and the angelic little girl he meets while in a black despair who asks him if he wants to buy anything from her shop. While this moment may border on easy sentimentality, it also provides a heart-felt residual belief in the essential goodness and generosity of humanity. Childhood for McDougall represents an important moment before dreams have been crushed and the rot has set in, and the reason why so many of his adult men have a tendency to regress – something echoed in Willie's final return to the deserted shipyard in which he plays on a discarded gangplank like a child. Significantly, it is Willie who is able to move on, his unemployment brings with it a recognition that he has spent all his adult life working in the same shipyard and in the final sequence of the film, while Carl is arrested for failing to turn up for duty after a night of heavy drinking, Willie boards a bus for London. On the journey he shares a drink with a young man who is clearly excited at the prospect of a new life, his expression of hope and comradeship providing a justification for Willie's own brave step forward.

In addition to their shared interest in masculine subjectivity and agency, *The Big Man* and *Down Where the Buffalo Go*, also allude in significant ways to wider social and political questions. Violence in McIlvanney's work is often consciously deployed as a metaphor for capitalism as a system that enacts its own forms of brutality on human beings. Consequently, Dan Scoular's predicament in *The Big Man* embraces a more fundamental conflict between the working-class community and the Thatcherite establishment. This takes the form of the clash of different value systems as embodied by Dan and Mat Mason, the ruthless, self-centred, criminal entrepreneur. Mason is a working-class boy made good, yet he has chosen to reject any of the values that Dan holds dear by subjugating all other considerations to the amassing of personal wealth and power. In a novel in which all trappings of bourgeois life are treated with contempt, Mason also represents an extreme version of the class traitor, defined by his material possessions, who has allied acquisitiveness with criminality. The relationship between the two men is essentially based on an economic transaction with Mason, the business man, trading Scoular, the pugilist, as a commodity. In this way Mason is no different from the mine owner who previously would have exploited Dan's physical labour down the pit, a state of affairs immediately understood by Dan's perceptive wife: 'He was letting others buy him for their purposes even though, from the little information he could give, he had no understanding of what those purposes were. He was selling his life in a market.'[26] Under Thatcherism the nature of the economy had changed and whereas the commodification of a figure like Tam Docherty was bound up in the politics of industrial production, Dan's labour is now directed towards the sphere of consumption, providing both entertainment for Mason's associates and a 'sporting' means for Mason to settle a business dispute with a fellow criminal in the process.

McIlvanney returned to the struggles of ordinary people attempting to resist the worst social and economic effects of Thatcherism in the collection of short stories, *Walking Wounded*. Alongside the familiar scenarios of surviving the monotony of life on the dole, dealing with domestic disintegration, break-up, negotiating the myriad of mundane injustices wrought by people on each other, McIlvanney introduces the new element of fantasy as a redemptive addition to the armoury of his 'walking wounded'. This is central to the final story in the collection, 'Dreaming', whose protagonist, Sammy Nelson, is an unemployed 17-year-old who immerses himself in a world of books, records, images and daydreams as a response to the grimness of small town life.[27]

By virtue of its cumulative depiction of the inhabitants of Graithnock, *Walking Wounded* allows McIlvanney to retain a potent, if residual, sense of collective experience as a bulwark against total social fragmentation. This is also reinforced by the links between his various fictions in which characters from one novel frequently appear in or are referred to in another. For example, Matt Mason is first introduced in *Laidlaw*, while in *Strange Loyalties* Jack Laidlaw investigates the death of Dan Scoular, killed in a mysterious hit and run that is obliquely linked in the novel to the death of Laidlaw's brother Scott. Laidlaw is also an acquaintance of Tom Docherty, grandson of Tam and the central protagonist of *The Kiln*. Ray Ryan suggests that by *Strange Loyalties*, McIlvanney's focus has become much more a contemplation of the state of the Scottish nation beyond the fictional communities of Graithnock and Thornbank. Consequently the 'web of interactions' or 'weaving of lives' that characterises the novels suggests a history which, unbidden, unfolds around those inhabiting Scotland. McIlvanney's corpus testifies to its integrity, wholeness and coherence; its existence is not dependent on the ratification of its individual citizens.[28] This ultimately allows McIlvanney's obsessions with the individual to exist alongside a concern with a collective national experience under attack from wider social and economic forces.

In *Down Where the Buffalo Go*, McDougall addresses the problem of unemployment primarily through the depiction of the death of the shipyards that had been Greenock's industrial life blood. The giant dockside cranes towering above the houses had already featured prominently in *The Elephant's Graveyard* and *Just a Boy's Game*, but this time the emphasis is on their static inactivity. Even more poignant is the huge engineering shed where Willie and a handful of other workers spend their last few weeks of employment, cleaning the idle machines – that potent metaphor for Thatcherite 'progress' – prior to their dismantling. The hollow emptiness of the space evoking the ghosts of a once great industry. One of Willie's more tragic work mates is an old fantasist, nicknamed the 'Trinkle Kid' (Alex McAvoy), who mimes the part of a western gunfighter forced to hang up his pistols when the redundancy notes come through. His fantasy life is presented as rather pathetic, reinforcing Carl's insistence that the allure of American culture as a means of escape is a hollow sham. The dying shipyard is contrasted with the frenetic activity in and around the submarine base on the Holy Loch, a forbidding metal structure resembling a floating factory from which helicopters constantly take off and land and sinister black nuclear submarines silently come and go. The presence of nuclear weapons on British soil constituted another major site of opposition to the Thatcher Government, led by groups such as the Campaign for Nuclear Disarmament. McDougall, however, does not make the concerns of the Peace Movement a direct focus, rather, the relationship between the local community and the American military personnel is presented in terms of economic dependency. The young American service men are a captive market for the local prostitutes – the opening sequence shows Carl 'raiding' the home of one local woman to arrest the AWOL serviceman in her bed. The lure the Americans have for the local women who take the ferry across to the US service club also embodies the kind of hope of a better life that had initially attracted Rachel to Carl. Yet once again this is ultimately shown to be a sordid and exploitative game, as evinced by the subplot of the woman who prostitutes her own young daughter, only to be left behind when the daughter goes off with both of the sailors they have been chatting-up in the bar. This contemporary manifestation of colonial exploitation combines with economic depression to form a double oppression of the locals, and by extension of the people of Scotland in general.

## COMMUNITY, ALLEGORY AND METAPHOR IN THE FILMS OF BILL BRYDEN

In contrast to McIlvanney and McDougall's intimate portraits of working-class struggle and despair, Bill Bryden's key works of the 1980s are much more overtly concerned with the larger questions of community and its relationship to the state. Despite its historical setting, *Ill Fares the Land* uses the famous evacuation of the remaining 36 inhabitants of the remote island of St Kilda on 29 August 1930 to make a number of points relevant to contemporary political and social concerns. For example, the parallels between the death of the island and the contemporary destruction of communities by the forces of Thatcherism are evident as Bryden himself has indicated: 'the image of the deserted village at the end of the film is a metaphor for the image of a deserted town or shipyard or industrial region which is the very depression we are faced with today.'[29] Bryden's portrait of St Kilda is of an idealised egalitarian republic with the island's parliament a democratic forum for collective consensual decision-making. The proto-socialist soul of this community is articulated by Donald Gillies (James Grant), the cragsman who is shown distributing the fulmar he has caught equally and fairly around the community. Gillies challenges his neighbour Willie MacDonald's (David Hayman) argument that the islanders must stop living in the past and embrace the modern world dictated by the wage economy with the blunt retort – 'I don't like the sound of wages.' Willie has emigrated to Glasgow for primarily economic reasons yet continues to be drawn back to the island he still regards as home. In addition to their socialist instincts, the community are also deeply religious; the communal readings from the massive family Bibles representing a major domestic ritual in the islanders' way of life. Spiritual preparation for evacuation is provided by the book of Exodus, the flight of the Israelites into

Egypt providing a poignant parallel to their own ordeal.[30]

If *Ill Fares the Land* can be seen as an oblique political comment on some of the issues confronting Scotland in the 1980s, *The Holy City* represents a much more audacious engagement with the present. Unsurprisingly, the perceived irreverence of a drama that mixed religion and politics (and which was broadcast by the BBC on Good Friday, 28 March 1986) generated a great deal of controversy. The editorial of *The Glasgow Herald* described the drama as 'a tawdry sham. It was Easter without Resurrection, a gospel without God.'[31] *The Holy City* begins with the new messiah – simply referred to as 'the man' – preaching to a crowd in a floodlit football stadium at night. His rhetoric has a powerful political resonance: he refers to 'the theft of a people's hope, the theft of a nation' alongside a social and economic tragedy signified by 'empty factories, unmined coal, deserted shipyards'. This is reinforced by the power-ful, if rather sentimental, iconography of the death of shipbuilding conveyed via recurring shots of idle cranes and rusting yards similar to that in *Down Where the Buffalo Go*. In one sequence, where 'the man' and his disciples march down the deserted dockside like a gang of western gunslingers heading for a showdown, Bryden even cuts in black and white images of the golden age of Clydeside shipbuilding to ram home his message. And while refusing any depiction of the crucifixion, the resurrection sequence of *The Holy City* features 'the man' standing on the end of a jetty in the shipyard, prophesying national redemption:

> The grouse will rise from his cover, and the thistle will sting at the touch. And the Clyde still flows quiet to the sea. But there will be ships built by your hands on its tide yet. I'll no be here for the labour, but I'll know the sight of a river in all its glory.

Whatever the rhetorical force, the romanticism of this sentiment overlooks the inconvenient fact that shipbuilding on the Clyde had been in a state of rapid decline since the end of the Second World War.

Unfortunately other aspects of Bryden's polemic in *The Holy City* are just as heavy-handed, particularly his inferred alignment of the economic forces of reaction with English imperialism. Throughout the film 'the man' is under intense surveillance by a group of English policemen, who – in stark contrast to the egalitarian Scottish characters – adhere to a rigidly hierarchical military model ranging from the 'officer class' head of the police to the cockney 'other rank'. They are united, however, by a shared ruthlessness, arrogance and racist hatred for 'Jocks' and 'Paddys'. In one scene as the policemen celebrate the impending arrest of 'the man', one of them remarks that 'Your Jock – even the one who has been educated or has crawled up the ladder – is somewhere between an urangutan, a jigaboo and a Paddy.' Yet Bryden's own conception of the English is hardly more sophisticated, as the following diatribe spoken by the sensitive and fair-minded Scottish policeman Inspector McBain (Richard Wilson) attests:

> The English mind is essentially one that justifies the means by the end. It may be too dull to see it and too self-righteous to suspect it. It is narrow and bigoted by nature. And it is bloated on the fat tradition of success. All people can to a degree deceive themselves when it is in their interest to do so. But this dull, prosperous people have a malign genius for it. They can deceive themselves into believing that blind hate for a race is a love of mankind: that massacres are the harbingers of the highest civilisation, that liberty of conscience is to think as they think. What did the man do? What crime did he commit? What if what he said was the truth?

The contrast between this vision of the oppressors and the fundamental decency and goodness of ordinary working-class Glaswegians could hardly be more crudely drawn. Despite its ambition and provocativeness, *The Holy City* ultimately lacks the kind of imagination, insight and subtlety – to say nothing of the sardonic humour – that gives Billy Connolly's famous comic monologue 'The Crucifixion', in which he also relocates Christ to Glasgow, far greater subversive power and poignancy.


## CONCLUSION: STILL A BOY'S GAME?

While the thematic and aesthetic complexities of *The Big Man, Down Where the Buffalo Go* and to a lesser extent *The Holy City* are testament to the creative vibrancy of 'Clydesideism', their shared reliance on a resolutely masculine focus does need to critically addressed. In McDougall's dramas, for example, women tend to be portrayed in largely unsympathetic terms: as downtrodden, bitter wives or smothering mothers, typified by the hard, pained faces of actors Jan Wilson and Katherine Stark. Ironically, the immaturity of McDougall's male protagonists is often obliquely related to the matriarchal underside that lurks beneath the overly masculine front of his fictions where men expect their wives to function as surrogate mothers. But ultimately McDougall has little or no interest in attempting to view the situation from the perspective of these women and consequently they remain a mystery, equally remote and closed off from the audience as they are from the immature male protagonists. Similar criticisms have been made of McIlvanney's work: Jeremy Idle noting that his female characters are invariably 'a mixture of brave stand-by-your man victims and whining snobs'[32], while Christopher Whyte curtly dismisses '[McIlvanney's] nostalgic paeans to a heroic masculinity for which post-industrial Scotland no longer (thankfully) has a place'.[33] Unlike McDougall, McIlvanney has not simply shrugged off or ignored such challenges. Rather, he has attempted to address the issue directly in his work. Consequently, the deconstruction of the myth of masculinity in *The Big Man* involves an attempt to begin, however tentatively, an examination of female consciousness. This has even found a positive response in some feminist critics – Beth Dickson argues that Dan Scoular's wife, Betty, occupies a meaningful presence in the novel.[34] While Dan's recognition of the struggle and hardship endured by his mother is regarded by Carol Craig as a significant correction to the idealised image of the obedient self-sacrificing wife represented by Jenny Docherty.[35]

While less overtly posed, the question of gender is arguably even more problematic in Bryden's work, which is more directly concerned with the idea of community than either McDougall or McIlvanney's. In *Ill Fares the Land* the idealised 'organic democracy' of St Kilda is an unashamedly patriarchal institution from which women are systematically disenfranchised. While the men debate the future of the community, the women work – their voice is silent, their will irrelevant. Moreover, it is Nurse Barclay, the incomer sent to St Kilda by the Scottish Office, who like the fallen Eve leads the Islanders out of their Eden and into a more brutal and exploitative world. The socialist vision of *The Holy City* is equally masculine in its orientation, from the crude utilisation of the gendered space of the pub to convey the heart and intellect of working-class Glasgow to the all-male community represented by the disciples. Bryden's messiah also lacks any of the ironic qualities or doubts of McIlvanney's 'big man' and those women who do appear in *The Holy City* are pathetic victims characterised by wantonness: the woman caught by her husband with a lover, the mother of the boy with the birthmark who promises to stop seeking solace in strange men if her son is cured, and the Mary Magdalene character who has five men on the go at once. All are weak, immoral creatures who are systematically excluded from the comradeship epitomised by the bond between the disciples and the equally male camaraderie of Hughie and his friends in the pub.

An alternative and refreshing challenge to Bryden's uncompromisingly masculine perspective is offered by John McGrath's three part mini-series, *Blood Red Roses*, broadcast in 1986. Adapted from the stage play successfully toured by 7:84 Scotland, *Blood Red Roses* tells the story of 'battling' Bessie McGuigan, a fearless and militant shop steward who takes on the might of an American multinational in an industrial dispute. After an initial victory, Bessie is subsequently made a scapegoat when the forces of international capital conspire to close the factory down a few years later. On one hand, *Blood Red Roses* conveys McGrath's disillusionment at the gradual erosion of class consciousness by the values of self-interest epitomised by the Thatcher

Government, but unlike in McIlvanney's fictions, the process is explicitly located in the context of the globalisation of advanced capitalism. McGrath also places Bessie's narrative – embracing a 34-year period from her childhood in the Highlands in the 1950s to her subsequent life in East Kilbride and then, after the factory has closed, in Glasgow – within a history punctuated by significant political events from the Suez Crisis of 1956, through a number of general elections culminating in the unequivocal endorsement of Thatcherism in 1983. These events are conveyed by way of television images, a medium that Bessie blames for contributing to the erosion of class solidarity among working people.[36] This historical dimension gives *Blood Red Roses* a more polemical force than any of the other works examined in this chapter by virtue of the explicit link made between the local and the global.

McGrath also examines Bessie's fight for justice within the context of her struggles as a wife and mother. Husband Alex, a full-time union official who had been the agent of Bessie's own political education, is portrayed by Gregor Fisher as a selfish, weak and thoughtless man who continually fails to provide his wife with the moral and practical support she needs. His commitment to the class struggle invariably takes precedence over the needs of his family – he misses the birth of one of his daughters because he is out campaigning for the Labour Party, for example – yet he still expects his wife to be a domestic skivvy, whatever work she may otherwise be occupied with. He also has an affair that hastens the break-up of the McGuigan family, with Bessie moving to Glasgow with her two daughters – who have inherited their mother's feisty temperament. The support provided by this community of women allows *Blood Red Roses* to end on an upbeat note with Bessie marching in the Glasgow May Day parade, a final image depicting the residue of solidarity. She is with a group of women, suggesting further that future struggle must learn from the mistakes of the past – including patriarchal oppression within left-wing politics.

But history had already rendered this optimistic denouement as impotent fantasy, and within a year Thatcher's Conservatives would resoundingly win their third general election in a row. And despite its narrative and ideological sophistication, *Blood Red Roses* embodies aspects that serve to further negate its appeal to traditional forms of working-class solidarity. As portrayed by Elizabeth McLennan, Bessie Gordon is a truly exceptional individual on a par with McIlvanney's male heroes. Her moral and physical strength gives her the means to dominate and overpower everyone who crosses her – from the boys at school and bullying supervisors at work to the scheming (and rather caricatured) upper-class English manager who runs the factory in East Kilbride. Bessie's Highland heritage provides her with an innate sense of justice and an irrepressible spirit, directly connecting her to the romantic tradition of Jacobite resistance perpetrated by Sir Walter Scott. This in turn renders her a variant on the figure of the 'noble savage', a Celtic amazon lured into a battle with the dark forces of modernity in the guise of multinational capital. It would appear that McGrath's pessimism in the face of the destruction of the values of community by the juggernaut of global capitalism can only be checked by creating a fantasy superwoman, a 'Mother Caledonia', ostensibly located in history yet ultimately appealing to that seductive realm outside historical process which Cairns Craig has so perceptively examined in relation to the Scottish novel.[37] But *Blood Red Roses* also brings us back to the fundamental centrality of gender in the discourse of Clydesideism and its response to Thatcherism. For what is Bessie McGuigan if not a symbolic neo-Jacobite response to the equally formidable figure of Margaret Thatcher as an embodiment of the power of the British state and the interests of multinational capital? In the imaginary struggle between these two female titans McGrath updates the concerns of his most celebrated work, *The Cheviot, the Stag and the Black Black Oil*, eliding the historical tragedy of Hanoverian oppression and its legacy with current nationalist concerns in Scotland. As a contribution to 'Clydesideism', *Blood Red Roses* offers a welcome challenge to the masculine dominance of the discourse, while suggesting that the category embraces a rather more complex, vibrant and multi-faceted tradition of socially committed cultural production than may sometimes be acknowledged.

## NOTES

1. Angus Calder notes that the first time he encountered the term Clydesideism was at the 1982 *Scotch Reels* event at the Edinburgh Film Festival. 'Workers Culture Popular Culture-Defining Our Terms', in *Revolving Culture: Notes from the Scottish Republic* (London: I. B. Tauris, 1994).
2. John Caughie, 'Scottish Television: What Would it Look Like?' in Colin McArthur (ed.), *Scotch Reels* (London: BFI, 1982), p. 121.
3. David McCrone, 'We're A' Jock Tamson's Bairns: Social Class in Twentieth Century Scotland', in T. M. Devine and R. J. Finlay (eds), *Scotland in the 20th Century* (Edinburgh: Edinburgh University Press, 1996), pp. 115–16.
4. Cairns Craig, '"Going Down to Hell is Easy": *Lanark*, Realism and the Limits of the Imagination', in Robert Crawford and Thom Nair (eds), *The Arts of Alasdair Gray* (Edinburgh: Edinburgh University Press, 1991), p. 91.
5. John Caughie, 'Representing Scotland: New Questions for Scottish Cinema', in Eddie Dick (ed.), *From Limelight to Satellite: A Scottish Film Book* (London: BFI/SFC, 1990), p. 16.
6. William McIlvanney, 'Stands Scotland Where it Did?', *Surviving the Shipwreck* (Edinburgh: Mainstream, 1991), p. 246.
7. Ian Spring, 'Image and Text: Fictions on Film', in Gavin Wallace and Randall Stevenson (eds), *The Scottish Novel Since the Seventies* (Edinburgh: Edinburgh University Press, 1993), p. 211.

8. William McIlvanney, *Surviving the Shipwreck*, p. 223.

9. Douglas Gifford, 'Interview with William McIlvanney', *Books in Scotland*, No. 30, Spring 1989, p. 3.

10. Ian Spring, *Phantom Village: The Myth of the New Glasgow* (Edinburgh: Polygon, 1990), p. 76.

11. Jeremy Isaacs, interviewed in *A Big Boy's Tale: A Profile of Peter McDougall, The Late Show*, BBC2 txd: 15 September 1993.

12. Cairns Craig, *The Modern Scottish Novel: Narrative and the National Imagination* (Edinburgh: Edinburgh University Press, 1999), p. 83.

13. Ibid. p. 82.

14. Gavin Wallace, 'Voices in Empty Houses: The Novel of Damaged Identity', in Wallace and Stevenson (eds), *The Scottish Novel Since the Seventies*, p. 221.

15. Duncan Petrie, *Screening Scotland* (London: BFI, 2000), pp. 134–40.

16. This was broadcast on Good Friday in 1986, the only time Bryden was to write and direct one of his own works for BBC Scotland during his tenure as Head of Drama.

17. Bill Bryden interviewed in *Radio Times*, 22 March 1986, p. 9.

18. William McIlvanney, *Surviving the Shipwreck*, p. 237.

19. Ibid. p. 236.

20. Ibid. p. 11.

21. Cairns Craig, *The Modern Scottish Novel*, p. 107.

22. Carol Craig, 'On Men and Women in McIlvanney's Fiction', *Edinburgh Review*, No. 73, 1986, p. 42.

23. William McIlvanney, *The Big Man* (London: Hodder and Stoughton, 1985), p. 174.

24. Ibid. p. 207.

25. Kenny Mathieson, 'Peter McDougall: A Boy's Game', *Cencrastus*, Winter 1987–88, p. 4.

26. William McIlvanney, *The Big Man*, p. 105.

27. Sammy Nelson's indelible sense of optimism is further enhanced in the 1990 BBC television version of *Dreaming*, adapted by McIlvanney, directed by Mike Alexander and featuring Ewan Bremner in his first major role.

28. Ray Ryan, *Ireland and Scotland: Literature and Culture, State and Nation, 1966–2000* (Oxford: Oxford University Press, 2002), p. 79.

29. Bill Bryden quoted by Jo Comino, 'Memoirs of Survivors', *City Limits*, 6–12 May, 1983, p. 13.

30. This image of a virtuous, non-conformist Christian socialism is similar to that of the portrayal of the Tolpuddle Martyrs in Bill Douglas's feature film *Comrades* (1987).

31. Editorial, *The Glasgow Herald*, 29 March 1986.

32. Jeremy Idle, 'McIlvanney, Masculinity and Scottish Literature', *Scottish Affairs*, No. 2, Winter 1993, p. 56.

33. Christopher Whyte, 'Introduction', in *Gendering the Nation: Studies in Modern Scottish Literature* (Edinburgh: Edinburgh University Press, 1995), p. xi.

34. See Beth Dickson, 'Class and Being in the Novels of William McIlvanney', in Wallace and Stevenson (eds), *The Scottish Novel Since the Seventies*.

35. See Carol Craig, 'On Men and Women in McIlvanney's Fiction', *Edinburgh Review*, No. 73, 1986.

36. A similar demonisation of television is elaborated by McGrath in 'Celebration, Spectacle, Carnival', *The Bone Won't Break: On Theatre and Hope in Hard Times* (London: Methuen, 1990).

37. See Cairns Craig, *Out of History: Narrative Paradigms in Scottish and British Culture* (Edinburgh: Polygon, 1996).

# CHAPTER 2

# A New Flowering of Creativity

## INTRODUCTION

But by the mid-1980s cultural expression in Scotland was developing in very interesting and productive ways. Alongside the old war-horses like McIlvanney, McDougall, Bryden and McGrath, a number of new creative individuals had also begun to make their innovative mark, giving substance to claims that a cultural renaissance in Scotland was underway. In the vanguard of this process were two Glasgow writers, Alasdair Gray and James Kelman, who began to redefine the imaginative scope and engagement of the Scottish novel in ways that were as audacious as they were inspirational. Around the same time, the reinvigoration of Scottish television drama was being spear-headed by the acclaimed playwright John Byrne, who had moved beyond the limitations of the theatrical stage to reach a wider national and international audience. Moreover, a distinctively Scottish contribution to a British cinema undergoing its own revival in the early 1980s was being attributed to the writer/director Bill Forsyth. Following in the progressive traditions of Scottish fiction, all four were united in their engagement with the lives and experiences of 'ordinary' individuals. However, in their own distinctive ways their work imaginatively transcends some of the limitations associated with 'Clydesideism': in particular its tendencies towards a rather narrow social realism, a sentimentality for a lost sense of working-class community, and a veneration of tough masculinity. Rather than mourning an idealised and rapidly vanishing urban industrial past, Gray, Kelman, Fortsyth and Byrne began to explore a broader range of social experience and narrative situations, and a more complex idea of contemporary subjectivity. Moreover, the work of all four shares a commitment to the creative re-imagination of urban Scotland, recasting the city of Glasgow as a modern metropolis rather than continuing to reproduce the limited and limiting 'no mean city' stereotype of urban deprivation and violence.

The first major publications by Gray and Kelman signalled nothing less than a watershed in the history of Scottish literary fiction. Gray's 1981 debut novel, *Lanark: A Life in Four Books*, published by Canongate, was hailed by Anthony Burgess as 'a shattering work of fiction in the modern idiom [by] … the best Scottish novelist since Walter Scott'.[1] More than a quarter century in the writing, *Lanark* is a rich and ambitious work that effortlessly combines realist and fantastical narrative modes to convey the (partly autobiographical) tale of the short life of a disaffected young Glaswegian, Duncan Thaw, that culminates in his suicide at the age of 22. Gray encases Thaw's story within the narrative of the eponymous Lanark, revealed as Thaw's alter ego in the afterlife, which is set in the dystopian city of Unthank, itself a fictionalised version of Glasgow. *Lanark* is also distinguished by a textual playfulness, most notably in the 'epilogue' in which Lanark the protagonist meets a version of Gray the 'author', his creator, and has an argument with him about his ultimate fate. This encounter is augmented by a series of footnotes, which in turn challenge and ridicule some of the claims of the author, and a list of plagiarisms in the margins of the text that identify the various literary influences and borrowings embedded in the novel. In both its inventive formal construction and its broad thematic scope that engages with post-war Glasgow's relationship to the forces of monopoly capitalism, *Lanark* sets the tone for Gray's subsequent fictions, the most important of which are novels *1982 Janine* (1984), *Something Leather* (1990) and *Poor Things* (1992).

The 'arrival' of James Kelman, if less immediately spectacular than that of Gray, was to prove no less important in terms of his impact on the Scottish literary scene. Kelman had already published two collections of short stories – *An Old Pub Near the Angel* (1973) and *Short Tales from the Night Shift* (1978) – before coming to critical attention with the 1983 short-story collection *Not, Not While the Giro* and the 1984 novel *The Busconductor Hines*, both of which were published by Polygon. Kelman had a close personal connection with Gray through their participation in the creative writing programme initiated by Philip Hobsbaum at the University of Glasgow in 1971. But in sharp contrast to his friend's penchant for mixing reality and fantasy, Kelman chose to focus as honestly as possible on the mundane minutiae of the lives of isolated individuals struggling to get by in an increasingly fragmented and indifferent society. But what really distinguished the vitality of Kelman's writing was the innovative approach to language. This involved a radical erasure of the rigid division between the use of standard English for the narrative voice and of vernacular for rendering working-class dialogue, liberating his prose from the pernicious, externally-imposed hierarchies of sophistication, meaning and cultural power. Like Gray, Kelman proved to be a prolific writer, producing four further novels, including the controversial Booker-prize winning *How Late it Was, How Late* (1994) and three further volumes of short stories. Having initially been championed by small Scottish publishers, both Gray and Kelman were subsequently signed up by major London-based companies, a recognition of their importance as writers which also served to give their work greater visibility and status within literary circles.

Meanwhile the idea of a distinctive Scottish cinema was also beginning to emerge, spearheaded by the efforts of Bill Forsyth. In the space of five years, Forsyth wrote and directed four original feature films: *That Sinking Feeling* (1979), *Gregory's Girl* (1981), *Local Hero* (1983) and *Comfort and Joy* (1984), and one television play, *Andrina* (1981), adapted from a short story by George Mackay Brown. Such sustained productivity was extremely unusual at a time when comparatively few films were being made in Britain, let alone Scotland, and this gave Forsyth a very high profile at a critical moment in British cinema history. After almost two decades making sponsored documentaries, Forsyth graduated into the realm of fiction with *That Sinking Feeling*, made on a tiny budget with the help of friends and colleagues and the participation of members of the Scottish Youth Theatre. A wry but essentially light comedy about a group of unemployed Glasgow teenagers who plot a daring heist involving the theft of ninety stainless steel sinks from a plumber's store, the film was well received at the 1979 Edinburgh Film Festival. This in turn helped Forsyth secure proper funding for *Gregory's Girl* from Scottish Television and the National Film Finance Corporation. At £200,000 even this was a very low budget affair, but the success of *Gregory's Girl* served to secure Forsyth's reputation as an innovative and distinctive *auteur* and paved the way for the more overtly commercial *Local Hero*, produced by David Puttnam and featuring Hollywood star Burt Lancaster in a supporting role.

A similar impact was being made in the realm of television drama by John Byrne, who burst onto the scene in 1987 with the BAFTA-winning drama series, *Tutti Frutti*, the tale of the ramshackle Scottish silver jubilee tour of ageing Glaswegian rock 'n' roll band 'The Majestics'. Another jewel in Bill Bryden's crown as head of the BBC Scotland drama department, the series garnered considerable critical acclaim, Hugh Herbert, the television critic of *The Guardian*, going so far as to suggest that *Tutti Frutti* had 'brought Scottish screen drama into the mainstream'.[2] Like Alasdair Gray, John Byrne was a graduate of the Glasgow School of Art who, before he began writing, had gained experience as a graphic artist and a set designer. He had created the innovative 'pop-up' book for the famous Highland tour of 7:84's production of *The Cheviot, the Stag and the Black, Black Oil* in 1973 and the animation sequences for Murray Grigor's irreverent travelogue, *Clydescope* (1974). Byrne's vivid visual sense was to add a further dimension to his subsequent work in theatre and television, but his reputation as a dramatist was secured with the celebrated *Slab Boys* trilogy. Based on his teenage experiences in the late 1950s, these plays convey the lure of American popular culture on the Scottish urban working class, a theme that was to explored further in *Tutti Frutti* and Byrne's other major television work, the drama series *Your Cheatin' Heart*, broadcast in 1990.

## DISAFFECTION AND INTENSITY IN THE FICTIONS OF JAMES KELMAN

In some ways it is James Kelman who provides the most obvious link with the concerns of the previous chapter, sharing with William McIlvanney the desire to render ordinary working-class experience appropriate subject matter for serious literature:

> I wanted to write as one of my own people, I wanted to write and remain a member of my own community … Whenever I did find somebody from my own sort of background in English literature there they were confined to the margins, kept in their place, stuck in the dialogue. You only ever saw them or heard them. You never got into their mind.[3]

But in his uncompromising attachment to realism, Kelman eschews the exceptional and admirable working-class heroes of McIlvanney. Rather, he utilises an intense and searing prose style (that has drawn comparison with Kafka, Beckett and Pinter) to concentrate on what he has termed 'the horror of ordinary life'. The central protagonists of his novels are the damaged and alienated victims of the brutality, fragmentation and indifference of capitalist society. Moreover, their struggle to get by is clearly circumscribed by the impossibility of altering their material or emotional circumstances. There is no residual sense of community, solidarity or of collective resistance that one might find in McIlvanney's novels. Instead Kelman's fictions ironically seem to confirm Margaret Thatcher's notorious claim that 'there is no such thing as society' – albeit in a profoundly negative sense. Consequently, Kelman's vision of working-class reality is distinguished not by retreat into existential dilemmas or creative fantasies, but rather by the endless and banal repetition of everyday events and acts: the rolling of cigarettes, making coffee, betting on horses and dogs, drinking in front of the television. The eponymous protagonist of *The Busconductor Hines* introduced the typical Kelman protagonist. Bored and alienated by a repetitive, monotonous and meaningless job, Rab Hines responds to his poor working conditions by sleeping in, bunking off, missing shifts, breaking rules and being booked by inspectors. While Tammas, the 20-year-old compulsive gambler of *A Chancer*, moves through life in a similarly indeterminate and impulsive manner, his existence is a game of chance and randomness in which fortunes necessarily fluctuate – one moment he can be pocketing considerable winnings, the next scavenging for change from the electric meter – and over which he can exert little or no control.

The desire to unflinchingly represent reality has been a prime motivational factor behind Kelman's innovative approach to language, an achievement hailed by Cairns Craig as a decisive breakthrough in 'the liberation of the voice' in Scottish fiction.[4] This vigorous reassertion of the vernacular in prose asserts 'the right to move without boundaries *between* the vernacular and Standard English, between the demotic and the literary'.[5] In Kelman's novels the relationship between the voice of the narrator and that of his central character is subverted by the erasure of the usual textual markers that conventionally signify such distinctions. Moreover, the narrative voice moves uninhibitedly and almost randomly across a range of positions and registers, from third to first person, from Standard English to demotic speech. The removal of clear markers between registers and perspectives serves to create for Craig a linguistic equality between speech and narration:

> The text, therefore, constructs a linguistic unity that resists the
> fragmentation and isolation that the novels chart as the experience
> of their characters. Unity of voice replaces unity of political or social
> purpose as the foundation of solidarity: the texts *enact* at a linguistic
> level what it points to as an absent world, a communality that
> transcends the absolute isolation of the individual human being.[6]

In this way, Kelman explores the existential substance of humanity in a very different way to McIlvanney. But while the paucity of meaningful choice and freedom may be severely circumscribed, Kelman's characters retain the ability to intellectualise their circumstances in their own terms using their own language. As the author himself stated in an interview with Duncan McLean:

> I don't think it's usual to meet books written from a working class
> experience that is total. Total in the sense that a character can be at the
> same time an intellectual and still be a *bona fide* member of the working
> class.[7]

Kelman's technique is forcefully conveyed in *The Busconductor Hines* in the following passage in which Hines worries about his son's education in a manner that encapsulates a deep understanding of the historical, political and cultural legacy of Glasgow and blatantly refuses to acknowledge a hierarchy of value:

> How d'you fancy a potted history of this grey but gold city, a once
> mighty bastion of the Imperial Mejisteh son a centre of Worldly
> Enterprise. The auld man can tell you about it. Into the libraries you
> shall go. And he'll dig out the stuff, the real mccoy but son the real
> mccoy, then the art galleries and the museums son the palaces of the
> people, the subways and the fucking necropolises, the football parks
> then the barrows on Sunday morning you'll be digging out old books
> and clothes and that ...[8]

But such positive insights are rare and the passage consequently shifts into a
counsel of despair, with Hines becoming increasingly trapped by his anxieties
and perceived failure as a father. As his situation deteriorates both at work and
at home, Hines immerses himself in a rapidly downward spiral of despair,
bordering on madness. This is painfully conveyed through his (often feverish)
interior mental activity, with thoughts going round and round in his head and
concepts endlessly interrogated from a number of angles:

> He had been getting himself into a state; and that is daft getting
> yourself into a state. You sit there getting worse and worse. What is the
> unnameable. That which is not to be articulated. Some things are not
> articulately. A horror of rodents is articulately. But the things that are
> not unnameable to be not said. What about them. They are not good.
> They are not good but must also be good.[9]

Kelman's preoccupation with chronic alienation is revisited in his subsequent
novel, *A Disaffection*, although this time his protagonist – 29-year-old school-
teacher Patrick Doyle – has a middle-class profession and is free from the
material insecurities affecting Robert Hines. Yet Doyle's disaffection is
if anything even more acute, bordering once again on the fringe of mental
illness. Doyle lives alone, a situation which serves to heighten his sense of
failure and loneliness, and his self-loathing is reinforced by his bourgeois
occupation, something he has come to despise as a act of class betrayal:

> Good teacher or bad teacher it made no difference. He was an article
> that was corrupt. He was representative of corruption, representative
> of a corrupt and repressive society which operated nicely and
> efficiently as an effect of the liberal machinations of such as himself,
> corruptio optimi pessima, not that he was approaching the best but just
> a person who had certain tools of the higher-educational processes at
> his command yet persisted in representing a social order that was not
> good and was not beneficent to those who have nothing. What right did
> he have to be treated differently to any member of the fucking

government or polis or the fucking law courts in general who sentence you to prison. Doyle had sold his rights.[10]

In this way Kelman annihilates any residual faith in the egalitarian Scottish myth of social mobility. As a university graduate, Doyle's alienation is given a more overtly intellectual cast than that of Rab Hines. Yet the cultivation of the mind has singularly failed to produce the means by which he can fulfil his potential as a human being. John Kirk observes that the voice of bourgeois hegemony is 'ruthlessly parodied' when Doyle attempts to compare himself to liberal intellectuals like Hegel and Hölderlin, or in the tortuous and feverish debate that goes on in his head following a casually racist remark by his brother Gavin.[11] Indeed, it is suggested that Pat's disaffection ultimately stems from his experience at university, making him complacent and self-satisfied:

> Patrick had stopped being bitter. What it did was just fucking stopped you from doing things. At uni it stopped him from doing things. If he had stopped being bitter he might have done things. What might he have done? He might have done things. Obviously he canni be expected to say what exactly these things are. But there are things he would definitely have done and that means he would not right at this fucking moment be a fucking damn bastarn schoolteacher, one who does fuck all in the world bar christ almighty nothing at all.[12]

Whatever powerful insights this provides into a very real sense of dislocation provoked by social mobility and the gradual erosion of community and belonging within advanced capitalism, one cannot ignore the almost total sense of defeat and desperation that permeates *A Disaffection*. Patrick Doyle may be able to intellectualise his situation in quite perceptive and profound ways, and he even enjoys a brief moment of life-affirming creativity when he enchants his brother's children with his tale of the magical pipes he has found and contemplates playing. But ultimately Doyle proves unable to resolve the contradictions of his predicament in terms of any meaningful action, or, as Ian A. Bell puts it, 'to find a perspective from which to renew himself and his predicament'.[13]

While Kelman's fictional world is unceasingly claustrophobic, confining his characters emotionally, intellectually and geographically, there are occasional glimpses of possible connections to other worlds and experiences however. Despite featuring his most desperate protagonist, an ex-con left blind after a self-inflicted altercation with policemen, *How Late it Was, How Late* signalled a new direction in Kelman's poetics of despair. Sammy Samuels' desperate attempts to regain some kind of meaningful control over what passes for a life are shot through with a pitch-black humour conspicuously lacking in Kelman's previous novels. Moreover, Uwe Zagratzki argues that *How Late it Was, How Late* invokes a blues idiom in that the blues has functioned to provide African Americans exactly the kind of symbolic resistance marking Sammy's predicament.[14] Sammy's blindness allows music to assume particular significance in his experience and consequently the narrative is punctuated with song lyrics, some of which he composes as direct comment on is own situation:

> When Samuels went blind he was thirty-eight
> He was thirty-eight years of age
> And the sun didn't shine
> No that old sun it didn't shine
> Yeh he's going back down the road one more time
> Poor boy
> Going back down the road one more time [15]

This connection with another cultural experience suggests that while Kelman's work may be relentlessly focussed on the specific details of life on the margins in contemporary Glasgow, rendered in a language that explicitly challenges metropolitan cultural hegemony, there is nevertheless an important internationalist impetus in his contemplation of the underdog.

But in the final analysis, the most characteristic aspect of Kelman's *œuvre* remains his intense and unflinching close-ups of the plight of those at the bottom of the heap. While this may provide a more honest analysis of contemporary alienation in Thatcherite Scotland, at the same time his novels offer little hope that poverty, exploitation and despair might be overcome. Rather, Kelman's protagonists remain isolated, rendering them incapable of forging and sustaining meaningful and nurturing relationships with other people as a bulwark against despair. It is consequently difficult to resist the conclusion that whatever his radical innovations in the sphere of language and in the poetics of despair and suffering, Kelman's fiction inevitably comes up against its own self-imposed limitations. As such, it runs the risk of re-animating the festering corpse of self-defeat that for many commentators had proved so debilitating to Scottish culture.

## THE 'LITERARY CATHEDRAL' OF ALASDAIR GRAY

In contrast to Kelman's sober and unflinching realism, Alasdair Gray's fiction has been marked by an imaginative audacity that recovers the creative energy of certain indigenous literary traditions. As Roderick Watson suggests,

*Lanark* 'allowed us to reassess the Scottish penchant for dealing with other realms, mixing metaphysical questions and fantastic inner experience with terror, black bawdry and political satire, all expressed with an extraordinary textual energy'.[16] One of the remarkable characteristics of Gray's debut novel was the sheer scope of its intellectual ambition, and in particular the ways in which it engaged with the big questions of Scottish history, culture and identity. As Douglas Gifford suggests, *Lanark* 'dramatically changed literary creative consciousness', by virtue of the way in which 'it thrust the idea of the entirety of Scotland again to the fore',[17] providing a kind of panoramic point of view in contrast to Kelman's extreme close-ups. The concerns at the heart of *Lanark* are replayed and augmented in Gray's subsequent novel, *1982 Janine* – a highly provocative and insightful rumination on the relationship between sex and politics conveyed via the pornographic fantasies and biographical reflections of a disaffected middle-aged Scotsman during a lone whisky-fuelled night in an anonymous hotel room. Both works share a concern with the experiences of emotionally cold, self-obsessed, sexually frustrated and socially disaffected protagonists struggling to make sense of their place in the world. The life trajectory of both Duncan Thaw and Jock McLeish, the protagonist of *1982 Janine*, is marked by the early loss of a mother and a fraught relationship with a father who identifies with the progressive, if rather naïve, post-war optimism of the welfare state. This contrasts with the son's cynicism, self-pity and negativity which poignantly embody that sense of betrayal and defeat that crystallised in the aftermath of the 1979 referendum defeat.

Both of Gray's novels are also linked through the inventive integration of realism and fantasy. The dual narrative of *Lanark* juxtaposes the realist life story of Duncan Thaw – through his experiences at school and then subsequently at the Glasgow School of Art to his eventually descent into madness and suicide – with the adventures of the lugubrious Lanark within the fantasy city of Unthank. Lanark's narrative functions as both a reincarnation of Thaw, and therefore a continuation of his life, but also as a series of repetitions or echoes that facilitate a richer understanding of the predicaments of both. Thaw and Lanark are essentially loners, characterised by insecurity and arrogance which obstructs their respective struggles to find contentment, love and sexual fulfilment. Both suffer from physical afflictions that are manifestations of deeper psycho-sexual problem – in Thaw's case chronic asthma and eczema, in Lanark's, the condition of 'dragonhide' in which the victim's flesh becomes gradually encased in a hard, armour-like covering. Neither character achieves any real measure of satisfaction in their lives: Thaw's unhappiness leads to insanity and suicide after he has possibly murdered a young woman while in a deluded state, while Lanark's search for sunlight results in only the briefest glimpse of his heart's desire. The fantastical realms of Unthank and the Institute also provide Gray with a means of locating his protagonist within an imaginative metaphor for the destructive effects of global capitalism in the post-war period. Lanark is initially depicted as a brooding intellectual who craves sunlight in the gloomy and perpetually twilight urban hell that is Unthank, before being transported via a huge mouth that opens in the ground to the Institute. In this sanitised bureaucratic domain Lanark is cured of his dragonhide, but quickly comes to perceive the Institute as yet another version of hell, based on a system of horrific exploitation in which the diseased inhabitants of Unthank provide the source of power and sustenance for this subterranean other-world. As Monsignor Noakes, a fellow inhabitant of the Institute, explains:

> Cannibalism has always been the main human problem. When the church was a power we tried to discourage the voracious classes by feeding everyone regularly on the blood and body of God. I won't pretend the clergy were never gluttons, but many of us did, for a while, eat only what was willingly given. Since the institute joined with the council it seems that half the continents are feeding on the other half. Man is the pie that bakes and eats itself and the recipe is separation.[18]

This indictment of the pernicious effects of advanced capitalism is subsequently amplified. Lanark's later return to Unthank finds the city transformed into a high-tech post-industrial metropolis run in the interests of a number of multinational industrial corporations. Over-crowded and politically unstable, Unthank is on the verge of revolution and threatened by massive pollution caused by the waste products of unregulated business. Persuaded by the Provost of Unthank, Lanark travels to the city of Provan to ask for assistance from the all-powerful council. Yet his farcical escapades at the gathering of world leaders reveals the 'Council' – a parody of the United Nations – to be at best an impotent talking shop and at worst yet another apologist for the interests and misdemeanours of big business. His mission ends, predictably, in failure and the novel concludes with Lanark, now an old man, awaiting his death on a hill, while the city of Unthank below is threatened by destruction in an apocalyptic conflagration of fire and flood.

In *1982 Janine*, Gray integrates reality and fantasy in a different way but to similar ends. Over the course of one night, Jock McLeish, a middle-aged, disgruntled alcoholic insomniac, passes the time by indulging in elaborate and misogynist sado-masochistic fantasies featuring a number of fictional and stereotypical characters including the 'Janine' of the title. Jock's fantasies are continually interrupted by repressed memories of his childhood and actual sexual relationships with real women. These are invariably painful recollections of unsatisfactory liaisons, including a protracted and loveless marriage to Helen and a brief but exploitative relationship with his first girlfriend, Denny. After a half-hearted suicide attempt, which results in a round of vomiting and a brief spell of unconsciousness, Jock is forced to face up to his various inadequacies – including his past failures and cruelties – and to take control of his destiny. The sexual fantasies and biographical flashbacks are also interwoven with deliberations on the history of Scotland. Like Jock's fantasy women, the nation is depicted as a willing victim of serial abuse: by English colonial oppression, by American imperialism that has led to the siting of nuclear bases near to Glasgow and by weak-willed and cowardly Scots like Jock himself – ('Scotland has been fucked. I mean that word in the vulgar sense of *misused to give satisfaction or advantage to another*. Scotland has been fucked and I am one of the fuckers who fucked her').[19] Jock is also revealed as a cynical Tory voter who works for a company which has profited greatly from cold war militarisation and economic recession. In this way national self-abuse is located as part of Scotland's historical problem. At one point Jock reflects on the extent of Scottish servility, ironically quoting a verse of Burns' 'A Man's a Man' before musing:

> The truth is that we are a nation of arselickers, though we disguise it
> with surfaces: a surface of generous, openhanded manliness, a surface
> of dour practical integrity, a surface of futile maudlin defiance like
> when we break goalposts and windows after football matches on foreign
> soil and commit suicide on Hogmanay by leaping from fountains
> in Trafalgar Square. Which is why, when England allowed us a
> referendum on the subject, I voted for Scottish self-government.
> Not for one minute did I think it would make us more prosperous, we
> are a poor little country, always have been, always will be, but it would
> be a luxury to blame ourselves for the mess we are in instead of the
> bloody old Westminster parliament. 'We see the problems of Scotland
> in a totally different perspective when we get to Westminster,' a
> Scottish M.P. once told me. Of course they do, the arselickers.[20]

The juxtaposition of this kind of socio-political and historical revelation with Jock's sordid exploitative fantasies and his painful memories of his actual sexual encounters inextricably bind the realms of the personal and the political even more tightly than they are in *Lanark*. At one key revelatory moment, Jock realises just how much he has in common with his fantasy victim 'Janine', both sharing, as George Donaldson and Alison Lee put it, a similar 'ontological space' as 'predictable actors in a script written by job, gender, country and class. Their performances have been measured by their conventionality, by their acceding to subjection by social norms.'[21]

It is only in confronting his shortcomings as a lover and as a man that Jock

McLeish is able to conquer his demons and to move forward positively in his life. The first stage of this is the resolution to resign from his job and with it his direct connection to the structures of oppression he has come to perceive.[22]

In locating the very personalised experiences of his Scottish protagonists within global socio-political forces, Gray's fiction represents a very effective embodiment of Fredric Jameson's concept of cognitive mapping.[23] Jameson draws on the history of map-making, from the diagrammatic construction of travellers' itineraries to the intervention of science that would facilitate the discovery of longitude and with it the ability of relating a specific location to the totalities of the earth's surface and beyond it to the stars. The mimetic limitations of mapping, transferring curved surfaces to flat charts, invokes the representational dimension of cartography, that all maps involve a form of creative distortion. In his theorising of postmodernity, Jameson applies these geographical ideas and insights to the aesthetic analysis of the complexities of contemporary social and political space. In a similar way, Gray's fictions embrace precisely this kind of ambitious link between the local and the global, articulated in terms of a particularly Scottish context. *Lanark* is replete with cartographic references, beginning with the young Thaw's map-making during his adventures in Kinloch Rua, referred to in the enigmatic final address that marks *Lanark*'s death. Thaw's career as an artist also involves a struggle to represent or 'map' the world around him, a process that is forever fraught with difficulties and obstacles. This links Mr Thaw's criticism of his 5-year-old son's representation of the sky as a flat blue line with the adult Thaw's inability to finish various grandiose paintings that constitute quasi-maps of biblical events such as the Creation and destruction of the world from Revelations. Central to this meditation on the problems of representation is the struggle for an all-encompassing perspective, a theme that encapsulates the ambition of Gray's fictional engagement with Scotland. Cairns Craig identifies a double perspective in *Lanark* that is most clearly articulated in the scene where Duncan Thaw contemplates such a reciprocal perspective as he looks out of his friend Aiken Drummond's window:

> From grey rooftops on the left rose the mock Gothic spire of the
> university, then the Kilpatrick hills, patched with woodlands and
> with the clear distant top of Ben Lomond behind the eastward slope.
> Thaw thought it queer that a man on that summit, surrounded by the
> highlands and overlooking deep lochs, might see with a telescope this
> kitchen window, a speck of light in a low haze to the south.[24]

Elsewhere, the painting of the Blackhill locks on the Monkland Canal leads Thaw to invent a double perspective, depicting the structures from both above and below – 'as they would appear to a giant lying on his side, with his eyes more than a hundred feet apart and tilted at an angle of 45 degrees'.[25] This then gives rise to a greater problem, that of framing the subject of the work within a suitably majestic context. Thaw turns to nothing less than the Book of Revelations for inspiration, indicating the scale of his ambitions that recur with the subsequent mural of the Creation, and indeed mirror Gray's own ambitions in the creation of *Lanark* itself. For Craig, the theme of double perspective not only relates the novel fundamentally to the schizophrenic tradition of Scottish writing but also to the problematic relationship between Scottish literature and history:

> We must be inside and outside at the same time: we must live in history and yet with the consciousness of being outside it. It is that desire for the impossible union that creates the double identity of Thaw-Lanark, for Lanark lives out Thaw's art, as Thaw, after his death, is allowed to live on through Lanark's life.[26]

The complexity of perspective is further highlighted by Gray's highly inventive formal technique, in particular his playful approach to narrative, the rich inter-textuality of his works and the self-reflexivity and the conscious manipulations of aesthetic traditions and formal devices.[27] But if this suggests that Gray's work can be labelled postmodernist, then it is in relation to Jameson's understanding of the category 'not as a style but as a cultural dominant',[28] inextricably bound up with the current moment of late capitalism. In other words, the postmodernity of *Lanark* relates to its profound and multi-faceted aesthetic engagement with the historical, the political and the social, rather than in its playfulness and use of pastiche. However, a further aspect of Gray's 'textual energy' is the copious illustrations that form a key component in many of his books. Since leaving Art School in the 1950s, painting had been Gray's primary form of creative expression and livelihood. And this immersion in the visual was to have a major impact on his subsequent literary career, both in terms of the intricate images that adorn the covers and accompany the text of his novels and short stories but also in his imaginative and sometime highly complex uses of typography. The most audacious examples of the latter include the 'epilogue' of *Lanark* and the 'ministry of voices' section in *1982 Janine* where Jock McLeish engages in a complex internal dialogue with a cacophony of voices in his head while attempting suicide.

But if the formal construction of Gray's fictions is complex and textually dense, the language he uses serves to naturalise the, often fantastical, events by way of its apparent but deceptive directness and simplicity. Philip Hobsbaum has argued that Gray's mode 'is similar to that of Defoe ... in that it invokes bizarre experience in a prose that seems ostensibly matter of fact, even, for part of the time, low pressure'.[29] Certainly, the specificity of Gray's language evokes a particularly Scottish view of the world in which the cloak of rationality and certainty masks the underlying complexities, contradictions and irrationalities of emotion and experience. The relationships of both Duncan Thaw and Jock McLeish to their parents and to authority figures in general are governed by such modes of communication. It is no coincidence that those authority figures are frequently versions of the Scottish parish minister or dominie such as Mr McPhedron in *Lanark* or 'mad' Hislop in *Janine*. These repressive Calvinist patriarchs serve to reflect the sense of guilt and shame that lies at the heart of the psycho-sexual complexes that Gray's protagonists suffer so much torment from. This delineation of this anguish is also frequently expressed in a disarmingly matter-of-fact way, as are the numerous humiliations that Thaw, Lanark and McLeish endure. All are victims of serial rejection, most notably Duncan Thaw who is still a virgin when he takes his own life, having been disappointed or wounded by every female he has desired.

But despite their many problems, both Duncan Thaw/Lanark and Jock McLeish are far from hopeless cases. While both use creativity as a refuge or escape from a world in which they are far less adept – Thaw's paintings, McLeish's fantasies – the fact that they are fundamentally imaginative beings provides the potential for such creative agency to be utilised in more productive ways. More than anything else, it marks one of the fundamental differences between Gray's and Kelman's fictions in terms of the potential for change that their respective social and political analyses embody. The allegory in terms of the need to creatively transform Scotland is strikingly obvious here. But the contemplation of creativity in *Lanark* further serves to comment on the making of the work itself. Thaw's story for the school magazine, about a boy who can hear colours, is rejected on the grounds that it is 'a blend of realism and fantasy which even an adult would have found difficult'[30] and is an ironic reference to the structure *Lanark* itself. While the tortuous and protracted painting of the 'Genesis' mural (based on a mural Gray painted in Greenhead Parish Church, Bridgetown, Glasgow, between 1958 and 1962) can be read as an oblique reference to the protracted creation of a novel that Gray had begun back in 1954.

## THE TROUBLE WITH MEN: BILL FORSYTH, JOHN BYRNE AND NEW IMAGES OF SCOTTISH MASCULINITY

The feature films and drama series of Bill Forsyth and John Byrne offer other ways in which the identity, predicament and emotional potential of the Scottish male have been re-imagined in more optimistic, positive and broadly humorous ways. As I have argued elsewhere,[31] Bill Forsyth's films draw upon certain traditions of a post-war European art cinema preoccupied with irony and a brooding obsession with the themes of loneliness, loss and isolation.[32] But these darker elements are overlaid with a wry, comic sensibility, predicated on the acute observation of human foibles which has allowed Forsyth to mock the immaturity and egotism of the Scottish male. Moreover, while concerned with the ordinary and unexceptional, Forsyth's films eschew any overt or traditional sense of working-class culture. With the exception of *That Sinking Feeling* and its back story of unemployment and social deprivation, his films deal with a Scotland that is essentially modern and classless. This is one of the reasons that *Gregory's Girl*, with its modest and apparently unassuming tale of a gawky 16-year-old school boy infatuated with a girl who is also the newest member of the football team, seemed so fresh and vibrant when it appeared in 1981 – just as the socio-economic consequences of Thatcherism were beginning to bite. As John Hill argues, the film posed an important challenge to certain familiar 'reductive' tropes of Scottish identity:

> The way in which *Gregory's Girl* challenges conventional Scottish imagery … is not by seeking to reveal an 'essential' or even distinctive, Scottish identity but by suggesting some of the ways in which 'Scottishness' may be inhabited. Indeed, one of the key sources of pleasure in the film is precisely its play with identities in the form of characters who fail to occupy their social roles in the expected ways. Adults behave like children, children behave like adults, boys behave like girls and girls behave like boys. While this has a certain link with the theme of 'escape' characteristic of British social realism, it is also the case that the desire to escape is not, in this case, motivated by poverty or hardship but by a wish to break free of the fixities of conventional social roles and identities (and especially those of gender).[33]

Forsyth had previously explored the comic potential of gender anxiety in *That Sinking Feeling* through the over-identification one of the gang has with becoming a woman in preparation for his role in the heist as a bogus cleaning lady. But *Gregory's Girl* takes this to a new level, constituting a sophisticated and finely observed study of gender roles and relations in the process. Primarily a study of male adolescent insecurity, the film explores various forms of teenage obsession. These range from Gregory's (John Gordon Sinclair) wistful infatuation with Dorothy (Dee Hepburn), echoed by the painful attempts by Andy and Charlie to chat up practically anything in a skirt, to a number of other exquisite character studies in sublimation featuring the channelling of libidinal energy into infatuations with photography, numbers or, in the case of the wonderfully ambiguous Steve (Billy Greenlees), cookery. While the boys are at the mercy of their hormones, the girls are portrayed as infinitely more knowledgeable, socially competent and self-aware, although just as interested in sex. Indeed, the film's denouement features the skilful manipulation of Gregory by a formidable female conspiracy as he is subtly but firmly diverted away from the crushing disappointment of being stood up by Dorothy, to a joyful date, and potentially serious relationship, with Susan (Claire Grogan). This notion of innate female wisdom even extends to Gregory's 10-year-old sister, from whom he seeks advice on how to deal with courtship rituals, personal grooming and hygiene. The contrived absence of their mother and father renders young Madeline a parental surrogate, magnifying and ridiculing Gregory's insecurity in the process.

Gregory's emotional awkwardness is augmented by his gangly physical appearance, which contrasts with the poise and control that Dorothy has over her body. She also dominates the touchingly naïve sports master, Phil Menzies, ignoring his protests that she can't join the trials for the football team and easily convincing him that she is the best player the school has. Much is made of the essential modernity and positive implications of having a girl play football, including the memorable musing by Eric, the photographer, of a gender-free future in which there will no longer be men or women – 'just a world full of wankers'.[34] Moreover, the contrivance of having a girl rescue the fortunes of the school football team in *Gregory's Girl* suggests a decisive lancing of the boil of national humiliation brought about by the débâcle of the Scottish football team's performance in the 1978 World Cup in Argentina. As such, Forsyth deftly undermines the mythic association between Scottish male potency and 'the beautiful game' in the process.

Male fascination with women as fantasy projections rather than flesh and blood individuals is also central to *Local Hero* and *Comfort and Joy*, suggesting that this is not merely confined to adolescence. A key moment occurs in the latter film when Alan 'Dickie' Bird (Bill Paterson), a Glasgow DJ whose kleptomaniac girlfriend has walked out on him just before Christmas, notices a pretty girl in an ice cream van while stuck in a traffic jam. She returns his smile and when the traffic starts moving again he decides on the spur of the moment to follow the van. This spontaneous action leads not to a romantic liaison, but rather an involvement in a dispute between two rival ice cream vendors. Like the teenage Gregory, Alan, who is in his late thirties, is a vulnerable and confused individual who lacks the insight to understand women and cope successfully with relationships. But rather than wandering around school corridors in a romantic day dream, Bird prowls the streets of Glasgow at dusk in his car like a private investigator from a classic *film noir*, giving his actions a hint of transgression. But Alan is no sexual predator and it is significant that his initial attraction towards the mysterious girl is quickly superseded by a need to mediate in the conflict between 'Mr Bunny' and 'Mr McCool'. In successfully brokering a reconciliation between warring factions of the same Scots-Italian family, Alan comes to terms with his existential crisis and the film ends with him back at work on Christmas Day. However, nothing materially has changed in his life, he still has to face the future without his beloved Maddie, and the final image of him alone at his work in an empty office underscores this fact. The bittersweet conclusion here is that survival depends on an acceptance of circumstances that men like Alan can do very little to alter. In this way *Comfort and Joy* serves to undermine the teenage optimism of *Gregory's Girl* that things will ultimately work out for useless guys because of the superior understanding and agency of women. While this may appear to ignore the real oppression of women by men, Forsyth does present a refreshingly alternative image of contemporary Scottish masculinity and gender relations to McIlvanney or McDougall. It is significant that Alan Bird conspicuously lacks recourse to the accusations of blame, naked aggression or stultifying self-pity of Carl and Willie in *Down Where the Buffalo Go* or Dan Scoular in *The Big Man*. And while Forsyth's female characters remain essentially unknowable, we are always aware that they are images, idealised projections, and that our inability to fully comprehend them is precisely a reflection of the failings of Forsyth's men to do so.

Like the allusions to the Wild West that one can find in Clydesideism, so the slightly sour sub-*noir* elements of *Comfort and Joy* are a reminder of the potent influence of American popular culture on the Scottish imagination. This transatlantic interface has been even more central to the work of John Byrne, and in particular the impact of 'Rock 'n' Roll', as an explicitly American cultural import, on working-class Scottish youth. The genesis of *Tutti Frutti* was Bill Bryden's idea for a drama series based on the story of a veteran Glasgow band, 'the Poets', who had had a chart hit in the 1960s and were still playing club gigs twenty years later. But Byrne used this to fashion a distinctive work in which he could elaborate his own preoccupations. Consequently 'The Majestics' tour that provides the narrative spine of *Tutti Frutti* immediately recalls George 'Spanky' O'Farrell's band in the third *Slab Boys* play, *Still Life*, who similarly trail around the country in a battered old baker's van in the vain hope of fame and fortune. *Tutti Frutti* opens with the funeral of Big Jazza McGlone, lead singer of the re-formed Majestics. McGlone's tragic death in a car crash has thrown the band's planned silver jubilee tour into doubt before it has even begun. But an opportunity to save the day is immediately presented in the shape of Jazza's younger brother Danny (Robbie Coltrane), who arrives at the funeral from self-imposed exile in New York. Danny is not only a musician, he is also his elder sibling's doppelganger, something that immediately triggers an idea in the devious mind of the Majestics' shady manager, Eddie Clockerty (Richard Wilson). Danny joins the band despite the misgivings of the other band members, guitarist Vincent Diver (Maurice Roëves), bassist Frank 'Fud' O'Donnell (Jake D'Arcy) and drummer Bomba McAteer (Stewart McGugan) and their faithful roadie Dennis (Ron Donachie). And so commences a tour of predominantly small and parochial Scottish towns before culminating in the band's 'triumphant' homecoming at the Pavilion Theatre in Glasgow. This is interwoven with a romantic plot line featuring Danny and former fellow art student, Suzi Kettles (Emma Thompson), who decides to accompany the band on tour. Yet within the confines of this orthodox narrative structure, Byrne fashions a drama that has a great deal to say about the state of contemporary Scotland, not least of all in the systematic way in which the national propensity for nostalgia is systematically taken apart.

*Tutti Frutti* replays the defining characteristics of Byrne's theatre work, which as Randall Stevenson notes:

> exploits as entertainment the humour which is a distinctive feature
> of Scottish urban life, in Glasgow especially, while also showing its
> origins in the need to escape from the oppressive monotony of daily
> life. Like their taste for sharp, fashionable clothes, the Slab Boys'
> comic invention and dextrous rhetoric and repartee create a bright,
> stylish surface for lives whose drab actuality they cannot fundamentally
> change.[35]

The members of the Majestics can be read as older versions of the kind of characters who inhabit the plays, retaining their verbal wit and creativity in the face of experience that has served to confirm the grim, mundane realities of life – even for ageing 'rock and rollers'. The most colourful character in this respect is undoubtedly Danny McGlone, who excels in his 'gift of the gab' particularly in his protracted attempts to woo Suzi Kettles. However, Byrne's women are equally adept in the verbal arts, as evinced in Janice Toner's (Katie Murphy) put-down of her louche boss, Eddie Clockerty, as 'a jumped-up haberdasher who thinks a prawn cocktail in a wimpy bar is a pretty lavish introduction to London night life'. Hugh Herbert has suggested that Byrne's 'punning and allusive' verbal style functions in terms of 'a comic chain of small misunderstandings ... dialogue and incident often consist[ing] of a series of accidentally or wilfully missed connections, used in an ironic counterpoint in painful situations'.[36] This distinctive juxtaposition of suffering and farce has been related by Byrne to his own teenage experiences with a mentally unstable and frequently institutionalised mother and the acute mixture of pain and absurdity this often entailed. As Adrienne Scullion has noted, the figure of the mother is as much a 'structuring absence' in *Tutti*

*Frutti.*[37] Danny's status as an 'orphan' is signified almost immediately by the shot of his parents' gravestone during the opening sequence at the funeral of his older brother. The stone immediately informs us that both McGlone parents are dead, the father having passed away in 1958. But more poignant is the close-up on the lower half of the inscription which reads 'Agnes Greenlees Died 1978 Devoted mother to James and Daniel', a palpable sense of loss that is confirmed by Danny at various points in the drama.

Director Tony Smith provides a visual counterpart to the internal dialectics of Byrne's language with his own absurd juxtaposition of muted naturalism punctuated by moments of visual excess. These incursions include the image of the Majestics' blue van in the funeral cortege, the guitar-shaped wreath, Big Jazza's yellow drape coat and Danny's arrival in a light blue suit – splashes of colour which rupture the grey sobriety of the Glasgow Eastern Necropolis, serving a similar emotional purpose to Lanark's constant yearning for sunlight. The band's silver jubilee tour is also set against the dowdiness of such unprepossessing backwater towns as Shotts, Methil and Buckie. These locations provide a very different kind of visual signifier of Scotland's industrial decline to the more familiar and obvious images of massive Clydeside shipyards, enormous rusting factories or the teeming fishing ports of Aberdeen or Peterhead. The refusal to mythologise working-class Scotland by recourse to spectacle presents an alternative image, unfamiliar to the cosmopolitan cognoscenti but all too familiar to the people who live in such unremarkable and under-represented environments and communities. Moreover, it also demonstrates Byrne's moral commitment to exploring and representing the extraordinary nature of the ordinary. The Majestics' concerts, held mainly in unfashionable social clubs or chintzy night clubs, also embody this unsentimentalised commitment to portraying Scottish working-class culture and in particular the lengths people will go to inject a little cheap glamour into their lives.

But the thematic heart of *Tutti Frutti* is Byrne's engagement with the gendering of Scottish culture. In particular, he exposes the failings of certain traditional conceptions of masculinity in order to bury the stereotype of the Scottish 'hard man' once and for all. This is achieved through a subtle exploration of the repertoire of masculinity and the complex relations between men and women. Ken Garner has noted that 'all of Byrne's plays simply use particular, modern environments to illustrate how these worlds create a distinctly male milieu of self-protecting trivial obsessions'.[38] At the heart of *Tutti Frutti* is a narrative tension generated around the figures of Danny McGlone and Vincent Diver. Clad in archetypal black leather and shades, the self-styled 'hard man of Scottish rock', Diver is a hard-drinking, egotistical and ultimately misogynist bully. He cheats on his wife Noreen with impunity, while emotionally manipulating his naïve 22-year-old mistress

Glenna who is only too eager to do his bidding. Vincent is not physically violent to women but he does resort frequently to verbal abuse, berating Noreen for her nagging and at one point chastising Danny for allowing Suzi to berate him with the assertion – 'if Noreen spoke to me like that I'd lamp her one'. Yet, at the same time, Vincent lacks the moral courage to either leave his wife or be open with her about Glenna. And his failure to reciprocate the love and affection given to him by women ultimately wreaks its destructive force, pushing Noreen to take one of her periodic non-fatal overdoses, and Glenna to go one stage further with her death leap into the River Clyde.

The destruction of the redundant model of the Scottish hard man is comically explored by way of the progressive comic damage wrought on the body of Vincent Diver. After burning his hand in episode one, Vincent subsequently head-butts a glass door, is involved in a car crash on the way back to Ardrossan, and is then is stabbed in the throat and testicles by a young woman in Buckie who believes him to be her estranged father. Vincent ends up bandaged, hospitalised (twice), confined to a wheelchair with a neck brace, before being forced to struggle to the Majestics' Glasgow gig on crutches. In this pathetic moment of need he stubbornly refuses the appeals of Noreen to get into her car who retaliates by selecting this moment to inform him that his low sperm count is the real reason why they were never able to have children, not her infertility.[39] This news is the final straw and Vincent slumps to his knees on the pavement, a pathetic figure whose reliance on fantasy is under-lined by his image as younger virile rock 'n' roller appears on countless television screens in a branch of Radio Rentals. But characteristically Vincent demands the last word, his final performance being to douse himself in alcohol before setting himself alight on stage at the band's climactic gig at the Glasgow Pavilion.

Danny McGlone is linked to Vincent in that he also suffers a series of physical knocks including a black eye and a burnt hand, both the result of off-screen incidents. But in contrast to Diver's hard man persona, Danny's masculine bluster and bravado are continually undermined as an act or a front. He may be introduced as a resurrection of his deceased older brother, but Danny ultimately represents a very different kind of masculinity to that personified by Big Jazza (whose notorious drink, drugs and carnal excesses are noted on more than one occasion) and, of course, by Vincent Diver. In this sense Danny can be seen not as the resurrection of his hell-raising brother, but as a reformed version of him: tender, sensitive, considerate and vulnerable. He is someone who has had to take failure on the chin, his time in New York having been spent barely eking out a living by playing piano in clubs and sharing a single room in a junkie-infested building. These qualities are further enhanced by Robbie Coltrane's performance, his large frame serving to emphasise his softness while in Jazza's case it had signified bodily excess.

Danny's relationship with Suzi Kettles is also set up in direct contrast to Vincent's interactions with women, particularly Glenna. Suzi can easily hold her own, making her own decisions, refusing to be lured prematurely into bed by Danny, and encouraging his positive qualities. Yet Suzi has her own problems. Her decision to accompany the Majestics on tour being a useful way of avoiding the unwanted visits paid to her by her violent husband, Stewart, a rich and respectable dentist whose anglicised tones and sadism mark him out as a greater villain than the proletarian Vincent Diver. Stewart's visits involve both physical and sexual abuse and when it is revealed that Suzi is pregnant (a poignant echo of Glenna's hysterical or phantom pregnancy), Danny's reaction is to offer to stand by Suzi and to be a father to the child. This confirms he has the necessary maturity and the commitment, conspicuously lacking on the part of Vincent, to successfully constitute a family. This 'resolution' also suggests a fundamentally new image of Scottish masculinity, based on reciprocation, mutual support and sustenance, and the ability to confront the demons of insecurity and loss.

## RE-IMAGINING GLASGOW

One common element uniting many of the fictions discussed above is a dynamic re-imaging of Glasgow that collectively has helped to transform the stereotypic and reductive 'No Mean City' image that has endured for much of the twentieth century. In a frequently quoted passage from *Lanark*, Duncan Thaw muses on the inadequate way Glasgow has been creatively imagined, remarking to his friend Kenneth McAlpin:

> [T]hink of Florence, Paris, London, New York. Nobody visiting them
> for the first time is a stranger because he's already visited them in
> paintings, novels, history books and films. If a city hasn't been used
> by an artist not even the inhabitants live there imaginatively. What is
> Glasgow to most of us? A house, the place we work, a football park or
> a golf course, some pubs and connecting streets. That's all. No, I'm
> wrong, there's also the cinema and library. And when our imagination
> needs exercise we use these to visit London, Paris, Rome under the
> Caesars, the American West at the turn of the century, anywhere but
> here and now. Imaginatively, Glasgow exists as a music-hall song and
> a few bad novels. That's all we've given to the world outside. It's all
> we've given to ourselves.[40]

While some critics have challenged Thaw's negative assessment, they are united in their praise for the way in which Gray sets out to create precisely the vibrant and imaginative vision of Glasgow that the passage alludes to. In *Lanark* he achieves this by creating a number of Glasgows, from the naturalistic backdrop to Thaw's narrative to the Kafkaesque gloom of Unthank and the radiant modern façade of Provan. Moreover, he locates these imaginary versions of Glasgow within a consideration of the impact of wider economic, political and social forces on the city over the course of the twentieth century through the device of metaphor. The panoramic complexity of the creative interrogation of Glasgow in *Lanark* is highlighted by the various critical responses to the issue. While Dorothy Porter argues that the Victorian city of Glasgow is the primary focus of Gray's temporal and spatial investigation,[41] Ian Spring suggests that the transformed Unthank of Book Four anticipates the myth and reality of the 'new' Glasgow of the 1980s – a city reinvented as the apotheosis of post-industrial chic and cultural heritage.[42] Such a plurality of interpretations is distinct from James Kelman's much more consistent and relentless depiction of Glasgow as a site of despair, isolation and a lack of purpose.

The idea of a 'new Glasgow' as a more modern and cosmopolitan city also permeates the work of both Byrne and Forsyth. In *Tutti Frutti* we are presented with the contrasting images of the grey, cramped proletarian housing estates where the various members of the Majestics live, and Suzi Kettles' bright and spacious West End Victorian tenement flat bedecked with Mackintosh trimmings and art works on the walls. The fact that Danny immediately elects to lodge with her – sleeping in the bath or on the couch – is an important element in his process of reintegration into his native city. His first dates with Suzi are spent in the Burrell Collection at Pollock Park (the second most popular tourist attraction in Scotland after Edinburgh Castle in the 1980s) and Mackintosh's famous Glasgow School of Art building, where they were both previously students. Both sites invoke the spirit of the resurrection of Glasgow as a city of culture. Moreover, the inclusion of the Art School not only recalls its cultural significance in *Lanark*, but the sequence in *Tutti Frutti* even features a panorama of Glasgow shot from the college followed immediately by a reverse angle shot of the college's distinctive architecture on Garnet Hill. The magnificent vista also inspires Danny to come clean about his life in New York, which was considerably less glamorous and rewarding than he had previously suggested, presenting the new Glasgow as an urban environment as potentially inspiring and vital as that of the 'Big Apple'.

Bill Forsyth had made numerous documentary films in, around and even about Glasgow prior to shooting *That Sinking Feeling*, which opens with the humorous disclaimer that the film is 'set in a city called Glasgow which should not be confused with any real town of that name'. But despite the repeated picturesque shots of the city-scape at dusk, the film perpetuates the traditional image of Glasgow as a grim and grimy landscape of tenements, high rise flats and waste ground. It is unsurprising that when one of the characters asks his friends what is their city known for, the replies are: 'drunks' ... 'muggers' ... 'multiple social deprivation'. In sharp contrast, the location of *Gregory's Girl* in the new town of Cumbernauld serves to efface geographical signifiers of class division from this portrayal of contemporary Scotland, presenting a clean and relatively affluent environment distinguished by modern housing, municipal public spaces and, of course, Scottish comprehensive education. The setting of *Local Hero* in an idealised and elemental highland coastal village represented a temporary retreat into a more stereotypical representation of Scotland for mass consumption. But with *Comfort and Joy* Forsyth returned to his native city, presenting it this time as a modern urban space of office blocks and busy freeways. There is also a sense of architectural diversity, Alan Bird's modern flat and his friend Colin's solidly bourgeois detached house contrasting with the meandering low rise schemes where Mr Bunny plies his trade. But as in *Tutti Frutti*, there is a sense of a confident new image of Glasgow emerging, in this case an urban environment that in many ways resembles a contemporary North American city, an association reinforced by Alan's tendency to drive everywhere.

Individually and collectively, the works of Kelman, Gray, Byrne and Forsyth opened up a range of fresh approaches and aesthetic strategies for the representation of Scotland and the creative engagement with contemporary experience. Moving beyond the limitations associated with the veneration of the urban, proletarian hard man, they not only focused in more honest ways on masculine vulnerability, but they also offered a range of different kinds of cultural analysis in the process: from Kelman's intense and empathetic dissection of everyday despair, to Gray's playful and profound contemplation of Scotland's place within historical, economic, political and social forces, Byrne's celebration of the restorative properties of popular culture and sharp verbal wit to Forsyth's wry and ironic contemplation of the shortcomings of the male psyche. Taken together, their various novels, films and television dramas give real substance to Angus Calder's invocation of the unleashing of a Carnivalesque creative energy in Scottish cultural production that dissolved the boundary between high and low culture and celebrated the virtues of participation, inclusiveness and diversity.[43] In offering an alternative sense of national identity based on a new-found confidence and sense of purpose, Alasdair Gray, John Byrne, James Kelman and Bill Forsyth were also to provide an inspiration for those new Scottish writers and film-makers who were to follow in their wake.

## NOTES

1. Anthony Burgess, *Ninety-nine Novels: The Best in English Since 1939* (London: Alison & Busby, 1984), p. 126.
2. Hugh Herbert, 'Tutti Frutti', in George W. Brandt (ed.), *British Television Drama in the 1980s* (Cambridge: Cambridge University Press, 1993), p. 191. The success of the series is also reflected in the fact that it was repeated on BBC2 within a year.
3. James Kelman, 'The Importance of Glasgow in My Work', in *Some Recent Attacks: Essays Cultural and Political* (Stirling: AK Press, 1992), p. 81.
4. Cairns Craig, *Out of History: Narrative Paradigms in Scottish and British Culture* (Edinburgh: Polygon, 1996), p. 193.
5. Ibid. p. 194.
6. Ibid. pp. 103–4.
7. Duncan McLean, 'James Kelman Interviewed', in Murdo MacDonald (ed.), *Nothing Is Trivial: An Anthology of Writing From* Edinburgh Review (Edinburgh: Edinburgh University Press, 1995), p. 111.
8. James Kelman, *The Busconductor Hines* (Edinburgh: Polygon, 1984), p. 90.
9. Ibid. p. 100.
10. James Kelman, *A Disaffection* (London: Secker and Warburg, 1989), p. 303.
11. John Kirk, 'Figuring the Dispossessed: Images of the Urban Working Class in the writing of James Kelman', *English*, vol. 48, no. 191, Summer 1999, p. 114.
12. James Kelman, *A Disaffection*, p. 53.
13. Ian A. Bell, 'Imagine Living There: Form and Ideology in Contemporary Scottish Fiction', in Susanne Hagemann (ed.), *Studies in Scottish Fiction, 1945 to the Present* (Frankfurt: Peter Lang, 1996), p. 231.
14. See Uwe Zagratzki, '"Blues Fell This Morning": James Kelman's Scottish Literature and Afro-American Music', *Scottish Literary Journal*, Spring 2000, vol. 27, no. 1.
15. James Kelman, *How Late it Was, How Late* (London: Secker & Warburg, 1994), p. 119.
16. Roderick Watson, 'Maps of Desire: Scottish Literature in the Twentieth Century', in T. M. Devine and R. J. Finlay (eds), *Scotland in the 20th Century* (Edinburgh: Edinburgh University Press, 1996), pp. 285–6.
17. Douglas Gifford, 'Imagining Scotlands', in Hagemann (ed.), *Studies in Scottish Fiction*, p. 33.
18. Alasdair Gray, *Lanark: A Life in Four Books* (Edinburgh: Canongate Publishing, 1981), p. 101.
19. Alasdair Gray, *1982 Janine* (London: Jonathan Cape, 1984), p. 137.
20. Ibid. pp. 65–6.
21. George Donaldson and Alison Lee, 'Is Eating People Really Wrong? Dining With Alasdair Gray', in *The Review of Contemporary Fiction*, vol. 15, no. 2, Summer 1995, p. 157.
22. This advocacy of purposeful action on both a personal and national level is also forcibly articulated in Gray's familiar slogan, 'Work as if you were in the early days of a better nation'.
23. Fredric Jameson, *Postmodernism: or, the Cultural Logic of Late Capitalism* (London: Verso, 1991), p. 51.
24. Alasdair Gray, *Lanark*, p. 275.
25. Ibid. p. 279.
26. Cairns Craig, '"Going Down to Hell is Easy": *Lanark*, Realism and the Limits of the Imagination', in Robert Crawford and Thom Nairn (eds), *The Arts of Alasdair Gray*

(Edinburgh: Edinburgh University Press, 1991), p. 104.

27. Nowhere is this more concentrated than in the 'epilogue' of *Lanark* in which our hero confronts a comic version of Gray as author-god, and in which we are presented with a list of the plagiarisms embedded in the novel (some of which are bogus) and a series of footnotes denoting another textual intervention this time calling into question some of the assertions made by the author in his heated discussion with his creation.

28. Fredric Jameson, *Postmodernism: or, the Cultural Logic of Late Capitalism*, p. 4.

29. Philip Hobsbaum, 'Alasdair Gray: The Voice of His Prose', in *The Review of Contemporary Fiction*, vol. 15, no. 2, Summer, 1995, p. 149.

30. Alasdair Gray, *Lanark*, p. 155.

31. Duncan Petrie, *Screening Scotland* (London: BFI, 2000), pp. 153–8.

32. These qualities are analysed by Allan Hunter, 'Bill Forsyth: The Imperfect Anarchist', in Eddie Dick (ed.), *From Limelight to Satellite* (London: BFI/SFC, 1990).

33. John Hill, *British Cinema in the 1980s* (London: BFI, 1999), p. 243.

34. A comic line to be subsequently incorporated by screenwriter John Hodge into the film version of *Trainspotting* (1996).

35. Randall Stevenson, 'In the Jungle of the Cities', in R. Stevenson and Gavin Wallace (eds), *Scottish Theatre Since the Seventies* (Edinburgh: Edinburgh University Press, 1996), p. 107.

36. Hugh Herbert, 'Tutti Frutti', in Brandt (ed.), pp. 184–5.

37. Adrienne Scullion, 'Feminine Pleasures and Masculine Indignities', in Christopher Whyte, *Gendering the Nation* (Edinburgh: Edinburgh University Press, 1995).

38. Ken Garner, 'Do Not Adjust Your Set', *The Listener*, 28 January 1988, p. 27.

39. John Byrne, *Tutti Frutti*, episode six, 'A-Wop Boppa Loo Bop, A-Wop Bam Boom ...'.

40. Alasdair Gray, *Lanark*, p. 243.

41. Dorothy Porter, 'Imagining a City', *Chapman*, no. 63, Spring 1991, p. 46.

42. Ian Spring, *Phantom Village: The Myth of the New Glasgow* (Edinburgh: Polygon, 1990), pp. 98–100.

43. Angus Calder, 'Introductory: Culture, Republic and Carnival', in *Revolving Culture: Notes from the Scottish Republic* (London: I. B. Tauris, 1993), p. 9.

# CHAPTER 3

# Broadening the Cultural Franchise

## INTRODUCTION

The elision of Scottish identity with working–class masculinity in the sphere of cultural representation frequently resulted in the political and economic tensions of the early 1980s being portrayed as a systematic assault on the values of an indigenous way of life by forces that were coded foreign, hier-archical, bourgeois and feminine. While some writers and film-makers responded to the consequences of change primarily through a negative prism of loss and confusion, others attempted to analyse the roots of the crisis as a consequence of internal complacency as much as of external assault. But despite displaying a welcome sensitivity to questions of gender relations, the predominant focus of the works of Alasdair Gray, John Byrne and Bill Forsyth was still very much on the trials and tribulations of men, with women still primarily consigned to the realm of 'otherness'. This depressingly one-sided tendency seemed to both accept and reflect the broader proposition that Scotland remained a more patriarchal society than England, a conclusion apparently confirmed by various data relating to occupational segregation, wage differentials, family demographics, educational attainment and political representation over the past century.[1] Or as S. J. Boyd puts it:

> The history of Scotland, in life and letters, is the history of a
> thoroughgoing Patriarchy. Even in the sphere of religion it is
> noteworthy that Calvinism ditched the Blessed Virgin Mary (an
> unofficial female deity in the Catholic world and generally more
> popular than her more distinguished relations), leaving us with only
> a stern judgmental father-figure whose avatars are omnipresent in
> Scottish literature.[2]

This state of affairs has been exacerbated by a historical tendency to ignore or undervalue the female contribution to the various arenas that constitute the public sphere, with women being consigned to the marginalised realms of domestic labour and child rearing.[3] Consequently the very real contribution made by women to, for example, political activity in Scotland has been considerably under-estimated. While the feminised realm of the domestic sphere – a site of consumption, leisure, creativity and the nurturing and restoration of self – has assumed an unprecedented importance in post-industrial society.

The masculine bias inherent in dominant cultural representations of Scotland began to be seriously questioned in the aftermath of 1979. In one important article, Carol Anderson and Glenda Norquay revealed the alarming extent of male domination, noting that the 'apparent absence of women is not even confined to the traditionally masculine preserves of criticism and political analysis, but extends to the more accessible area of creative writing'.[4] Anderson and Norquay trace this state of affairs back to the inter-war Scottish literary renaissance and in particular to the reaction against the Kailyard, which opposed the feminised values of the 'cabbage patch' with those of an aggressive intellect, virile and predominantly masculine. This version of Scottishness, which finds its epitome in the tropes of Clydesideism, is rooted in male comradeship, the football match, the pub and an exaggerated use of Scots vernacular, emphasising a no-nonsense and vigorous masculine attitude to which women have no legitimate recourse. Yet such an appeal to masculinity has been rendered anachronistic by changing sex roles in modern society. Consequently the tenacity of such an outmoded perspective in the face of real social change is ultimately related by Andrerson and Norquay to Beveridge and Turnbull's 'inferiorisation' thesis, by which 'colonised' Scots continue to over-invest in a masculine version of Scottish national identity in opposition to a feminised Englishness. This in turn has inevitable consequences for the gendering of Scottish culture:

> If men need to see Scottishness in terms of virility, they must also find
> a role for women in their schema. As a correlative to their own actively
> masculine identity, women are seen as objects which romantically
> symbolise the nation. In this role women are inevitably constrained.
> In seeking his own identity, therefore, the male Scot contributes to the
> process of women's inferiorisation.[5]

This is supported by David McCrone's assertion that the project of giving voice to the distinctive and self-contained essence of a Scottish national culture had consistently relegated women to mere guardians of the moral and family values of the nation:

> It is ... no coincidence that those identities diagnosed as archetypically
> Scottish by friend and foe alike – the Kailyard, Tartanry and

Clydesideism – have little place for women. ... there is no analogous
'lass o' pairts'; the image of Tartanry is a male-military image (and kilts
were not a female form of dress); and the Clydeside icon was a skilled,
male worker who was man enough to 'care' for his womenfolk.[6]

Such marginalisation frequently serves to obscure significant achievements
within cultural production. As various critics have pointed out, there is an
important if somewhat neglected tradition of Scottish women's writing which
includes such figures as Catherine Carswell, Rebecca West, Nan Shepherd,
Willa Muir, Naomi Mitchison, Jessie Kesson, Muriel Spark and Liz
Lochhead.[7] This in turn has provided an important historical context for
considering the emergence of a new generation of Scottish women writers in
the 1990s that served to complement and broaden the creative and insightful
engagement with contemporary Scotland initiated by their male counterparts.

The respective domains of Scottish television drama and cinema have
proved more resolutely male, however, with female writers and directors
conspicuous by their absence. Moreover, works for both large and small screen
that did focus on female experience by and large tended to reinforce the
connections between women, landscape and elemental forces and the past.[8]
The situation began to change in the 1990s however. In television the
watershed was the appointment in 1994 of Andrea Calderwood, an ambitious
but relatively inexperienced young producer, as the new Head of Drama at
BBC Scotland. This initiated a period of female ascendancy within the department, confirmed when Calderwood was succeeded by Barbara McKissack.
Calderwood was to play a key role in the development of the career of Scottish
film-maker Lynne Ramsay, now regarded as one of the most exciting and
visionary writer/directors in British cinema. However, it is salutary to
recognise that Ramsay's 1999 debut, *Ratcatcher*, was only the second Scottish
feature film to be written and directed by a woman, following veteran
documentarist Margaret Tait's sole foray into fiction, *Blue Black Permanent*,
in 1992.[9] But the increase in production activities in the 1990s, particularly in
the field of short films, has created opportunities for a number of young
Scottish female directors, writers and producers, promising a greater diversity
of voices and representations in the future.

## A NEW FEMALE PRESENCE IN SCOTTISH LITERATURE

The arrival of a vibrant new female presence in Scottish writing was marked
by the emergence of two writers who, in their own distinctive ways, were to
become as significant as the 'arrival' of Gray and Kelman a decade earlier. In
their novels and short stories, Janice Galloway and Alison Louise (A.L.)

Kennedy addressed the experiences, problems, hopes and fears of women from a perspective that was unequivocally contemporary and urban. Galloway was the first to appear with her debut novel, *The Trick Is to Keep Breathing*, published by Polygon in 1989. This uncompromising work tackles head-on the question of damaged female identity through the travails of Joy Stone, a young drama teacher in the midst of a breakdown following the accidental death of her lover in a drowning accident on holiday. Joy's loss is compounded by her personal circumstances, which are circumscribed by questions of gender and power. Her dead lover Michael, a fellow teacher, was married with children and had only recently left his family to move into a flat on a run-down council estate with Joy. But as the lease was in Michael's name, Joy now has to deal with the possibility of eviction. Her insecurities are exacerbated further by the fact that her best friend Marianne has moved to America. Moreover, those significant others who remain are either unable to provide the support and understanding she requires – Marianne's mother, Ellen, her teenage lover, David – or are more intent on exploiting her vulnerability – her bullying 'sister', Myra, Tony, the lecherous boss from the bookies where Joy works on a Saturday. Consequently, Joy's attempts to reassert some control over her rapidly disintegrating life are manifested in various forms of compulsive and self-destructive behaviour, and before long finds herself being referred to a psychiatric hospital.

The intense interiority and sense of anguish conveyed in *The Trick Is to Keep Breathing* is coupled with the kind of obsessive attention to detail that also characterises James Kelman's fiction, suggesting a shared commitment to rendering often ignored aspects of everyday reality. As Galloway herself has noted:

> I enjoy fiction that asks me to look at where I am in the world. It's the kind I write too. I don't feel I'm addressing *issues*, I feel I'm looking at everything. My job is to go out there and be very honest about what I bring as well. I let my protagonists encounter things that to me are real – as felt – as possible.[10]

Alone in her barely furnished council flat, desperately attempting to salvage any scraps of self-worth from the deluge of loathing that has overcome her, Joy Stone's predicament recalls the similar plight of Kelman's damaged male characters. Yet while certain aspects of her circumstances resemble that of fellow teacher Patrick Doyle, the ways in which Joy's struggle for identity and meaning are manifest are largely determined by her gender. There is no male equivalent in Kelman of the anorexia and bulimia that exacerbate Joy's mental and physical deterioration, no corollary of the abusive relationship with Tony or of the uncertainties of the relationship with Myra who may actually be her mother rather than her sister. And there is certainly no equivalent systematic negation that Joy experiences, culminating in the devastating sermon at Michael's memorial service:

THOUGH THE SORROW IS
UPPERMOST IN OUR HEARTS. AS
WE CLOSE, LET US THINK OF
WHAT MICHAEL FISHER
BROUGHT TO OUR LIVES. BUT
MORE ESPECIALLY IN THESE
MOMENTS OF SILENCE

> and his arms began to
> Stretch out towards the front
> rows

EXTEND OUR SYMPATHIES, OUR
HEARTS AND OUR LOVE

> the arms stretching further
> like Jesus commanding
> Lazarus

ESPECIALLY OUR LOVE

> a split-second awareness that
> something terrible was about
> to about to
> > happen

TO HIS WIFE AND FAMILY

Half-way into the silence for Norma Fisher, my arms were weightless. The rest came piece meal as the moral started to compute.

1. The Rev Dogsbody had chosen this service to perform a miracle.
2. He'd run time backwards, cleansed, absolved and got rid of the ground-in stain.
3. And the stain was me.

I didn't exist. The miracle had wiped me out.[11]

Such a systematic erasure of self, which is manifest in various aspects of Joy's behaviour, can only be seen in relation to the operations of a social system where the identity of 'mistress' has a similar meaning and value to that of 'prostitute'.

The typographical construction of the above extract also demonstrates the creative way in which Galloway uses textual devices to reinforce and illustrate the ideas, feelings and experiences explored in her prose. This experimentation has been related by more than one critic to the influence of Alasdair Gray[12] and in particular to his own vivid tale of psychic dissolution, *1982 Janine*. Like Gray, Galloway utilises a variety of typographical devices to convey the fragmentation of Joy Stone's self. These include the use of italics for the sections dealing with Michael's death; intermittent bits of text that bleed and disappear into the margins of the page; the lists, letters and extracts from magazines and the dialogues with doctors and other authority figures that are presented in script form. For Cairns Craig the babble of extraneous discourses that pervade Joy's world serve to:

> both displace and substitute for any assertion of her own identity. Joy, whose body is withering in anorexia and who has ceased to menstruate, has become a tissue of other people's discourses, her own voice barely registered, left outside the body of the text and 'bleeding' into the silence beyond its boundaries.[13]

But against the odds Joy does begin towards the end of the novel to re-establish some tentative control over her life and she is spurred on by a new sense of purpose. *The Trick Is to Keep Breathing* ends with Joy at home alone. But in sharp contrast to the opening scene of her sitting alone in a cold dark room, this time the central heating is on, the Christmas tree lights are shining brightly and she has a glass of whisky in her hand. She ponders learning to swim as a metaphor for re-entering life: 'I'm gawky, not a natural swimmer. But I can read up a little, take advice. I read somewhere the trick is to keep breathing, make out it's not unnatural at all.'[14] This leads to Joy uttering the magic words, 'I forgive you', a final acknowledgement both of herself and of the self-harm she has inflicted. This small victory is a vital acknowledgement of self, a necessary precursor for Joy to begin the arduous task of rebuilding her identity as a woman and as a human being.

Galloway's second novel, *Foreign Parts* (1994), continues the focus on insecurity and identity but by shifting the focus to the question of female friendship. Cassie and Rona are two women in their early forties on a motoring holiday in France. Armed with a guidebook for travellers on a low budget, the two tour around the towns and countryside of Normandy and the Loire valley but conspicuously fail to connect with the proscribed experience conveyed in the guide. Rather, their journey becomes a confrontation of their failure as tourists and – in the case of the less assured Cassie – as human beings: 'We are neither real nor proper: just fraudulent moochers in other people's territory, getting by on the cheap.'[15] It is from Cassie's perspective that the narrative is constructed, although the prose oscillates between first and third person in a technique that once again recalls Kelman. The women's experiences in France are also punctuated by Cassie's memories of previous holidays with her first long-term boyfriend, Chris – a relationship marked by a gradual erosion of her sense of self – and with subsequent lovers. Paralleling the recalled demise of the relationship with Chris is the developing connection between Cassie and Rona. They have also been on holiday a number of times together in recent years and share a strong bond of mutual affection. At times Cassie's feelings for Rona seem to hint at erotic attraction, but this appears to be motivated more by curiosity than some kind of profound revelation about Cassie's sexuality. Towards the end of the holiday the two get drunk and discuss past relationships, living without men, missing sex and the social- isation process that ensures the reproduction of heterosexual relationships despite gender antagonism. Finally, Cassie plucks up the courage to make a bold, if not entirely unexpected, proposition:

> The paint on the ceiling throbs through the gloom. I watch it pulsing, feeling my own heartbeat in my wrists, my mouth opening and closing no reason I am aware of. And I hear my own voice saying
>
> You know what we could do Rona?
>
> We could make a go of it ourselves. Look after each other. A big flat on the Southside maybe: one with corniced ceilings, a tiled close and a drying green. Imagine. Cut costs, save fuel, half the time you spend washing up; enjoy stimulating conversation and witty exchange at any time of the day or night with an in-house companion. What d'you think Rona?
>
> Rona?
>
> The horrible stillness knows I have gone too far. Waiting for an answer that does not come.
>
> Rona?
>
> A mild rasping noise, like a drill several streets away. Only it is night and there are no workmen. The mild rasping noise repeating in lungfuls. I look over. Rona leans against the wall, propped up in the candlelight. Snoring.[16]

Despite this failure to fully connect, the final scene on the beach looking out over the English Channel does signal a possible new beginning when the friends meet a young Algerian student who asks Cassie if Rona is her sister: 'she looks at me, I look at her. Oui, I say. Ma sœur'.[17] The novel subsequently ends with the two women embracing – a quiet, brief moment as powerful in its own way as Joy Stone's moment of personal forgiveness – before they resume the business of skiffing stones into the sea.

In a particularly insightful analysis of Galloway's writing, Glenda Norquay identifies the term 'bricolage' – one of the first foreign signifiers Cassie and Rona encounter after arriving in France – as an appropriately rich metaphor for exploring the essence of Galloway's technique as 'a writer who explores states of brokenness and fragmentation'[18] primarily through the technique of fractured narratives. Norquay suggests that to take apart a narrative also implies an attendant process of reconstruction, which alludes to the restorative and essentially positive aspect of Galloway's often painful explorations of female identity. In addition to providing a metaphor for the building of a new text from fragments, bricolage also means 'rough repair', which is equally appropriate to Galloway in that her fictions bring about such an effect at the level of central protagonists who are in the process of finding new meaning. Third, the metaphor also alludes to the reworking of cultural meanings, and in particular the remaking of myths of gendered and national identities which Galloway negotiates in both *The Trick Is to Keep Breathing* and *Foreign Parts*. It is this sense of thematic complexity and aesthetic sophistication that gives Galloway's fiction its insight into the substance of women's lives and the subtle operations and negotiation of various structures of power and inequality that continue to define contemporary existence.

The question of female subjectivity is also at the heart of A. L. Kennedy's major works of fiction which, like Galloway's, are often concerned with personal journeys of rediscovery – while contemplating more overtly the lineaments of desire and identity. After first catching the attention of readers and critics with her 1990 collection of short stories, *Night Geometry and the Garscadden Trains*, the Dundee-raised Kennedy subsequently moved to Glasgow, and the city came to assume a significant place in much of her work, although often more obliquely than in Galloway's fiction. But arguably the most distinctive aspect of Kennedy's writing lies in the insightful and challenging ways in which she is prepared to tackle the complexities and contradictions in relationships between women and men, or as Alan Freeman puts it, 'the struggle to construct and sustain the human subject in contemporary life'.[19] Her explorations of female identity, in an often unequal and unforgiving world, consistently find meaning in what often appear as strange, extreme or controversial relationships, arrangements and situations. These meditations are rendered in a complex prose style frequently characterised by the carefully directed use of free indirect speech and thought. Kennedy facilitates intimate access to her characters' interior thought processes, while simultaneously drawing attention to the constructed nature of the writing through the utilising of certain self-reflexive narrative techniques. The result is a more illusive or flamboyant prose style than Galloway, in which the creative imagination of protagonists achieves a new level of significance.

Kennedy's first novel, *Looking for the Possible Dance* (1993), explores a number of different problematic relationships with men negotiated by the novel's central protagonist Margaret Hamilton. The significant others include an emotionally demanding boyfriend, a lecherous and spiteful boss, and (most interestingly) an adored and adoring father. Margaret's dilemma concerns the intertwined problems of coming to terms with the death and memory of the father who raised her after her mother left when she was a baby, and of fully committing herself to Colin, whom she seems to genuinely love but pushes away when his emotional needs become too great. The narrative is structured around a series of elliptical flashbacks as Margaret travels from Glasgow to London in a journey that begins as an opportunity to escape from the double blow of losing both job and boyfriend in quick succession. On the train she strikes up a connection with James Watt, a crippled boy or man of indeterminable age, an encounter that leads her to reassess her options and own emotional needs. Consequently, on arriving at Euston station she immediately calls Colin to tell him she will be back on Friday, marking a major decision to repair a relationship that had apparently fallen apart and to return to a injured lover (crippled in his own way by a violent encounter with a vicious loan shark who has him nailed to floor) whose needs for the first time are manifestly greater than hers.

The intensity of Margaret's relationship with her father is signified in the opening scene outside a Methodist dance hall in which he urges Margaret not to waste her life as he has done, and that finding a way to live – the 'possible dance' of the title – is what is really important. As a child, Margaret experiences a direct contrast between the warmth, love and reassurance provided by her father and an experience of school that is depicted in typically Calvinist terms as an institution for brutalising children into accepting their place in the social order. Later she recalls the intensity and exclusivity of the bond with her father which forced her to keep her relationship with Colin a secret. This is prompted as much by Margaret's own sense of responsibility and duty to her father rather than by any intimations of jealousy or attempts to regulate his daughter's life on his part however. Dorothy MacMillan argues that one of Kennedy's great achievements in creating this relationship is that 'the proper physicality of the love between a father ("daddy") and daughter is conveyed without embarrassment or excess'.[20] At one point Margaret recalls a moment when her father came into her bedroom:

'Princess? There's my Princess. You asleep?'
    He was whispering so low that Margaret could barely hear him and she could tell that he was really speaking to himself. He let a path of light into her room, walked forward and the closed it off behind him. He came over gently to let his weight tug down one side of the bed. She didn't move, didn't open her eyes, knowing that he wanted her to be there, but nothing else. That was nice in a way; not as good as talking, but nice.[21]

The passage also hints at Margaret's father's own deep emotional needs and investment in the relationship, something which later comes to the surface when, on learning that Margaret intends to return to England after finishing university, he breaks down in tears and pleads with her to stay. This is also the only moment when he vents anger and bitterness at having been abandoned by his wife and left with the responsibility of bringing up his daughter alone – 'She didn't die, she fucking left me. Did you think I would tell you that? Your mother was a fucking slut? She ran away the first chance she got because I was no bloody good?[22] Such vulnerability has also engendered a heavy emotional responsibility on his daughter:

> He always did such nice things for her, but still kept that place inside him that stayed beyond her reach. She couldn't stop him being lonely, or pacing his bedroom floor, waiting for something she didn't understand to appear along the line. She hadn't helped him with that, or with much else. A bit of a useless daughter, really, if she thought about it.[23]

Kennedy revisited the terrain of fathers and daughters in her screenplay for the 1997 feature film *Stella Does Tricks*, directed by Coky Giedroyc, which draws in part on an earlier short story, 'Friday Payday' published in the 1995 collection *Now That You're Back*. This time, however, the focus is parental abuse: protagonist Stella being a teenage Scottish prostitute in London who has exchanged life with her father in Glasgow for an equally exploitative surrogate relationship with her domineering middle-aged pimp, Mr. Peters. But while the narrative premise may appear to fall back on a more lurid perspective on an overly close father/daughter bond, the film is not without its own subtleties and surprises. As in *Looking for the Possible Dance*, Stella's relationship with her father Francis, a third-rate stand-up comedian, is conveyed through a series of flashbacks, which reveal a great deal of ambivalence involving memories of both fondness and revulsion. In contrast to his puritanical sister Aileen, Francis is shown to be a loving and indulgent parent who helps to nurture Stella's own vivid imagination. But he is also manipulative and nasty, most chillingly rendered in the imaginary sequence in the church where from the pulpit he launches into a stand-up routine which involves an account of her own daughter's rape. The site of the sexual abuse is Stella's father's pigeon loft, an almost surreal structure reminiscent of a fairy tale tower which turns out to be more of a prison. However, Stella does enact her own revenge by setting fire to the tower, dressed in fairy wings and carrying a magic wand, in a symbolic reclamation of her childhood innocence. The recourse to fantasy provides the older Stella with a means of both dealing with the complexities of the past but also of maintaining a space beyond the control of Peters. As Charlotte Brunsdon notes, her 'imagination, is her most significant attribute, and through giving Stella the ability to fantasise the film seems to figure her as enunciator, and attempts to break with the tradition of naturalist representation of the prostitute as victim'.[24]

Fantasy is used in a particularly innovative and audacious manner in Kennedy's second novel, *So I Am Glad*, published in 1995. This work ostensibly returns to familiar territory in featuring a central female protagonist who is experiencing problems with forming relationships. Jennifer Wilson, a Glaswegian radio announcer, uses sex as a way of avoiding real intimacy in her life, including a penchant for sado-masochistic practices with her previous boyfriend Steven. She even muses on her reputation thus:

> You should be aware of my principal characteristic which I choose
> to call my calmness. Other people have called it coldness, lack of
> commitment, over-control, a fishy disposition. I say that I'm calm,
> a calm person, and usually leave it at that.[25]

Jennifer admits to being emotionally empty and has chosen to live quietly in a shared flat with three strangers. The reasons for her predicament are gradually revealed to reside in certain traumatic childhood experiences with parents who argued and had boisterous sex in front of their daughter, forcing her to retreat into herself as a coping strategy. But the audacious twist in the novel is provided by Kennedy's solution to Jennifer's problems. A mysterious stranger turns up in the flat who seems to have lost his memory and has no idea why he is there or where he has come from. Even more intriguing to Jennifer is his strange appearance:

> The kitchen is really quite gloomy by this time and it should be
> difficult to see Martin, but in fact he is far more visible than he has any
> right to be. When he opens his mouth for any length of time there is a
> pale gleam which reminds me insanely of the light from a self-sealing
> envelope if you peel it apart in the dark. An unnatural, static blue flash.
> His hands and face are simply burning.
> That's exactly what he looks like. But with a silver burning, a
> chemical flame, fluctuating in and out of colour, running like mercury
> and then disappearing into air. When he moves, shadows boil away
> from him, they roll under the furniture, hiding from his hands.[26]

The mystery man begins to recover his memory and reveals himself to be none other than the seventeenth-century French soldier, philosopher and poet, Savinien de Cerano de Bergerac. Despite the audacity of the claim, Jennifer chooses to believe the stranger and gradually begins to relax and to let down her guard as the relationship between them begins to develop. The inevitable consummation is postponed due to various twists in the plot, and when they do finally admit to their feelings and have sex, this is rendered in very elusive terms – 'we stayed in the room in the big house and were full of finding out'.[27] But while Jennifer discovers new meaning in her life, Savinien's sense of temporal and cultural displacement becomes intensified and as the problems of reconciling different codes of conduct from different places in different centuries begins to take its own toll he has an urge to return home to France. In Paris Savinien seeks out traces of his past and his writings in various antiquarian books and in the Bibliothèque Nationale before returning to the town where he originally died being swallowed up by the ground.

The audacious deployment of fantasy, within an otherwise realist depiction of contemporary urban life and emotional problems, gained *So I Am Glad* a great deal of critical praise. Sarah M. Dunnigan argues that while Kennedy's *œuvre* concerns 'the emotionally and politically disenfranchised and dis-possessed, it also aims to discover the means of (re) enchantment'.[28] While Moira Burgess concludes her historical survey of Glasgow in fiction with an enthusiastic endorsement of Kennedy's literary achievements as nothing less than the introduction of magic realism to the Glasgow novel.[29] As with Alasdair Gray, this expansive use of the powers of the imagination to shed new light on the contemporary human condition is augmented and reinforced by an innovative approach to narrative construction. *So I Am Glad* takes the form of a self-reflexive first-person account in which Jennifer addresses the reader directly in a playful yet confessional style, which also makes references to the account she is herself writing. This involves not just flashbacks but also anticipated developments in the narrative yet to transpire, the deliberate concealment of certain information, and the downplaying of aspects of her narrative, such as the revelations about her childhood experiences. The self-consciousness of this approach allows the protective strategies Jennifer has put into place to be gradually peeled away, revealing a character who has, through the fantastical powers of her narrative, moved on from her initial predicament to find a new footing on which to build a satisfying emotional life. In this way Jennifer's narrative trajectory not only echoes that of Margaret in *Looking for the Possible Dance* but also those of Janice Galloway's heroines Joy Stone and Cassie in asserting the need for women to find and assert a viable and stable sense of identity.

## CINEMATIC REPRESENTATIONS: SUBJECTIVITY AND LANDSCAPE

The serious expression and exploration of female experience within film have been even more marginal than in the realms of the novel. One important landmark in this unforgiving terrain is the fortuitous collaboration between the writer Jessie Kesson and film-maker Michael Radford. Born in 1916, Kesson had grown up in poverty in the rural North East but had begun publishing stories in various Scottish magazines in the 1940s. Her first novel, the autobiographical *The White Bird Passes*, appeared in 1958, followed by *The Glitter of Mica* five years later. But she remained a rather minor figure within the annals of Scottish literature. This was to change with the appearance in 1980 of Radford's BBC adaptation of *The White Bird Passes*. The poetic and moving dramatisation of a deprived childhood was appended by a 30-minute interview with Kesson bringing her life story up to date. It also paved the way for a subsequent collaboration between Radford and Kesson, a project dealing with her wartime encounter with some Italian prisoners of war on the Black Isle where she was living and working as a cottar's wife. The film and novelised versions of *Another Time, Another Place* subsequently appeared in 1983 to great acclaim. In particular, Radford's sensitive depiction of a young woman trapped by a combination of geographical and emotional isolation proved a welcome alternative to the more familiar cinematic images of self-pitying and confused men. Oppressed by an unresponsive husband and an insular community, Janie's intense craving for life is brought into sharp focus by the eruption of the outside world in the shape of the exotic Italian prisoners, culminating in a brief but disastrous sexual liaison with one of them. Aided by Phyllis Logan's understated performance, Radford creates a palpable sense of Janie's subjectivity by privileging her perspective within the film's construction. The spectator is invited to share her emotions as they progress from wonderment and incomprehension to desire and ultimately guilt via a combination of numerous close-ups on her face, various furtive looks and glances and the refusal of subtitles when the strangers speak in Italian.

But despite this central focus on the lineaments of female desire, Radford's film was attacked in certain quarters for reinforcing the patriarchal bias of mainstream cinema. For example, Connie Balides argues that '[w]hile appearing to present the woman's story from her point of view and from a culturally specific position [the film] makes the same mistakes as the dominant cinema in the place it gives to woman'.[30] Balides suggests that the pattern of looks in *Another Time, Another Place* robs Janie of the dominant specularity she is supposed to hold by reproducing an objectifying male gaze. Radford presents Janie's naked body for erotic contemplation three times in the film: alone washing herself after a hard day on the threshing mill, undressing knowingly before getting into bed with her husband, and in a fantasy sequence where she appears naked in front of the Italians.[31] Yet despite such criticism, it was clearly Radford's intention to evoke Janie's own sense of her body as a signifier of both her desire and her vulnerability, rather than pandering to sexist codes of representation. The question may be more to do with cinema's need to show rather than tell, or of the difficulties of representing female nudity. What such controversy does raise however is the more fundamental problem of the lack of women film-makers and the consequences this has for women to adequately represent themselves within the medium of cinema.

Another issue raised by *Another Time, Another Place* is the familiar association of women and landscape, something which cannot be reduced to a gender perspective. While Kesson rhapsodises about the restorative power of the land in her novel, Radford's use of low grey skies, endless winter rain and the ploughed fields of the Black Isle convey Janie's sense of oppression and melancholy longing as well as hinting at her youthful fertility. This link between body and land is also central to Margaret Tait's 1993 film, *Blue Black Permanent*, the first Scottish feature to be written and directed by a woman. The narrative concerns a daughter's struggle to come to terms with the haunting legacy of a mother who died by drowning. It is also revealed that the woman's grandmother was also claimed by the sea and that this prior tragedy ultimately led to her own mother's possible suicide. While the enduring lure of water, which has long been associated with female reproductive power and 'otherness' and as such a challenge to male supremacy, is explored by Tait in an interesting way *Blue Black Permanent* ultimately fails to capture the raw force of nature, rendering the Orcadian seascapes, and ultimately the drama itself, as rather flat and lifeless.

The use of landscape as a mirror of emotional states is more successfully conveyed in Alan Rickman's 1998 adaptation of Sharman MacDonald's play *The Winter Guest*. The film is shaped by a profoundly feminine sensibility characteristic of a Scottish writer who had chosen to work primarily in England, prompting Peter Zenziger to suggest that MacDonald's 'escape from a male-dominated Scottish culture shows in the almost complete absence of adult men in her plays'.[32] Set in a small Scottish seaside town, *The Winter Guest* revolves around four pairings of characters, at the centre of which is the rather fractious relationship between Frances and her mother Elspeth (played by real-life mother and daughter Phyllida Law and Emma Thompson). Frances mourns her dead husband and plans to leave for Australia while Elspeth, fearful of her own mortality, attempts to rekindle the bond between them that has clearly been lost. Meanwhile Frances's lonely son Alex meets the beguiling and sparky Nita who helps him to exorcise the ghost signified by the photographs of his dead father. The other characters include two pre-pubescent schoolboys, Sam and Tom, who skip school and explore the frozen coastline, and the elderly eccentrics Lily and Chloe, who spend their lives attending funerals. In different ways each of the dyads allows the exploration of themes of uncertainty, loss, the fear of mortality and the emotional complexity of close relationships. But feminine subjectivity and agency are also central to the structuring of *The Winter Guest*, explored most effectively in the struggle between mother and daughter to perceive and then to seize the opportunity to reconnect in such a way as to also (re)affirm each as a living, autonomous and desiring individual. While it is Nita's fearlessness – running out on the ice, pursuing Alex and then confronting to need to put away his father's pictures – that provides Frances's son with his own opportunity for growth. This creative use of landscape as a place of liminality is not only a recurring feature in Sharman MacDonald's work but, as Susan Triesman notes, 'the edge of the sea – where nature offers a meeting place for new understanding … is also an important trope in woman's writing and in feminist theory'.[33]

In contrast to the bourgeois introspection and artful lyricism of *The Winter Guest*, a rather more prosaic, but no less sensitive, exploration of female struggle is presented by May Miles Thomas in her debut film, *One Life Stand* (2000). This study of the relationship between a single mother and her teenage son is located, as Tony McKibbin notes, in a Glasgow 'not only beyond industrialisation, but also beyond the urbanised misery of industrial collapse' where the old certainties of class and status are no longer relevant'.[34] Miles Thomas represents a post-Thatcherite world marked by casualised employment and social fragmentation where there is no recourse to solidarity and collective struggle. Consequently, the focus on the emotional and psychological relationship mother and son is all the more intense and poignant. *One Life Stand* commences with mother and son beginning their respective new jobs – Triese (Maureen Carr) in a call-centre specialising in tarot card readings, and John Paul (John Keilty) with a modelling agency which is (unbeknown to his mother) also pimping him out as a male escort to middle-aged women. Triese is an immediately recognisable prematurely aged but dedicated mother in her late thirties, ground down by her circumstances, her 18-year-old son still relying on her for all his domestic needs. Triese also has to deal with the problems of the adult men in her life, including John Paul's estranged father, Jackie (Gary Lewis), who despite having a new partner and child elsewhere still regards his ex-wife as a source of petty cash and sympathy and with her boss, the lascivious but kind hearted Shazz (Archie Lal), who showers her with attention and compliments which she is unable to comprehend, let alone enjoy.

Triese's primary motivation is to ensure that John Paul is able to have and take the kind of opportunities that have passed her by – a predicament heartbreakingly crystallised in the scene where having presented him with a mobile phone, she poignantly asks 'Who can I call?' The extent of her own self-denial is revealed when, having rejected the rather crude advances of Shazz on a works night out, Triese returns home to an empty flat and lies down on her son's bed. Relations between the two have deteriorated and John Paul has begun spending time, ironically, with another lonely middle-aged woman he has met through his escort work. John Paul moves out and the film ends with a brief moment of Triese, alone in her flat, the tacky ornament she received at work for being employee of the month prominently positioned. Throughout, *One Life Stand* adopts a more intense and analytical realism to its subject. This is reinforced by Miles Thomas' black-and-white images which, combined with stillness of her camera and frequent close-ups, draws attention to the faces of the characters in order to reveal something of the emotions and the understandings behind the visage. This conveys a powerful sense of the frustration, the loneliness and the lack of meaning beyond nurturing that circumscribes Triese's existence. Yet at the same time, the diminutive Maureen Carr's performance contains an inner-steel and resilience, ensuring Triese is never reduced to the status of victim.

## THE VALUE OF COMMUNITY: THE TELEVISION DRAMAS OF DONNA FRANCESCHILD

If the novel and the feature film proved appropriate forms for the exploration of female subjectivity, the different aesthetic possibilities of television drama suggested alternative ways of representing contemporary female experience. In this respect the dramatist Donna Franceschild has consistently posited the importance of community as both a site of creativity and an important source of support for both women and men alike. Moreover, the fundamental political values of community are also aligned with shifting gender roles and employment patterns in contemporary society, maintaining a strong sense of a female imperative in the process. Having worked primarily as a playwright since the late 1970s, the American-born Franceschild had pursued a career as a playwright in London. But a major turning point came in 1990 when her play, *And the Cow Jumped Over the Moon*, set in a women's cancer ward in Glasgow, was performed at the Traverse Theatre in Edinburgh in 1990 before going on a Scottish tour. The drama was not only adapted for broadcast by BBC Scotland the following year, but it also marked an engagement with Scotland that was to take Franceschild's work to a new level. As she explains:

> One of the problems I'd had as a playwright was that I hadn't really found a voice to write in. Although I was writing about English people, I was never really at home creating English characters. I felt more comfortable writing about the Scots. They were more direct than the English so I could take things from my own childhood and put them in the voices of Scottish characters without any cultural clash.[35]

The first of Franceschild's major commissions was the six-part series, *Takin' Over the Asylum*, broadcast at peak time on BBC2 in 1994. This also marked her first collaboration with director David Blair, inaugurating what was to become a very fruitful creative partnership. The central protagonist of *Takin' Over the Asylum* is the hapless hospital radio DJ 'Steady' Eddie McKenna, who had appeared as a supporting character in *And the Cow Jumped Over the Moon*. The new drama begins with Eddie (Ken Stott) being thrown off the hospital radio station he has worked on for eight years before following his subsequent struggles to set up a similar station in St Judes, a large Glasgow psychiatric hospital. McKenna also has a day job as a double-glazing salesman, a position he desperately needs to enable him to look after his dependent grandmother, a domineering Lithuanian émigré who gives him constant grief about being single at the age of 38. The initiative at St Judes inevitably involves a number of the patients and *Takin' Over the Asylum* subsequently focuses on the impact on a handful of these characters, drawing out their talents and providing them with a new sense of purpose. In the process Eddie is also forced to face up to his own personal problems, including his alcohol dependency and his failure to fulfil his ambitions to be a professional DJ. Consequently the radio station becomes a nurturing and restorative environment, providing a stark contrast Eddie's experiences at Twin View, the double-glazing company run by the patently unhinged Mr Griffin, which embodies the worst aspects of ruthless contemporary capitalist culture. Griffin is a devotee of the most brutal kind of ambitious, competitive individualism, articulated via an addiction to management speak and the constant urging of his employees to sublimate everything in their lives to the mantra of sell, sell, sell. Eddie's boorish colleague, McAteer, represents the inevitable outcome of this culture, avaricious and mortgaged up to the hilt, he is a bully, prepared to push anyone aside to get what he wants.

If the world of Twin View represents the dystopian consequences of the Thatcherite revolution in a bold and unsubtle fashion, St Judes, on the other hand, suggests an alternative set of possibilities. The hospital may be a resource-starved public institution dealing with the casualties of modern society, but it retains a vital sense of social concern, human empathy and mutual support – values that have all but vanished in the brave new world of enterprise free markets and consumer choice. Franceschild also draws a crucial distinction between the aggressive, hyper-masculine values of the sales team at Twin View and the feminised, caring ethos of St Judes. In this way Eddie and the other male patients are symbolically coded feminine, presented as vulnerable, emotional and often self-sacrificing individuals who continually run the risk of being hurt in their dealings with the outside world. Eddie's own propensity to self-sacrifice – giving his grandmother £3,000 to help her return to Lithuania, stepping aside to allow Campbell to take a job at Radio Scotland despite his own long-cherished ambitions in this area – are of the kind that are more commonly associated with women than men.

Franceschild's 1986 series *A Mug's Game* returned to similar themes of self-sacrifice and community through the central character of Kathy Cowan (Michelle Fairley), an employee of a failing fish farm on Loch Fyne. Still only 30, Kathy's responsibilities as a wife, mother and daughter – to a self-pitying unemployed husband, two difficult children and a domineering mother respectively – have put intolerable pressure on her, yet she continues to be the rock at the centre of her family. She also gave up a career as a promising young musician to look after her father after he became ill. Kathy's situation becomes even more complicated when she unwittingly attracts the attention of both her new boss, Martin McCaffrey (Ken Stott), a ruthless manager who has been brought in to 'save' the company; and his nephew Con (Sean Harris), a wayward 20-year-old from Belfast expelled by the IRA for his anti-social activities. Con's arrogant self-centred attitude to life makes him a rather unsympathetic character who refers to Kathy's commitment to her family as 'a mug's game' while pursuing her at least in part as a way of antagonising his despised uncle. But at the same time Con is also a talented musician, which rekindles Kathy's own sense of alternative possibility. This also has a sexual component in that when her husband finally walks out, Kathy lets Con take her to bed. In a previous conversation with her sexually voracious friend Denise (Katy Murphy), Kathy had let slip that she has never had a good sex life and the coupling with Con starts off being no different. However, in one of the key moments in the drama, Con lets his guard down and, admitting his own inexperience, asks Kathy to show him what to do. In taking control of the sex Kathy begins to learn the importance of satisfying her own neglected needs as a woman and as a human being. The other major theme reprised from *Takin' Over the Asylum* is the corrosive effect of capitalism, in this case the slow destruction of the community brought about by the 'downsizing' at the fish farm. While a far more complex and contradictory character than Griffin, McCaffrey distances himself from the human consequences of his decisions by recourse to abstract economics and business plans. Ironically his departure is brought about when Kathy sabotages the nets and frees the salmon – at one point she compares her own predicament to that of a confined, farmed salmon aware of the freedom and heroic life cycle of its wild cousin – and despite the impending closure of the factory, *A Mug's Game* ends with Kathy and Con playing together at a fund-raising event for the Trade Union. This rather utopian image of solidarity, reminiscent of the contrived up-beat ending of John McGrath's *Blood Red Roses*, sits somewhat uncomfortably with Kathy's more subtly realised personal journey towards fulfilment and is motivated more by the need for dramatic closure than a realistic assessment of the community and its future.

The political concerns of Franceschild's earlier work were brought centre stage in the 2003 series *The Key*, easily her most ambitious project to date.

This family saga charts the experiences of three generations of Glasgow women and their involvement in left-wing politics from the rent strikes and lock-outs of the First World War to the advent of New Labour in 1997. While such a serious engagement with the historical role of women in the public sphere provided a rich and long-neglected dramatic subject, *The Key* ultimately failed to live up to its promise despite the skills of its writer/director team and the benefits of a strong cast. The main problem was one of length: this ambitious panorama was squeezed into a woefully inadequate structure of three one-hour episodes and consequently suffered from the inevitable compression of narrative events and character development. Not only are the complex personal, social and historical issues rendered unnecessarily melodramatic by the sudden temporal jumps and the twists and turns of an over-determined plot, but the major political struggles of the twentieth century are rendered as little more than agit-prop sloganeering and the simplistic and clichéd depiction of humane and enlightened trade unions, oppressive bosses and duplicitous politicians. Had *The Key* been given a more appropriate structure of six episodes, the ambition clearly contained within the project might have been realised as a serious analysis of political and social history to rival *Days of Hope* or *Our Friends in the North*. But despite its shortcomings, *The Key* is a reminder of Franceschild's commitment as a dramatist to a political and a social understanding of women's lives and history, all the more important given the current tendency towards individualistic stories and risk-averse commissioning within television.

## CONCLUSIONS: GENDER AND NATION

The marginalisation of women in Scottish culture has created a situation where female creativity is inevitably linked to gender in ways that never pertain in the case of their male counterparts. In this way, female cultural expression becomes caught in a version of the Scottish predicament, forever restricted to a narrow and obsessive focus on gender identities and issues. Yet many writers and film-makers have challenged this by transforming such assumptions into new creative possibilities. Janice Galloway, for example, has acknowledged that gender, national identity and class have all unquestionably contributed to the formation of a particular world-view. But her primary purpose as a writer is to challenge rather than confirm expectations of the consequences such attributes have on her characters and their experiences. Galloway has also posited an important link between the marginalisation of a national voice with a similar process of exclusion based on gender:

> I want to write as though having a female perspective is *normal* which is
> a damn sight harder than it sounds. I don't think people tend to regard

'women's priorities' as in any way normal: so-called *women's issues* are still regarded as deviant, add-on, extra. Not the Big Picture ... And to reprioritise, to speak through your norms are the ones that matter, is what's happened to Scottish writing as well recently. Scottish writers have started writing as though their language and national priorities signify, whereas for years we took on the fiction that they didn't.[36]

The vexed question of identity is also articulated by A. L. Kennedy's fictitious Scottish writer, Monagh Cairns who, in the short story 'Warming My Hands and Telling Lies', informs a young admirer that '(T)he better Scottish writing gets, the less it will matter. The work will improve itself, it won't be competing with anything other than the best it can produce. It will be international.'[37] This sentiment can apply equally to the labelling of work by gender and Kennedy has been particularly successful in creating fictions that resist such reductiveness through the assertion of the essential individuality of her characters, whose identities as female or Scottish are significant but never wholly determining. Kennedy has the ability to engage with the national while maintaining a strong sense of the personal and the individual. Indeed, as Alison Smith argues, 'For a woman to write fiction with such authority, range and humour, and to be able to be so unconcerned about gender, is a real step forward. The margins have been pushed back.'[38]

Elsewhere such margins have been challenged in a more radical way through the assertion of the essential fluidity and contingency of identity. Jackie Kay's 1998 novel *Trumpet* tells the story of a famous jazz musician, Joss Moody, the son of a Scottish mother and an African father who, on his death, is revealed to be a woman who has successfully passed for man for more than fifty years. In this way the novel both problematises and relates concepts of identity based on race, gender, nationality or even sexuality (Joss is never regarded as a lesbian in drag). This in turn draws on Kay's own complex identity as a black lesbian woman adopted and brought up by white Glaswegian parents, a topic first confronted and explored in her celebrated 1991 collection of poetry, *The Adoption Papers*. In *Trumpet*, Kay utilises a fragmented narrative structure dominated by the perspectives of Joss's wife Millie and their adopted son Colman, which are supplemented by a series of responses to the revelation of Moody's identity. These include the perspectives of the doctor who confirmed his death, the funeral director who prepared his body, Big Red McCall, Joss's friend and drummer, and Sophie Stones, a tabloid journalist intent on milking the sensationalism of the story for all it is worth. Alison Lumsden argues that this mode of narration provides an appropriate prism through which the 'evasive fluidity' of the (absent) subject can be effectively conveyed:

the multiple narratives allow the reader no fixed position by which Joss's constructed identity may be contained; rather, the at times competing perspectives imply that his/her life and death can never be safely delimited through standard teleological narrative modes.[39]

Gender thus becomes more a question of performance than biology, something that, as Lumsden notes, is reflected in the mutability of other characters, most notably Colman, a mixed race orphan born in Scotland who on being adopted changed his name and who at the age of 7 moved from Glasgow to London. The metaphor of identity also finds its apotheosis in the free and improvisational form of jazz, restlessly searching for new aesthetic possibilities and expressions of feeling, however transient or elusive.

But ultimately Kay invokes an important sense of connection between human beings, providing points of necessary stability within this sea of apparent indeterminacy. Colman finally gains some sense of comfort through tracking down Joss's mother Edith – who gives him a photograph of young 'Josephine' Moore aged 7 – and plucking up the courage to read the letter which his father had written to him as he lay dying. This recounts the arrival of Joss's own father in Scotland, a story that crucially emphasises bonds that transcend blood, linking Colman, Joss/Josephine and John Moore within the overarching narrative of diasporic identity which has necessarily involved a sense of mutability: 'That's the thing with us: we keep changing names. We've all got that in common. We've changed names, you, me, my father. All for different reasons. Maybe one day you'll understand mine.'[40] This suggests that despite the fluidity of identity, meaningful connections and points of identification still matter. Compared to many of their male counterparts, writers like Janice Galloway and A. L. Kennedy address a sense of national consciousness and identity in much more diffuse and implicit ways. Yet while national identity may not be writ large, it does inevitably intrude, primarily through highly mediated structures of feeling. In *Looking for the Possible Dance*, despite having gone to university in England, Margaret perceives the landscape around her as increasingly 'foreign' as the train beings her closer to London: 'The walls by the side of track are very strange now, grey brick and black brick and honey brick … Margaret stares out at trees of an alien green and reminds herself that her ticket is a return.'[41] While in *Foreign Parts*, Rona and Cassie are positioned as outsiders in a foreign landscape, they are considerably more comfortable in their national identity than Cassie's former boyfriend Chris, who disavows his Scottishness in order to impress some locals in Turkey. When challenged on this by Cassie, his response is typically domineering and aggressive, giving credence to Glenda Norquay's suggestion that, 'the structures of colonialisation lead patriarchy to assert itself more forcefully in men whose political context has disempowered them'.[42]

The sea change in gender relations has also been reflected in the political and economic developments that have transformed Scotland in the past twenty years. The changing role of women in Scottish politics is just one signifier of the progressive direction of such change. While in 1979 only one Scottish female MP was returned to Parliament – representing a mere 1.4 per cent of Scottish seats – by the first elections to the new Scottish Parliament in 1999 this had increased to 37 per cent. For David McCrone, this was consistent with other profound shifts in gender relations in Scotland in which 'masculinist cultures of work, politics and leisure were on the defensive. Workers were now mainly women. Girls were outperforming boys in the classroom.'[43] McCrone's assertion is supported by John McInnes who draws upon a European study of attitudes to gender, work and the family to suggest that Scottish attitudes towards gender (on the part of both men and woman) were slightly more egalitarian in terms of levels of support for the idea of equal rather than separate roles for men and women compared to the rest of the UK or Europe. MacInnes suggests that the perception of a crisis in masculinity should be seen more in terms of a crisis in the material circumstances of men brought about by wider processes of change, rather than a question of gender identity:

> The macho Scotsman, like his counterparts across Europe, is not yet a dying breed, but he is trapped in the quicksand of social and economic change. The 'crisis' of masculinity is only the obverse of the significant material success of feminism in bringing greater equality between men and women.[44]

One of the recurring features of the female narratives examined in this chapter is the attempt to dispel or limit vulnerability in the assertion of selfhood. These fictions may explore the trials and tribulations faced by particular women in their lives, but the emphasis more often than not is on a kind of quiet triumph over adversity, often achieved through the intimacy and security provided by relationships to others. This contrasts significantly with the fictions examined in the previous chapter which saw men beginning to express (and accept) the existence of vulnerability, rather than raging against perceived threats to their masculinity. But more often than not this still remained at the expense of real and meaningful intimacy and human connection.

## NOTES

1. Arthur McIvor, 'Gender Apartheid?: Women in Scottish Society', in T. M. Devine and R. J. Finlay (eds), *Scotland in the 20th Century* (Edinburgh: Edinburgh University Press, 1996), p. 206.

2. S. J. Boyd, 'A Man's a Man: Reflections on Scottish Masculinity', *Scotlands*, No. 2, 1994, p. 103.

3. See, for example, Esther Breitenbach, 'Out of Sight, Out of Mind? The History of Women in Scottish Politics', *Scottish Affairs*, No. 2, Winter 1993.

4. Carol Anderson and Glenda Norquay, 'Superiorism', *Cencrastus*, New Year 1984, no. 15, p. 8.

5. Ibid. p. 10.

6. David McCrone, *Understanding Scotland: The Sociology of a Stateless Nation* (London: Routledge, 1992), p. 190.

7. See Douglas Gifford and Dorothy McMillan (eds), *A History of Scottish Women's Writing* (Edinburgh: Edinburgh University Press, 1997); Carol Anderson and Aileen Christianson (eds), *Scottish Women's Fiction 1920s to 1960s: Journey's Into Being* (East Linton: Tuckwell Press, 2000).

8. Examples include *I Know Where I'm Going* (Michael Powell and Emeric Pressburger, 1944), *The Brothers* (David MacDonald, 1947), *Another Time, Another Place* (Michael Radford, 1983) and *Blue Black Permanent* (Margaret Tait, 1992).

9. Tait's film was produced by Barbara Grigor who, along with Paddy Higson, provided an important female presence in the nascent Scottish film industry of the 1980s.

10. Janice Galloway, Interview with Cristie Leigh March, *Edinburgh Review*, No. 101, 'Exchanges', Summer 1999, p. 3.

11. Janice Galloway, *The Trick Is to Keep Breathing* (Edinburgh: Polygon, 1989), p. 79.

12. See Janice Galloway, 'Different Oracles: Me and Alasdair Gray', in *The Review of Contemporary Fiction*, Vol. 15, No. 2, 1995.

13. Cairns Craig, *The Modern Scottish Novel: Narrative and the National Imagination* (Edinburgh: Edinburgh University Press, 1999), p. 193.

14. Janice Galloway, *The Trick Is to Keep Breathing*, p. 235.

15. Janice Galloway, *Foreign Parts* (London: Jonathan Cape, 1994), p. 150.

16. Ibid. p. 251.

17. Ibid. p. 259.

18. Glenda Norquay, 'Janice Galloway's Novels: Fraudulent Mooching', in Aileen Christianson and Alison Lumsden (eds), *Contemporary Scottish Women Writers* (Edinburgh: Edinburgh University Press, 2000), p. 131.

19. Alan Freeman, 'Realism Fucking Realism: The Word on the Street – Kelman, Kennedy and Welsh', *Cencrastus*, No. 57, Summer, 1997, p. 7.

20. Dorothy McMillan, 'Constructed Out of Bewilderment: States of Scotland', in Ian A. Bell (ed.), *Peripheral Visions: Images of Nationhood in Contemporary British Fiction* (Cardiff: University of Wales Press, 1995), p. 96.

21. A. L. Kennedy, *Looking for the Possible Dance* (London: Secker & Warburg, 1993), pp. 101–2.

22. Ibid. p. 66.

23. Ibid. p. 104.

24. Charlotte Brunsdon, 'Not Having It All: Women and Film in the 1990s', in Robert Murphy (ed.), *British Cinema of the 90s* (London: BFI, 2000), p. 172.

25. A. L. Kennedy, *So I Am Glad* (London: Jonathan Cape, 1995), pp. 4–5.

26. Ibid. pp. 12–13.

27. Ibid. p. 208.

28. Sarah M. Dunnigan, 'A. L. Kennedy's Longer Fiction: Articulate Grace', in Christianson and Lumsden (eds), *Contemporary Scottish Women Writers*, p. 154.

29. Moira Burgess, *Imagine a City: Glasgow in Fiction* (Glendaruel: Argyll Publishing, 1998), p. 314.

30. Connie Balides, 'Another Time Another Place: Another Male View?', *Cencrastus*, Spring 1984, p. 41.

31. Kesson has suggested that most of the sex in her novel occurs within the (nameless) protagonist's head. Yet her writing remains unequivocal about the potential force of female desire: 'Never before had she felt so desirable. Knowing in that moment how Eve must have felt, waking up in the trance of her creation, to look into the dark appreciative eyes of Adam.' Jessie Kesson, *Another Time, Another Place* (London: Chatto & Windus, 1983), p. 62.

32. Peter Zenziger, 'The New Wave', in Randall Stevenson and Gavin Wallace (eds), *Scottish Theatre Since the Seventies* (Edinburgh: Edinburgh University Press, 1996), p. 135.

33. Susan C. Triesman, 'Sharman MacDonald: The Generation of Identity', in Christianson and Lumsden (eds), *Contemporary Scottish Women Writers*, p. 54.

34. Tony McKibbin, 'One Life Stand', *Cencrastus*, No. 69, 2001, p. 32.

35. Donna Franceschild in conversation with Steve Clarke, 'Lives that Leap from the Screen', *The Daily Telegraph*, 27 January 1996.

36. Janice Galloway, Interview with Cristie Leigh March, *Edinburgh Review*, No. 101, 'Exchanges', Summer 1999, p. 1.

37. A. L. Kennedy, 'Warming My Hands and Telling Lies', *Now That You're Back* (London: Jonathan Cape, 1994), p. 165.

38. Alison Smith, 'Four Success Stories', *Chapman*, Nos 74/75, Autumn/Winter 1993, p. 192.

39. Alison Lumsden, 'Jackie Kay's Poetry and Prose: Constructing Identity', in Christianson and Lumsden (eds), *Contemporary Scottish Women Writers*, p. 87.

40. Jackie Kay, *Trumpet* (London: Picador, 1998), p. 276.

41. A. L. Kennedy, *Looking for the Possible Dance*, pp. 236–7.

42. Glenda Norquay, 'Janice Galloway's Novels: Fraudulent Mooching', in Christianson and Lumsden (eds), *Contemporary Scottish Women Writers*, p. 140.

43. David McCrone, *Understanding Scotland: Sociology of a Nation* (London: Routledge, 2001), p. 29.

44. John MacInnes, 'The Myth of the Macho Scotsman: Attitudes to Gender, Work and Family in the UK, Ireland and Europe', *Scottish Affairs*, No. 23, Spring 1998, p. 121.

# CHAPTER 4

# Ducking and Diving in the Nineties

## INTRODUCTION

In addition to the belated engagement with questions of gender and the specificity of female experience and subjectivity, Scottish writers and film-makers in the 1990s also began to deal in new ways with the new social realities that were the direct consequence of the Thatcherite revolution. As Will Hutton argues, the policies of economic deregulation and the promotion of market principles promoted by the New Right had served to create a more divided and unequal society in Britain. Rejecting traditional conceptions of stratification based on social class, Hutton articulates a model that draws particular attention to the pronounced sense of insecurity and instability that came to characterise employment patterns and consequently the life experience of the population at large in the new market society. By the mid-1990s only 40 per cent of the British adult population were in what could be termed secure employment, the group Hutton terms *privileged*. A further 30 per cent – the *marginalised and insecure* – occupied either fixed-contract, part-time or casualised work, typically characterised by the absence of effective job protection, pension rights, sickness benefit, etc. The remaining 30 per cent – *the disadvantaged* – were either unemployed or economically inactive.[1] The consequence of the end of welfare capitalism for Hutton has been the marketisation of society, which has brought with it a number of interconnected negative consequences of communal decay and excessive self-interest. In addition to the erosion of the old stable identities of class, employment and community, this social revolution also began to undermine that symbolic building block of the traditional Conservative conception of the 'good society', the family.

This new social backdrop has provided rich material for writers and film-makers. Unlike the earlier fictions of McIlvanney, McDougall, Gray and Kelman, these new works also reflect the perceptions of a younger generation who do not have the same recourse to the myths of a more stable, egalitarian and humane past. Consequently, they dramatise and interrogate the very different kind of situations, encounters, problems and opportunities that had come to structure the lives of young Scots in a world dominated by the onward march of global capitalism. This is consistent with Irvine Welsh's stated interest in 'what the 'Thatcher's Children generations of forty and under of the working class get up to – how they survive in the current economy and society'.[2] One positive consequence of the Thatcherite revolution, however, was the fostering of a new sense of entrepreneurial energy and creativity in the realm of culture that was directed towards a critical response to the wider consequences of Tory reform, rather than a vindication of the profit motive. The emergence of a new wave of socially-committed Scottish writing in the early 1990s owed a great deal to such entrepreneurial activity in the field of independent publishing. Taking their inspiration from the kind of DIY fanzines that had emerged in the punk era, these new publishing initiatives – such as the Clocktower Press, founded in 1990 by Duncan McLean and James Meek, and Rebel Inc. a similar initiative started by Kevin Williamson two years later – tended to concentrate on the production of limited circulation magazines featuring short stories, poems and extracts from novels by new Scottish writers.[3] But while the cultural centre of gravity of the earlier break-through led by Gray and Kelman had been Glasgow, by the early 1990s the focus had moved to the East coast: the Clocktower Press, for example, was based in South Queensferry just outside Edinburgh, while Rebel Inc. was also published in the Scottish capital. And despite the limitations of such small ventures, exposure in the pages of Clocktower and Rebel Inc. helped to bring a number of aspiring writers to the attention of the legitimate – and more mainstream – publishing world and with it to a considerably larger readership.[4]

## IRVINE WELSH: THE VIEW FROM THE SCHEME

A key starting point for understanding the impact and significance of Irvine Welsh is the earlier innovations of James Kelman, whose achievements as a chronicler of the those at the margins of society and as a committed advocate of the use of non-standard English provided acolytes with both a thematic and a formal direction. Welsh's 1993 debut novel, *Trainspotting*, was immediately distinguished by, on one hand, its focus on the experiences of a group of young junkies and wasters (very much part of the excluded 30 per cent of the new society), and on the other by an uncompromising use of working-class Edinburgh vernacular as its primary narrative voice. While unflinching in the depiction of the squalid depravities and exploitative self-interest that characterise the everyday life of heroin addiction, *Trainspotting* nevertheless succeeds in creating a palpable empathy for its rag-bag ensemble of characters and an understanding of their motives for becoming involved with such a destructive substance as heroin. Significantly, Welsh also moves beyond the limitations of previous depictions of the Edinburgh drug scene, such as Peter McDougall's television drama *Shoot for the Sun*, by directly acknowledging the pleasures involved:

> Take yir best orgasm, multiply the feeling by twenty, and you're still fuckin miles off the pace. My dry, cracking bones are soothed and liquefied by ma beautiful heroine's tender caresses. The earth moved, and its still moving.[5]

Yet at the same time Welsh refrains from any faux romanticisation of the drug culture. As Jenny Turner notes, his achievement is 'to affirm without being affirmative, to recognise without giving the stabilising stamp of approval that the act of recognition generally, if fallaciously, entails'.[6]

Once again the link between form and content is central and in particular the apparently direct access *Trainspotting* provides to the lives, the experiences, the thoughts and the actions of its (socially marginalised) young protagonists. For Robert Morace, Welsh's use of language creates 'a world that offers no introduction and no apology, a world that simply resents itself on its own terms, in its own words and with its own frame(s) of cultural reference'.[7] Following Kelman, Welsh reaffirms both the validity and necessity of the vernacular to convey both first-person subjectivity and third-person narration as a means of challenging the hegemony of standard English – the language of a political and cultural establishment from which his characters are estranged. This strategy also asserts a declaration of independence and equality, the right to convey ideas, emotions and interactions in the language through and in which these are experienced and lived. Yet in focusing on a doubly marginalised social group – members of a deviant, criminalised subculture of the Scottish working class – Welsh does more than simply assert the rights of a linguistic alternative to Standard English. As Alan Freeman points out:

> With its serially published episodes and many voices, *Trainspotting* embodies in its form not just the local system of working-class Edinburgh dialect, without compromise to a supposed standard position in language; it also enacts the tension within this system, between different social registers, divergent discourses within which to interpret reality. As a consequence, at the heart of Welsh's linguistic virtuosity lies a crucial feature of language, the evolving, uncertain relations between signifier and signified.[8]

Freeman demonstrates this in relation to the multiple nicknames the various characters use for each other in different circumstances to convey the subtleties of power relations between them, the frequent recourse to (often elaborate) scatology, and the general prevailing of pattern over meaning in speech. This linguistic instability further conveys characters cut off from a meaningful past or a hopeful future, but rather are 'consigned to an endless present, a sequence of discrete, divided moments of experience, the post-industrial, punk generation repudiates their human potential, confirming their severance from continuity'.[9]

While clearly connecting with Kelman's project, Welsh can also be regarded as reacting against the aspects of the former's use of language and of his depiction of the 'horror of everyday life'. Welsh's vivid representation of his particular stratum of Edinburgh society undermines the familiar reductive binary conception of Glasgow – the locus of an authentic, working-class Scottish identity – contrasted with an Edinburgh that is necessarily inauthentic, bourgeois and Anglo-centric.[10] Moreover, as Nicholas Williams notes, 'just as Welsh has stripped his literary language of its pretensions to "high art" (English) respectability, he undoes the compensatory vision of Scottish authenticity'.[11] In addition to questioning the very authenticity that Kelman frequently appears to invoke, Welsh also bestows upon his characters a greater sense of humour and creative potential in the teeth of the obvious deprivations and obstacles they face. While Pat Doyle in *A Disaffection* is the study of a self-pitying man going under, Mark Renton fights back from the brink through a combination of life-affirming intelligence and wit. Like Doyle, Renton is a genuine native intellectual, constantly reflecting on the profound dilemmas and contradictions that give substance to human exist-ence. But he is also self-reliant and enterprising, virtues that provide him with the wherewithal to survive in an increasingly harsh and unforgiving world. When off the junk he is also highly mobile, travelling regularly to London where he is involved in a complex benefit scam – allowing Renton to ultimately move on in a more purposeful manner than the rather sudden and enigmatic departures that bring Kelman's novels *A Chancer* and *How Late it Was, How Late* to their respective conclusions.

One of the most powerful aspects of *Trainspotting* is its projection of the specific social milieu of Edinburgh housing schemes blighted by a mixture of poverty, complacence and the erosion of any meaningful sense of community. The protagonists are defined by their relationship to leisure – moving from the legitimate world of the pub to the criminalised domain of the shooting gallery – rather than by employment. Indeed, the only member of the central group with a 'proper job', Gavin Temperley, ironically works for the DHSS, while others such as Spud and Renton actively seek to avoid being forced to take a job. Their existence is financed by a combination of state benefits and various forms of minor criminal activities. One of the ways in which Welsh explores this social world is through the dialectic between individual and community, a relationship that focuses some of the central tensions at the heart of the social, economic and political changes of the last two decades. While Mark Renton occupies a privileged position within the narrative in terms of the number of episodes featuring his first-person narrative, parts of the novel are recounted by other characters including Simon 'Sick Boy' Williamson, Francis Begbie, Danny 'Spud' Murphy, Rab 'Second Prize' McLauchlin, Davie Mitchell and Kelly. Robert Morace argues that this ensemble structure ensures 'that the reader can never enjoy the luxury of either forgetting the other characters or subordinating their stories and voices to Mark's narrative'.[12] In addition, there are also a number of sections narrated in the third person that serve to enhance the creative tensions between object and subjective viewpoints, between Standard English and Leith vernacular and between the individual and the community. Yet the 'community' at the centre of *Trainspotting* has nothing of value binding it together. What connections do exist are a combination of shared personal history, the cycles that govern living with drug dependency, or even the bonds of fear – in the case of Begbie and his intimidatory relationship to the rest of group. The nexus of self-interest is brought home in chilling fashion in the scene where Lesley's baby daughter is found dead in her cot, the pain and trauma of which can only be displaced by an immediate heroin hit. This places Renton, by virtue of the fact that he is the only one with any gear, in a temporary position of power, confirming his earlier assertion about there being 'nae friends in this game. Jist associates'.[13]

In addition to the corrosive influence of junkie culture on any meaningful sense of community, the other major cancer at the heart of the world of *Trainspotting* is that old chestnut, Scottish working-class masculinity. As befits the nihilistic world of the novel, the insecurity, self-loathing, abuse and exploitation defining the psyche of the Scottish 'hard man' is given a characteristically harsh twist by Welsh. While Renton is not immune from such forms of behaviour – the most shocking example being when he fucks his pregnant sister-in-law in the toilet after his brother's funeral – the primary exponents of cruelty in *Trainspotting* are Sick Boy and Begbie. The former is perhaps the most nakedly self-interested of the gang, and he ends up pimping young girls who are addicted to smack – leading Alan Sinfield to argue that the entrepreneurial and upwardly mobile Sick Boy represents the values of Thatcherism in Welsh's fictional world. But the real centre of masculine malevolence in *Trainspotting* is occupied by Francis Begbie, a violent psychopath who terrorises his friends, beats up his pregnant girlfriend and engages in random acts of ultra-violence against innocent individuals in bars and on the streets. Begbie is a lumpen traditionalist who shuns heroin in favour of alcohol and violence, but as a variant of the 'hard man' all traces of any residual code of honour are long gone. Indeed, Welsh uses Begbie as a graphic manifestation of the Scottish male's myopic capacity for self-destruction, and self-hatred. Renton reflects on the endemic problem his 'friend' embodies:

> Ah hate cunts like that. Cunts like Begbie. Cunts that are intae baseball-batting every fucker that's different; pakis, poofs, n what huv ye. Fuckin failures in a country ay failures. It's nae good blamin it oan the English fir colonising us. Ah don't hate the English. They're just wankers ... Ah hate the Scots.[14]

Renton's intellect also provides the means for Welsh to reflect more broadly on the historical baggage retarding Scotland's development as a mature and confident society. In particular, he explores aspects of the internal colonial history of the British Isles and its legacy in the running sore of religious sectarianism. The product of an Edinburgh Catholic mother and a Glaswegian Protestant father, Mark Renton is a living embodiment of this cultural schism. As a staunch Hibs fan, Renton identifies with his maternal culture, while his older brother Billy has followed his father into the sectarian world of the Orange Order and its espousal of 'Queen and Country'. Billy is also in the British Army – an embodiment of that symbol of stable Unionist incorporation, the 'Scottish Soldier'. When he is subsequently killed on patrol in Northern Ireland, the bitter irony is not lost on Renton who notes that his brother 'died an ignorant victim ay imperialism, understanding fuck all about the myriad circumstances that led tae his death'.[15] In contrast, Renton has no doubts who the real culprits are: 'His death wis conceived by these orange cunts, comin through every July wi thir sashes and flutes, fillin Billy's stupid heid wi nonsense about crown and country n aw that shite.'[16] The blight of sectarianism and racism has blinded Scotland to its own subservience, feeding ancient hatreds and further corroding the opportunity for progressive and nurturing change. The two are directly linked in the scene when Stevie is beaten up by a bunch of Hearts fans who then proceed to racially abuse an Asian and her two small children. Spud is also aware of the underlying causes of the problems suffered by his mixed-race Uncle Dode, whose father was a West Indian sailor: 'Ah sortay jist laugh whin some cats say that racism's an English thing and we're aw Jock Tamson's bairns up here ... It's likesay pure shite man, gadges talkin through their erses.'[17] Renton's oedipal rage against the Unionist culture of his father on the other hand is examined by Dermot Kelly in terms of an attack on the outdated legacy of imperialism in a postcolonial age:

> Renton's conflicted personality mirrors the uneasy relationship
> between the two cultures in urban Scotland and his confused minority

consciousness is yet fertile ground for a dialogue with the majority culture. Irvine Welsh's achievement in *Trainspotting* should be celebrated in these days of devolution for showing, as MacDiarmid predicted, that cultural awakening would start from the residual difference of the incompletely assimilated immigrants.[18]

So while Mark Renton may conspire to make his escape with no foreseeable means of returning the only way forward, Welsh generates an analysis and initiates a dialogue that suggests the glimmer of a more positive future for Scotland.

Welsh continued his exploration of the relationship between Scotland's imperial legacy and damaged masculinity in his second novel, *Marabou Stork Nightmares* (1995), although this time within a much more sustained and ambitious contemplation of subjectivity. The novel charts the life of Roy Strang from his childhood in the Edinburgh scheme of Muirhouse to his adult involvement with the notorious Hibs casuals, a gang of ruthless football thugs who thrive on violent encounters with rival fans. At the centre of the narrative is Roy's participation in a brutal gang rape of a young woman and the subsequent guilt he suffers culminates in him ending up in a coma after a botched suicide attempt. The various events are recounted by Roy from his hospital bed and oscillates between his semi-conscious sensations on the verge of regaining consciousness, flashback memories of the stages of his life, and a fantasy narrative involving the hunting of the hideous Marabou Stork. The later sections are conveyed in a kind of pastiche of boy's own imperialist adventure stories alluding to the operations of Roy's unconscious mind, with the stork – which massacres the helpless flamingos – the symbol of Roy's profound sense of guilt and self-loathing over the rape of Kirsty:

> I realised what we had done, what we had taken. Her beauty was little to do with her looks, the physical attractiveness of her. It was to do with the way she moved, the way she carried herself. It was her confidence, her pride, her vivacity, her lack of fear, her attitude. It was something even more fundamental and less superficial than these things. It was her self, or her sense of it.[19]

Yet when his brutalised victim turns up at the hospital to enact her revenge on the comatose Roy, it becomes clear that his recollection is unreliable – she reminds him of how he sodomised her while using a mirror to both see her face and to force her to look at him during the ordeal. Roy's narrative has charted a growing sense of guilt, initially triggered by the high profile 'Zero Tolerance' campaign against sexual violence that was mounted in Edinburgh during the 1990s. The guilt and the nightmares continue to haunt him even after he moves to Manchester and has a brief but happy relationship, largely fuelled by ecstasy and clubbing. But in the end, Roy returns to Edinburgh and attempts suicide by taking a paracetamol overdose and placing a plastic bag over his head.

The shocking act of retribution that concludes *Marabou Stork Nightmares* – Kirsty cuts off Roy's eyelids and his penis, stuffing it in his mouth and leaving him to suffocate – has attracted a great deal of criticism. Berthold Schoene-Harwood argues that not only does this silence Roy precisely at the moment he has gained insight – facing up to the fact that the Stork is himself – but it also places Kirsty in the masculine-defined role of avenger, denying any alternative feminine response to violence:

> Universalising the insidious dynamics of patriarchal power as some kind of irremediable, generic by-product of human nature, *Marabou Stork Nightmares* concludes with a total eradication of sexual difference. Woman is deprived of her potentially subversive heterogeneity and becomes a completely predictable mirror image of man. Violently driven out of the Dark Continent of her hitherto inscrutable alterity, she finds herself compelled either to become or – more ominously perhaps – to enter the colonised, systematically enclosed Africa of man.[20]

The sheer excess of this resolution conveys a further weakness in Welsh's writing in terms of his predilection for graphic, and often rather cheap, shock beyond the more everyday banal brutality of scheme life. Moreover, this tendency sits uncomfortably alongside, and even undercuts, Welsh's ability to humanise his subjects, allowing a broad readership to empathise and understand the motives of complex characters like Mark Renton or Roy Strang. In *Trainspotting* Welsh also provides a more empathetic space for female subjectivity via the passages narrated by Kelly. Her inclusion may be primarily a means by which Welsh demonstrates the misogynistic and insensitive ways in which men routinely treat women, but Kelly nevertheless remains a strong and positive character. Kelly not only demonstrates her own ability for retaliation, she also aspires to something more fulfilling and is taking a degree at Edinburgh University as a means of self-advancement. Unlike the feckless Renton who dropped out of his degree course at Aberdeen after a year, Kelly possesses the determination and force of character to succeed. Welsh's interest in the failure of men to understand and connect outside a narrowly defined and heavily policed sense of strictly heterosexual homosociality is further explored via the question of homosexuality. In *Trainspotting* Renton allows himself to be picked up by an old Italian man in a porn cinema in London, while in *Marabou Stork Nightmares* this is through

Roy's relationship with his gay half-brother Bernard. Christopher Whyte has denounced Welsh for perpetrating the strict delineation between an essentially heterosexual Scottishness and homosexual otherness,[21] however, Zoe Strachan provides a more positive assessment of the way in which characters like Mark Renton are tolerant and even empathetic towards homosexuals.[22] In this way, Welsh not only attempts to posit a vital alternative to the queer-hating paranoia of Scottish hard man, but he also retains an amoral sense of difference within his depiction of the Scottish schemes.

## ALAN WARNER: TOWARDS A NEW HIGHLAND MYTHOLOGY

The contemporary Scottish writer most frequently linked with Welsh is Alan Warner. His 1995 debut novel *Morvern Callar* – the story of a young woman who escapes the limitations of her life in a West Highland town for the hedonistic Spanish rave scene – drew immediate comparisons given Welsh's association with drug and club culture. However, a more substantial point of connection lies in Warner's own acknowledged debt to James Kelman,[23] an influence most obviously apparent in their respective use of language and fascination with the mundane detail of the rituals of everyday life. Yet as with Welsh, Kelman also provides Warner with something to react against, in particular his refusal to 'tell stories'.[24] Consequently, Kelman's suspicion of bourgeois narrative is conspicuously discarded in the inventive and often fantastical narratives that distinguish *Morvern Callar* and Warner's other novels, *These Demented Lands* (1997), *The Sopranos* (1998) and *The Man Who Walks* (2002). Also apparent in Warner's work is an eclectic range of national and international literary influences from Gogol to MacDiarmid, Camus to Stevenson. While Welsh has at times colluded with his media image 'as some kind of *idiot savant* who had learned to write by reading comics and listening to Iggy Pop',[25] Warner has adamantly asserted in various interviews his profound interest in and engagement with serious literature, while rejecting, with equal force, his easy co-option into the so-called 'Chemical Generation' of fashionable young writers.

Like Welsh, Warner creates a coherent and consistent fictional world, in this case centred around a small West Highland town, 'the Port' (a version of Oban) and its hinterland. The essentially rural world of Warner's fictions distinguishes his works from the inner city associated with Welsh and Kelman, yet life in the Port is still determined by the same economic and social forces as urban existence. Indeed, the rural backdrop can serve to render the fragmentary pressures of post-industrial society even more acutely.

Warner consequently depicts a world marked by the conspicuous consumption of various forms of leisure – be it music, films, fashion, drinking, clubbing or drug taking. However, this is framed by a crazed hedonistic pursuit of pleasure that is clearly a response to the quiet desperation of a rural population subject to the chill winds of economic and social insecurity, within a set of opportunities limited by circumstance and geography. The eponymous heroine of *Morvern Callar*, a 21-year-old who works in the local Superstore understands the process by which people become trapped by the machinations of global capitalism:

> Cause of tallness I had started part-time with the superstore when thirteen, the year it got built. The superstore turn a blind eye; get as much out you as they can. You ruin your chances at school doing every evening and weekend. The manager has you working all hours cash in hand, no insurance, so when fifteen or sixteen you go full-time at the start of that summer and never go back to school.[26]

This critical perspective is further fed by her stepfather, Red Hanna, a railway man and staunch trade unionist who tells Morvern that 'there is no point in having desire unless you've money'.[27] In Warner's novels it is primarily young women who perceive the limitations of such an existence and who seek something more fulfilling and sustainable. A common response is the journey, which in *Morvern Callar* and *These Demented Lands*, takes the form of a kind of mythic odyssey that serves to reinvigorate and transform not only the life of the protagonist but by extension the mythopoeic representation of rural Scotland itself.

*Morvern Callar* begins with the eponymous heroine discovering the dead body of her boyfriend, setting the cool detached tone that was to distinguish Warner's debut:

> He'd cut His throat with the knife. He'd near chopped off His hand with the meat cleaver. He couldn't object so I lit a silk cut. A sort of wave of something was going across me. There was fright but I'd daydreamed how I'd be.[28]

Morvern's narrative is related in the rhythms and quirks of her distinctive inner voice, naïve and uneducated, she conspicuously lacks the self-awareness and probing intellect of Irvine Welsh's protagonists. She is more attuned to the sensations and surface details that comprise the substance of her world – be it painting her nails, smoking a cigarette, recording compilations of music – than in exploring or conveying her emotions. As Sophy Dale puts it: 'the effect is of a narrative voice at once denying emotion by refusing to discuss it, but suffused with wonder at the feeling of water on the skin or the play of light on the hills'.[29] In her detachment from much of the social interaction going on around, Morvern recalls Meursault from *The Outsider*. Camus' description of his own protagonist – 'an outsider to the society in which he lives, wandering on the fringe, on the outskirts of life, solitary and sensual'[30] – is also appropriate to Warner's heroine. Moreover, it is Morvern's hunger for experience that marks her out among the assortment of eccentrics who seem to populate the Port, mirroring Meursault's own enjoyment of everyday experience despite his apparent indifference to bigger emotional and moral issues. It is with the same detached coolness that on discovering her boyfriend has left the text of the novel he wants to be his legacy, she decides to pass the work off as hers on sending it to a publisher. But as suggested above, Morvern's is more than an existential dilemma, her desire to escape is also fuelled by the underlying sense of economic and social brutality surrounding her, the kind of harshness that exists among the poor, the disadvantaged and the desperate. This is hinted at through gossip in the Mantrap nightclub concerning the nastiness of men, in the excessive and border-line psychotic behaviour of some of the town's 'characters' and in the insensitive and exploitative manner of the random sexual encounters that occur in the Port.

Morvern's distinctive subjectivity also gives the novel an elliptical quality with regard to its temporal dimension. While some scenes are extended via the exploration of sensation, at other moments the narrative jumps forward without any clear rationale. Following the initial Christmas/Hogmanay section we fast-forward to Summer time with the information that 'All was as per usual till open-starlight-days, then actual heatwave comes to the port.'[31] While her second visit to Spain comprises a period of four years, condensed into a mere twenty-six pages of painting toenails, tanning, raving and swimming alone in the sea at night, culminating in a kind of epiphany:

> I turned facing the sea. You heard a drip come off my hair. I closed my eyes there in the quietness just breathing in and breathing in. I hadn't slept for three days so I could know every minute of the happiness that I never dared dream I had the right.[32]

The final section of the novel features Morvern's attempt to get back to the Port, wandering along the frozen railway line at night and stopping off at the village where her boyfriend grew up, before culminating in a typically enigmatic manner: 'I placed both hands on my tummy at the life there, the life growing right in there. The child of the raves. I put my head down and closed my mouth. I started walking forward into that night.'[33] Morvern herself is an orphan and we never find out anything about her real parents. Her stepmother also remains an enigma, she is dead and buried on the nearby island to which she travels at the start of *These Demented Lands*. This decision is motivated by a piece of information Morvern receives at the end of the first novel, positioning the latter as a direct sequel. And significantly, on the way to the island the ferry sinks, forcing her to swim to shore.

*These Demented Lands* in part comprises Morvern's written account of what subsequently happens to her on the Island she travels to, culminating in the birth of her daughter. Her narrative is interspersed with a second manuscript, that of the mysterious Aircrash Investigator who is also resident in the Drome Hotel, located next to the graveyard where Morvern's stepmother is buried and managed by the demonic John Brotherhood, a former gun runner. The novel conveys a new engagement with textuality in terms of the construction of the main text from other texts. There is also an editor's note and a fragment torn text from what we later discover is the Aircrash Investigator's manuscript incorporated into Morvern's narrative: 'it was only months later I'd read His pages'.[34] This textual dualism immediately recalls such potent touchstones of the Scottish literary tradition as Hogg's *Confessions of a Justified Sinner* and Stevenson's *The Master of Ballantrae* as well as Alasdair Gray's own reworking of this tradition in *Lanark*. Warner also extends his interest in creating a vibrant new mythic vision of Scotland through Morvern's Odyssey to and then across the unidentified island. *These Demented Lands* shifts the balance much more towards the mythic, the necessity of which is affirmed by the Argonaut when he tells the Aircraft Investigator 'When our myths fade we must revitalise them. Understand?'[35]

Not only does Morvern's strange encounters recall those of Homer's Odysseus or Lewis Caroll's Alice, the Island itself is posited as a kind of netherworld reminiscent of Unthank in *Lanark*. Indeed, just as Duncan Thaw commits suicide by drowning before his reincarnation as Lanark, so the sinking of the ferry at the beginning of *These Demented Lands* can be read as death, a crossing to the other side. Morvern's odyssey is doubled by that of the Aircrash Investigator's journey, the vivid image of him with a propeller strapped to his back and a jellyfish on his head mimicking a crown of thorns clearly evoking Christ's road to Calvary. However, the birth of Morvern's child at the climax of the novel, accompanied by fire imagery rather than water, would appear to posit a new beginning:

> A window exploded then the curtains in the dining room tore outwards and erupted. The fire burned along the roof towards the pine plantation and through my tears I saw a string of trees lift up in a rush of fire, windows burst out and the roof tiles curled above the kitchens where I'd turned on the deep-fat friers earlier: full power, wet tea-towels over.
>
> Soon, all the way down, the blockade of pine plantation was alight and, as my child was born in a burst of blood and the forester whirled

her free, the smeared face of an ancient prophet or seer came close to mine, smearing a mucousy blood across one of my tits, nipple erect in smoke-driven breeze while the inferno of trees fell ...[36]

Morvern and her daughter are subsequently placed in a coffin pulled by Charlie the shirehorse, an allusion to the flight to Egypt. The final image is of flashing semaphore lights on the hillside, a 'chaos of blinkings, dyings and flourishings like God's Christmas tree: the entire sky seemed to be doing press ups'.[37] This ending not only recalls the apocalyptic destruction of Unthank, Warner also has Morvern sign off with Gray's signature 'Goodbye'.

Warner returns to the terrain of female subjectivity in *The Sopranos*, the tale of a group of vivacious fifth-year Catholic schoolgirls who are also members of the school choir. During a visit to Edinburgh, ostensibly to take part in a singing competition, the girls embark on a hedonistic binge of shopping and drinking. The thrilling encounter with the city serves to highlight the limitations of their usual existence: 'Their senses were in a kind of overload: all the colours and motion simultaneously. Their heads were moving fast, from side to side to take sights in so they looked each other hardly ever in the face as they talked.'[38] In this way Warner returns to the question of opportunity and human potential in relation to young working-class women whose limited choices rarely extend beyond low-paid insecure work and motherhood.

In contrast, *The Man Who Walks*, a return to the contemplation of a mythic Scotland, focuses resolutely on masculinity. The protagonists – the epony-mous 'Man' and his nephew, 'The Macushla' – are not only male, but examples of the kind of rough, unpredictable and border-line psychotic confined to the background of Warner's previous novels. In contrast to instinctive women like Morvern Callar, both characters are idiosyncratic versions of the organic intellectual – the nephew, for example, owns an eclectic library of books and peppers his inner speech with a mixture of literary allusions and obscenities: 'That reminds me, the nephew thought. Must re-read T. S. Eliot's Notes Towards a Definition of Culture, yacuntya, as he sipped a gush more lager.'[39] The narrative of *The Man Who Walks* is built around yet another journey, with the nephew on the trail of his Uncle who has killed the nephew's four pet budgies and stolen the World Cup kitty from the Mantrap. This takes him north to Ballachullish and Fort William before ending up at the site of the Battle of Culloden near Inverness. Along the way, Warner interrogates various Highland myths – from the tale of the vanished Roman legion to the murder site of Colin Campbell, the Red Fox – while simultaneously creating his own new mythology comprising ancient family gatherings and legendary occult manuscripts to a new film production of Stevenson's *Kidnapped*, featuring a black Alan Breck. The novel culminates with the Nephew, his knee caps having been smashed by the real villains, crawling alone around a piece of wilderness which turns out to be a movie set recreating the aftermath of the Battle of Culloden, the landscape littered with artificial corpses. In this way Warner once again contemplates the creative powers of myth and imagination as weapons against the economic, emotional and spiritual poverty of post-industrial society while critiquing the limitations of exploitative kitsch.

## WELSH, WARNER AND CINEMATIC ADAPTATION

Both Welsh and Warner's works are saturated with references to cinema culture. *Trainspotting* begins with Renton and Sick Boy watching a Jean Claude Van Damme video, while in Warner's novels there is an implied tension between reading and watching films, with Morvern Callar more interested in videos than 'His' manuscript. Consequently, it is no surprise that the work of both has proven rich and popular material for filmic adaptation. A major watershed in Scottish cinema in the 1990s was the critical and commercial success of the Edinburgh-set thriller *Shallow Grave*.[40] At the triumphant screening of the film at the 1994 Edinburgh Film Festival, the creative team behind the production announced that their next project was to be an adaptation of *Trainspotting*. This proved to be an even greater phenomenon than its predecessor. Fully funded by Channel Four to the tune of £1.7 million, the film was also given an unprecedented high-profile £1 million marketing campaign in the UK by distribution company Polygram. The commercial instincts of both companies were vindicated with *Trainspotting* proving the most profitable British release of 1996, earning more than £12 million in the domestic market and over $72 million internationally. The key selling points for the film were a combination of the cult status of the original novel, the risqué subject matter and an attractive ensemble cast of talented young actors, some of whom were on the verge of major stardom. They included Ewan McGregor, cast in the central role of Mark Renton, Robert Carlyle (Begbie), Jonnie Lee Miller (Sick Boy), Ewan Bremner (Spud), Kevin McKidd (Tommy) and Kelly MacDonald (Diane).[41] But the impact of *Trainspotting* also lay in the way in which director Danny Boyle, writer John Hodge and their creative collaborators had transformed Welsh's novel into something distinctively cinematic. As they had done previously with *Shallow Grave*, the film-makers eschewed the kind of gritty naturalistic aesthetic associated with such contemporary hard-edged subject matter in British film, drawing instead on the stylish techniques of a tradition of American independent cinema.

Bursting into life with Renton's dash along Edinburgh's Princes Street, the police in hot pursuit, accompanied on the soundtrack by the frantic beat of Iggy Pop's 'Lust for Life' and Renton's own emblematic mantra:

> Choose life. Choose a job. Choose a career. Choose a family. Choose a fucking big television. Choose washing machines, cars, compact disc players and electrical tin openers. Choose good health, low cholesterol and dental insurance. Choose fixed interest mortgage repayments. Choose a starter home. Choose your friends. Choose leisurewear and matching luggage. Choose a three piece suite in a range of fucking fabrics. Choose DIY and wonder how you are on a fucking Sunday morning. Choose sitting on that couch watching mind numbing, spirit crushing game shows, stuffing fucking junk food into your mouth. Choose rotting away at the end of it all, pishing your last in a miserable home, nothing more than an embarrassment to the fucked up selfish brats you've spawned to replace yourself. Choose your future. Choose life. But why would I want to do a thing like that? I chose not to choose life. I chose something else. And the reasons? There are no reasons. Who needs reasons when you've got heroin![42]

The subsequent filmic narrative is built around a series of largely studio-based set pieces charting Renton's experiences of junk dependency and attempts to kick the habit. This is punctuated by his brief romance with Diane, his move to London to escape the inevitable downward spiral of life in Edinburgh, and the final drug deal that provides Renton with a more meaningful means of escape. Boyle renders this by way of one hand the playful self-reflexivity of the French *nouvelle vague* and its refraction through the British films of Dick Lester (*A Hard Day's Night*, *Help!*, *The Knack*) and the 'New Hollywood' of Martin Scorsese and Quentin Tarantino. This contributes much to the film's sense of zest and is manifest in the temporal manipulations, freeze frames, intrusive editing, split screens, on-screen subtitles, as well as giving an edge to some of the performances. This is leavened, however, with a more ominous neo-expressionist undertone of low camera angles and garish colour schemes – the vivid reds, greens, oranges and blues in Mother Superior's drug den recreating the palette of Francis Bacon. Murray Smith dubs the film's aesthetic 'black magic realism', distinguished by 'a concentration on the most dismal aspects of realist *mise en scène*, in order both to draw a kind of gallows humour from them, and to lay the groundwork for a miraculous transformation of them'.[43] A key sequence in this respect features Renton's attempts to retrieve his opium suppositories from a filthy toilet, culminating in his disappearing into the bowl and diving for pearls through clear blue water. While for Smith, this is motivated in part by the transformative effects of drugs, it also reinforces a certain inclination towards what he terms 'aesthetic redemption':

The film depicts poverty realistically, but in a way that encompasses possibilities of escape as well as stories of entrapment. Moreover, *Trainspotting* exploits the aesthetics of film (set design, lighting, visual composition, musical scoring, and so forth) to draw a kind of vitality from grinding poverty.[44]

Another defining aspect of *Trainspotting* is the use of music, the soundtrack bringing together such luminaries of the 1970s' drug counterculture as Iggy Pop and Lou Reed with a roll call of the hippest bands associated with 1990s 'Britpop' and club culture including Blur, Pulp, Sleeper, Elastica, Leftfield, Primal Scream and Underworld. This not only provided another layer that could be used to sell *Trainspotting* to a young contemporary audience, but it also confirmed its status as a 'British' cultural product as opposed to the more narrowly conceived Scottish frame of reference defining Welsh's original novel. Indeed, Murray Smith locates the film firmly within a nexus of British cultural issues around music, art, football and sexual identity, as much if not more than the more local focus of the problem of heroin addiction and the rise of HIV in Edinburgh during the 1980s.[45]

In addition to making Renton more central to the filmic transformation of Welsh's narrative (and in the casting of McGregor, distinctly more handsome than the acne-scarred red head of the original text), the other major alteration is in the use of Edinburgh dialect. In this respect Welsh's concentration on the specificity of the working–class Leith speech gives way to a more accessible, if still strongly accented, variant of standard English that reflects the intended broad audience for the film. The enhanced commodity status of the film can also be related to the more intensive way in which it ponders the culture of consumption compared to the original novel. Both are concerned with a social world defined primarily in terms of leisure as opposed to work, consumption rather than production, be it legitimate forms such as pubs, clubs, five-a-side football or the illicit activities of the shooting gallery. Yet the transformation of Renton in the film takes him from his rejection of the trappings of consumer culture to an enthusiastic embracing of it, as signified by his final speech in the movie that repudiates almost word for word his opening monologue. Alan Sinfield argues that in this way Renton takes on the Thatcherite impulse that Welsh had bestowed upon Sick Boy: 'by destroying the distinction between them, the film cancels Renton's leftish rebellion, making Thatcherite selfishness the "natural" way, on or off heroin, to live'.[46] Or as Claire Monk has noted, *Trainspotting* 'addresses a generation of Thatcher's children for whom the conflation of subcultural dissent and entrepreneurial capitalism holds no contradictions'.[47] For all its warnings about the ultimate dangers of heroin, *Trainspotting* is a resolutely upbeat film, sanitising and rendering some of the novel's darker excesses more palatable for mass consumption.[48] One of capitalism's great strengths has been its ability to neutralise dissent by turning it into yet another commodity form, and arguably Welsh had been subject to this very process or branding when the style magazine, *The Face* dubbed him 'the poet laureate of the Chemical Generation'.

A contrasting depiction of life at the margins of society is provided by the film *My Name Is Joe* (1998), written by Paul Laverty and directed by Ken Loach. The narrative here revolves around an unusual and mis-matched relationship between Joe Kavanagh (Peter Mullan), a recovering alcoholic who runs a local no-hoper football team, and Sarah Downie (Louise Goodall), a local health visitor. The two meet through Sarah's clients Liam (David Mackay) and Sabine (Annemarie Kennedy) a young couple with a baby son struggling to keep their family unit together. Joe also has a paternalistic interest in Liam who is a member of his team, and he intervenes when the couple fall foul of a ruthless dealer and gangster, McGowan (David Hayman). But in agreeing to act as a drugs courier for McGowan, Joe alienates Sarah and sends his own life spinning once again out of control. But in this way *My Name is Joe* tackles head-on the ways in which the lives of those at the bottom of the heap are profoundly circumscribed by restricted opportunity and choice, presenting a very different and bleak picture to the playful high jinx of *Trainspotting*. And while Mark Renton ultimately has the ability to move on, Joe is presented as a man whose life entails an on-going struggle to keep above water and off the booze. Moreover, Liam and Sabine are also trapped in vicious cycle of drug dependency, leading ultimately to his suicide. As in that other Loach/Laverty collaboration, *Sweet Sixteen*, there seem to be no choices available to those at the bottom of the heap in post-industrial Scotland. Liam is unable to leave Glasgow, despite Joe giving him £300 with instructions to do so, deciding that the only way out is death. As John Hill suggests, 'there is something remorseless about the way in which the narrative imposes its determinist grip … A sense of pessimism dominates almost completely. Moreover, unlike previous films, there is no character who might offer a more politicised perspective on events.'[49]

One of the most exciting new Scottish film-makers to emerge at the end of the 1990s was Lynne Ramsay, whose debut feature, *Ratcatcher*, proved a considerable critical success, opening the Edinburgh Film Festival in 1999. Three years later, Ramsay followed this auspicious start with an adaptation of Alan Warner's *Morvern Callar*. In sharp contrast to the American-inspired aesthetics of *Trainspotting*, Ramsay's cinema is squarely in the traditions of the European art film as defined by the likes of Robert Bresson, Bill Douglas and Terence Davies. *Ratcatcher* had been distinguished by its intense, impressionistic concentration on the isolated subjectivity of its central protagonist and on small details – sights, sounds, emotions, interactions – characteristics shared by Warner's novel and its similar fascination with Morvern's sense of detachment and obsessive fascination with the surface of her world. Tony McKibbin also links Ramsay's two films through their shared examination of a moral attentiveness on the part of the respective protagonists who both experience a certain culpability for the death of someone close to them,[50] and it is significant that Morvern's boyfriend, referred to only as 'Him' in the novel, is, in Ramsay's adaptation, given the name James Gillespie after ill-fated young protagonist of *Ratcatcher*. Ramsay cast the English actor Samantha Morton as Morvern, a performer with a proven track record in playing rather enigmatic young women.[51] Morton's detached coolness contrasts effectively with the garrulous and slightly gauche persona of Lanna, played by newcomer Kathleen McDermott. Her inexperience effectively conveys Lanna's small-town directness and unease, particularly when outside the familiarity of her familiar geographical and social domain. Unlike Morvern, Lanna is comfortable joining in the tacky and vulgar poolside games at the hotel in Spain and in chatting up the lads in the clubs, whereas she lacks the curiosity that drives Morvern's desire to find a more 'authentic' Spain. Lanna later refuses to leave the Port again with Morvern, claiming she is happy on home ground – 'it's the same crap everywhere – so stop dreaming'.

Ramsay's adaptation of Warner sets out in part to reclaim a female perspective – a reaction to the reservations expressed at the almost voyeuristic way in which the novel presents Morvern's sexual behaviour, in particular the homoerotic undertones of scenes between her and Lanna. The construction of the character is also resolutely cinematic. Linda Ruth Williams compares *Morvern Callar* to Michelangelo Antonioni's 1975 feature *The Passenger*, which Morvern actually watches at one point in the novel.[52] In both, the central protagonist attempts to fundamentally change his/her life by assuming the identity of a dead man, in Ramsay's we are presented with a protagonist whose presence is continually called into question. This is signified visually in the opening scene where we first see her, lying on the floor next to her boyfriend's corpse, the flashing Christmas tree light illuminating Morvern's face then plunging it back into darkness, repeated in the later sequence in the Spanish nightclub. The effect is a simultaneous presence/ absence, now you see her, now you don't, underlining Morvern's ethereal qualities. The audience's access to Morvern as a character is therefore a complex and ultimately distanced one. Williams suggests that the viewer is 'placed in a peculiar position of sharing her solipsism while never knowing what is driving it',[53] a perspective reinforced by the way in which the camera continually frames Morvern in thresholds, particularly doorways. The use of music also reinforces this effect – with the audience briefly sharing Morvern's auditory sensations of the music on the compilation tape her boyfriend left, only for it to cut to the distanced, tinny and muffled sound of someone else's Walkman.

## DAVID KANE: THE POST-INDUSTRIAL ROMANTIC COMEDY

In addition to the straight adaptations of Welsh and Warner for the big screen, a further significant engagement with the central issues of this chapter has been made by the writer/director David Kane within the distinct but linked domains of television drama and cinema.[54] Kane's major breakthrough came when he won the Lloyd's Bank National Screenwriter's award for *Shadow on the Earth*, subsequently filmed in 1988 as a BBC 'Screen Two' production. Set in 1961, the film explores the deep-rooted anti-Catholic bigotry of Central Scotland via its allegorical story of a group of young children in a West Lothian mining village who become convinced that the strange albino man who regularly watches the night sky through his telescope is an alien. Kane followed this with *Dream Baby* (1989), the sparky tale of an unemployed young girl (Jenny McCrindle) living in Edinburgh's notorious Craigmillar estate who pretends to be pregnant as a means of escaping her predicament – extorting money from the two men who think the child is theirs to fund a round-the-world trip with her friend. *Dream Baby* demonstrated the acuteness of Kane's sensitivity towards questions of gender – which in the overtly masculine focus of Scottish drama made his contribution all the more refreshing. *Dream Baby* is also set against a backdrop of pressing social issues including life on the dole, Scottish resistance to the iniquitous poll tax – a misguided and hugely unpopular policy that ultimately led to Margaret Thatcher's downfall – and the emerging problem of intravenous drug use on Scottish housing schemes. After writing two major drama series,[55] Kane realised his ambitions to direct his own scripts in 1995 with *Ruffian Hearts*. Scheduled by the BBC as part of 'Love Bites', a trilogy of thematically-linked dramas, Kane's bitter-sweet romantic comedy received an enthusiastic critical reception and subsequently paved the way for his graduation into the realm of cinema with the 1999 feature *This Year's Love*.[56]

One of the immediate distinguishing characteristics of Kane's major works are their multi-character, ensemble approach of a kind that tends to be confined to soap operas and popular TV drama series such as *This Life* and *Cold Feet*. Even the film version of *Trainspotting*, which vigorously exploited the image of its ensemble cast in a high profile marketing campaign, eschews the multi-perspective structure of Welsh's original novel in favour of a unambiguous reliance on the centrality of Mark Renton, and on Ewan

McGregor's emerging star quality. *Ruffian Hearts*, on the other hand, gives almost equal weight to its central core of eight characters, linked by the unusual tenement in Garnett Hill that five of them occupy – a Glasgow version of the bohemian Manhattan loft conversion. *This Year's Love* features a tighter narrative structure that more directly recalls Max Ophuls' classic self-reflexive meditation on love, *La Ronde* (1951). Opening with the wedding of Danny (Douglas Henshall) and Hannah (Catherine McCormick), two young Scots in London, this marriage is a mere 35 minutes old before Danny finds out that Hannah has slept with his best man and immediately storms out of the reception. At Heathrow he gets drunk and subsequently meets Marey (Kathy Burke), an airport cleaner. Meanwhile Hannah is chatted up in a Camden pub by Cameron (Dougray Scott), a scruffy Scottish artist who preys on women who place messages in the lonely hearts column. Then Cameron's flat-mate Liam (Ian Hart) meets Sophie (Jennifer Ehle), an unemployed single mother, and so the merry-go-round commences. All three couplings inevitably come unstuck and the narrative jumps one year on. Marey meets Cameron at an auction where he is selling one of his paintings, Sophie hooks up with Danny after getting a tattoo at his shop, while Liam encounters Hannah at a singles event, becomes besotted with her and moves into the spare room in her flat. Hannah for her part has entered into a liaison with a woman called Alice (Emily Woof) and when Liam catches the two of them together in bed, he tries to kill himself in remorse. As the various relationships fall apart, once again, the wheel turns and we flash forward another year. This time Cameron and Sophie and Marey and Liam begin ill-fated relationships. In contrast, Danny and Hannah end up reuniting and flying off on honeymoon, so completing the narrative cycle. The effect of Kane's ensemble approach is to place greater emphasis on the shared, rather than the individual, experience of the ups and downs of love and romance. This strategy necessarily points up the social context in terms of the extended network of interactions that give dramatic structure and texture to both films. In Kane's world, society may have been radically transformed but its enduring existence is positively affirmed. Both *Ruffian Hearts* and *This Year's Love* are populated by distinctive and individual characters, but it is the wider and continually changing and necessary communal framework of interconnections that is Kane's ultimate concern, giving his work a social conscience conspicuously lacking in most romantic comedies.

This central concern with the social is enhanced by a consideration of the ways in which Kane's romantic comedies engage with other aspects of urban post-industrial society. The distinctive inner-city locations in his films function as an intrinsic part of the drama, spaces in which particular forms of domestic, leisure and economic interaction predominate. The Camden Town of *This Year's Love* is described by Jonathan Romney as a place 'where people collide in a faux-carnival setting',[57] an environment of up-market bars and grubby bedsits, market stalls and bookies, in which the style-conscious young rub shoulders with the detritus of humanity. While embracing the contradictions and stark contrasts of the post-industrial inner city, the location also conveys a palpable sense of energy and a possibility for renewal and change that are absent in the more socially homogenous environments of the housing estate or the suburb. But what is also significant is the absence in Kane's films of any residual whiff of nostalgia for a more stable, industrialised past of the kind that is such a feature of the 1980s' TV dramas of Bryden, McDougall and McGrath. The consequences of such fluid and unstable forms of living affect Kane's protagonists in different ways. Some adopt thick-skinned strategies, turning insecurity to their own advantage and exploiting the weaknesses of others. Some survive by holding on to their dreams through expressing their creativity, while the over-sensitive, notably Liam in *This Year's Love*, inevitably end up as society's casualties. Yet the general sense of these dramas is that life goes on and people find ways of getting by – occasionally finding love and happiness, however temporary. In this way Kane also rejects the sense of hopelessness and defeat that permeates Ken Loach's narratives of despair in *My Name is Joe* and *Sweet Sixteen*.

While the cultural identity of *Ruffian Hearts* is unquestionably Glaswegian, *This Year's Love*, on the other hand, features the interactions of three Scots, a Liverpudlian, and two Londoners from opposite ends of the social scale. Yet the accent of the film itself is distinctly Caledonian, retaining a hard-edged comic sensibility that is darker, more acerbic and ultimately more socially concerned that most of the British romantic comedies to which it has been compared.[58] Moreover, the distinctly 'Scottish' perspective of *This Year's Love* serves to reconfigure class conflict along devolutionary lines with the familiar – if essentially problematic – association between Scottishness and the virtues of proletarian culture contrasted against the values of a bourgeois and Anglocentric British culture. This is brought into sharp relief in the two sequences where Scottish men are brought into contact with Sophie's world of class privilege. Danny's rage against the hypocritical decorum of the bourgeois cocktail party leads him to demand that Sophie make up her mind who she is and where she belongs. This scene also reveals Danny's own deep insecurities (acknowledging a national character flaw) and contrasts with the way in which Cameron's ill-mannered if refreshingly honest behaviour during his meeting with Sophie's patrician parents is played squarely for laughs. It is instructive that Sophie's brief liaison with Liam, a working-class Liverpudlian, involves no such confrontation of social difference, rather their incompatibility revolves around her dissatisfaction with his immaturity and sexual inadequacies. Moreover, the proletarian, demotic empathy, embodied in the performances of Douglas Henshall and Dougray

Scott in the film as a whole, provides a telling contrast with the bourgeois, polished and ultimately rather smug English persona of Hugh Grant, the actor most iconically associated with the British romantic comedy.

## REFLECTING POST-INDUSTRIAL REALITIES

The fictions considered in this chapter constitute a new engagement with the social, economic and political realities of the 1990s. The lives, perceptions and expectations of 'Thatcher's children' proved markedly different to those of their parents and grandparents. Gone are the expectations of stable communities, jobs for life, security and predictability. These have been replaced by uncertainty, instability and transience, generating a deep sense of anxiety. On the other hand, the more fluid structures characterising post-industrial society have presented new opportunities and possibilities for those able to perceive them. The fictions of Irvine Welsh, Alan Warner and David Kane respond in different ways to this new world, and in particular the indeterminate and transitory quality of life as experienced by their youthful protagonists. Welsh's insightful focus on the anomic side of contemporary urban existence tends towards a rather pessimistic assessment in that the only means of transcendence for his characters is through exile or death. In contrast, Kane's faith in the ability of people to muddle through is bolstered by his affirmation of the communality of experience and in the redemptive qualities of love and romance – however temporary and transient particular relationships may prove to be. While Warner constructs a new mythology of Highland Scotland, based once again on a sense of mobility as a creative and affirmative challenge to the social, economic, emotional and psychological damage wrought by post-industrialisation. In addition to a shared concern with the individual/community dialectic, the question of gender remains a central issue in the work of all three. Once again, Welsh's explorations of Scottish masculinity tend towards the pessimistic, resurrecting the Scottish hard man in a new and more atavistic form. While his implied (but largely unexplored) sympathies for a female alternative to the dead end of masculinity are taken up instead by Warner and Kane, both of whom demonstrate a new and more forceful commitment and sensitivity to the role and experience of young women in contemporary Scottish society. In moving beyond both the sour harridans of Peter McDougall and the fantasy projections of Bill Forsyth or Alasdair Gray, this fundamental acknowledgement of the importance of women by male writers and film-makers is a testimony to the impact of feminism and the cultural achievements explored in the previous chapter.

## NOTES

1. Will Hutton, *The State We're In*, revised edition (London: Vintage, 1996), pp. 105–10. Christopher Harvie cites a 1998 Scottish Council Institute report identifying a tripartite division into what it terms 'settled Scotland, insecure Scotland and excluded Scotland', in which the factors of location, age and health played a significant role in conjunction with that of occupation. Christopher Harvie, *Scotland & Nationalism: Scottish Society and Politics 1707 to the Present*, third edition (London: Routledge, 1998), p. 214.

2. Steve Redhead, *Repetitive Beat Generation* (Edinburgh: Rebel Inc., 2000), p. 142.

3. See Duncan McLean, 'Time Bombs: A Short History of the Clocktower Press', Introduction to McLean (ed.), *Ahead of Its Time: A Clocktower Press Anthology* (London: Jonathan Cape, 1997).

4. Gordon Legge's debut novel, *The Shoe*, was published by Polygon in 1989.

5. Irvine Welsh, *Trainspotting* (London: Secker & Warburg, 1993), p. 11.

6. Jenny Turner, 'Sick Boys', *London Review of Books*, 2 December 1993, p. 10.

7. Robert Morace, *Irvine Welsh's Trainspotting* (New York: Continuum, 2001), p. 25.

8. Alan Freeman, 'Ghosts in Sunny Leith: Irvine Welsh's *Trainspotting*', in Susanne Hagemann (ed.), *Studies in Scottish Fiction 1945 to the Present* (Frankfurt: Peter Lang, 1996), p. 254.

9. Ibid. p. 257.

10. In Welsh's fiction Glaswegians very much occupy the position of 'Other'.

11. Nicholas M. Williams, 'The Dialect of Authenticity: The Case of Irvine Welsh's *Trainspotting*', in Tom Hoenselaars and Marius Buning (eds), *English and Other Languages* (Amsterdam: Rodopi, 1999), p. 230.

12. Robert Morace, *Irvine Welsh's Trainspotting*, p. 53.

13. Irvine Welsh, *Trainspotting*, p. 6.

14. Ibid. p. 78.

15. Ibid. p. 210.

16. Ibid. p. 221.

17. Ibid. p. 126.

18. Dermot Kelly, 'Trainspotting: Papish Punk – Proddie Rock', *Cencrastus*, No. 66, p. 33.

19. Irvine Welsh, *Marabou Stork Nightmares* (London: Jonathan Cape, 1995), p. 190.

20. Ibid. p. 156.

21. See Christopher Whyte, 'Masculinities in Contemporary Scottish Fiction', *Forum for Modern Language Studies*, XXXIV No. 3, July 1998.

22. See Zoe Strachan, 'Queerspotting', *Spike Magazine*. www.spikemagazine.com

23. 'I don't think I could have had the courage to write if I hadn't glanced over a single page of Kelman', Sophy Dale, 'An Interview with Alan Warner', *Edinburgh Review*, No. 103, p. 126.

24. Sophy Dale, *Alan Warner's Morvern Callar* (New York: Continuum, 2002), p. 17. Warner also benefited greatly from his acquaintance with Duncan McLean, whose short story collection, *A Bucket of Tongues* (London: Secker & Warburg, 1992) had suggested the possibility of contemporary Scottish fiction with a rural setting.

25. Andrew Crummy, 'Irvine Welsh', http://www3.sympatico.ca/simsg/bio.htm

26. Alan Warner, *Morvern Callar* (London: Jonathan Cape, 1995), p. 10.

27. Ibid. p. 45.

28. Alan Warner, *Morvern Callar*, p. 1.

29. Sophy Dale, *Alan Warner's Morvern Callar* (New York: Contiuum, 2002), p. 13.

30. Albert Camus, 'Afterword', *The Outsider* (London: Penguin Classics, 2000), p. 118.

31. Alan Warner, *Morvern Callar*, p. 76.

32. Ibid. p. 210.

33. Ibid. p. 229.

34. Alan Warner, *These Demented Lands* (London: Jonathan Cape, 1997), p. 16.

35. Ibid. p. 163.

36. Ibid. pp. 210–11.

37. Ibid. p. 215.

38. Alan Warner, *The Sopranos* (London: Jonathan Cape, 1998), p. 97.

39. Alan Warner, *The Man Who Walks* (London: Jonathan Cape, 2002), p. 199.

40. See Duncan Petrie, *Screening Scotland* (London: BFI, 2000), pp. 191–9.

41. Murray Smith pulls no punches in his acknowledgement of the film's impact and the enormous cultural significance of *Trainspotting* 'as a lightning rod for debate across a wide array of social, cultural and aesthetic matters; including "ladishness", male sexual inadequacy and musical and footballing obsessiveness'. *Trainspotting*, BFI Modern Classics (London: BFI, 2002), p. 11.

42. John Hodge, *Trainspotting* (London: Faber & Faber, 1996).

43. Murray Smith, *Trainspotting*, p. 75.

44. Ibid. p. 33.

45. It is also instructive that Smith tends to describe the particularly Scottish aspects of both film and novel – in particular the use of dialect – as 'regional' rather than 'national', reinforcing the British (as opposed to Scottish) frame of reference.

46. Alan Sinfield, *Literature, Politics and Culture in Postwar Britain*, second edition (London: Athlone, 1997), p. xxvii.

47. Claire Monk, 'Underbelly UK: The 1990s Underclass Film, Masculinity and the Ideologies of "New" Britain', in Justine Ashby and Andrew Higson (eds), *British Cinema Past and Present* (London: Routledge, 2000), p. 285.

48. One difference concerns the speech Renton makes in the pub about hating the Scots for allowing themselves to be colonised by the English and consequently blaming everything on the coloniser. In the film, this rant is in response to Tommy's patriotic enthusiasm for the countryside, 'the great outdoors', that makes him feel proud to be Scottish, but which Spud regards as 'not natural', as he takes another swig from his can of beer. While the original implied a critique of Scottish masculinity, Renton's speech in the film invokes a critique of a deeply rooted tradition of visual representation that reduces Scottish national identity to the picturesque depopulated vistas of mountains and lochs.

49. John Hill, 'Failure and Utopianism: Representations of the Working Class in British Cinema of the 1990s', in Robert Murphy (ed.), *British Cinema of the 90s* (London: BFI, 2000), pp. 182–3.

50. See Tony McKibbin, 'Singular Ethics: Lynne Ramsay's Morvern Callar', *Cencrastus*, No. 74, 2003.

51. Indeed, McKibbin notes Morton's 'capacity for autism, for playing characters for whom language can't hope to express their thoughts'. Ibid., p. 30.

52. Linda Ruth Williams, 'Escape Artist', *Sight and Sound*, October 2002, p. 24.

53. Ibid. p. 23.

54. While a student at Dundee's Duncan of Jordanston Art College Kane was inspired to start writing by the presence of John Byrne as writer in residence.

55. The over-ambitious eco-thriller *Jute City* (1991), and *Finney* (1993) a gritty tale set in the criminal underworld of Newcastle.

56. Made on a budget of £4 million, ten times the cost of *Ruffian Hearts*, this represented a

significant elevation for Kane in terms of his aesthetic ambition and his potential audience.

57. Jonathan Romney, *The Guardian*, 19 February 1999.

58. Robert Murphy links *This Year's Love* with *Four Weddings and a Funeral* (Mike Newell, 1994), *Jack and Sarah* (Tim Sullivan, 1995), *Sliding Doors* (Peter Howitt, 1997), *Martha – Meet Frank, Daniel and Laurence* (Nick Hamm, 1998) and *Notting Hill* (Roger Michell, 1998). See Robert Murphy, 'Citylife: Urban Fairy Tales in Late 90s British Cinema', in Murphy (ed.), *The British Cinema Book*, second edition (London: BFI, 2001).

# Part II

# Themes and Traditions

# CHAPTER 5

# A Walk on the Dark Side

## INTRODUCTION

One of the most striking features of Scottish cultural production of the past twenty years is an unsettling sense of nastiness permeating both literary and cinematic works. As Angus Calder remarks, 'the Scotland of recent fiction has been a grim and dangerous place'.[1] On a superficial level, this phenomenon can be seen as the latest manifestation of the familiar themes of desperation and violence that are central to the Clydeside 'hard man' tradition. But such a preoccupation with a darker and more destructive side of the human condition not only asserts distance from the respectability and refinement of bourgeois, Anglo-centric high culture. It can equally be regarded as a reaction to the cloying sentimentality and whimsy of a Kailyard tradition that continues to hold sway in certain quarters within Scottish culture. Under-pinning such atavistic expressions is a deeply rooted and distinct tradition of Scottish Gothic that can be traced back to a fascination with the macabre and the supernatural characterising Shakespeare's *Macbeth* and subsequent influential works by Robert Burns, James Hogg and Robert Louis Stevenson. Moreover, the power of this tradition still holds sway in the Scottish cultural imagination and can be discerned in a range of important contemporary novels and films.

The wider Gothic tradition in literature is a broad and complex field embracing a diverse range of authors and historical 'movements'. Its origins are frequently associated with the novels of Horace Walpole, Anne Radcliffe, M. G. Lewis, Mary Shelley, Charles Maturin and others, written between 1760 and 1820 and featuring tales of sinister castles, embattled heroines and predatory foreign aristocrats. Also significant are the later decedent fictions of the Victorian *fin-de-siècle*, notably Stevenson's *The Strange Case of Dr. Jekyll and Mr. Hyde*, Oscar Wilde's *The Picture of Dorian Gray* and Bram Stoker's *Dracula*, which are more concerned with various macabre and uncanny physical transformations. But the category Gothic has also been applied more widely to embrace the ghost story, the horror film and certain aspects of postmodern fiction. Despite this range and diversity, David Punter suggests that the heart (as opposed to the body) of the Gothic tradition can be characterised in relation to a fundamental concern with the issues of paranoia, barbarism and the taboo, bound together by a preoccupation with fear.[2] Such expressions can be related to and motivated by particular socio-historical contexts. Kelly Hurley, for example, regards the Gothic as 'an instrumental genre, re-emerging cyclically, at periods of cultural stress, to negotiate the anxieties that accompany social and epistemological transformations and crises'.[3] The nineteenth-century high water mark of the Gothic can consequently be posed in terms of a move from a reaction to the rationality of Enlightenment thought to an engagement with the anxieties generated by late Victorian scientific discourse ranging from Darwinism to social anthropology, sexology and pre-Freudian psychology.

Considerations of the Gothic also stress specifically national components. Cannon Schmitt, for example, identifies the ways in which Englishness comes to be embodied in the figure of the female in Gothic fictions, who is imperilled by a foreign, contaminating presence. In this way 'threatened femininity comes to stand in metonymically for the English nation itself, a generalisation of Gothic narrative with imperial as well as domestic consequences'.[4] Moreover, this sense of national vulnerability intensifies with imperial expansion and the attendant incorporation of 'aliens', Schmitt arguing that:

> comparative and negative definitions of English selfhood are invoked
> with greater frequency as the Empire comes into contact with and
> subdues more and more foreign peoples. And, somewhat paradoxically,
> an internationalisation of the foreign occurs that results in an uneasy
> awareness of a hybrid, deeply fractured and contradictory self.[5]

The Gothic therefore comes to be regarded as symptomatic of the way in which identity is forged negatively, defined against what it is not. The consequent process of policing the boundary between self and 'Other' gives rise to an internal anxiety that renders the national subject split and incapable of achieving self-identity. But despite the national specificity of his thesis, Schmitt is careful not to claim any essential correspondence between Englishness and the Gothic, which has been related to other national contexts and histories such as the American South.

It is also germane to a consideration of Scottish culture, and Schmitt's invocation of psychic division at the level of the national subject is a particularly relevant and significant issue in this context. For the most potent figure of Scottish Gothic is the diabolic and uncanny figure of the double, or doppelgänger, which Karl Miller claims 'stands at the start of that cultivation of uncertainty by which the literature of the modern world has come to be distinguished'.[6] While the double has a potent and durable presence, manifest across a wide range of cultural contexts and writers from Hoffman to Dostoevsky, Poe to Wilde, it is also central to such major Scottish writers as James Hogg and Robert Louis Stevenson. Indeed, Miller's starting point in his seminal study of the phenomenon is Hogg's 1824 novel, *The Private Memoirs and Confessions of a Justified Sinner*, a work which in turn influenced Stevenson, most obviously in *The Master of Ballantrae* and *The Strange Case of Dr. Jekyll and Mr. Hyde*. Despite being set in London, the latter tale, arguably the most singularly defining cultural representation of human duality, is imbued with a potent sense of the split personality of Stevenson's home city of Edinburgh.[7] While John Herdman remarks:

> that such a small country as Scotland should have contributed ... two
> of the foremost masters of the double is a remarkable fact, but though
> the ultimate reasons for this heightened Scottish awareness of duality
> may lie deep in the national psyche and history, a proximate causation
> in the schematic polarities of Calvinist theology can scarcely be in
> doubt.[8]

The centrality of fear – that fundamental feature of the Gothic – to Calvinist theology and its pervasive influence on the Scottish imagination is a vital consideration here. Cairns Craig suggests that 'the potency of fear' central to Scottish culture itself embodies a duality that turns on the ambiguity of the term 'fearful'. On one hand, this refers to 'the fear-stricken submission to a greater power', that of a vengeful Calvinist God. While on the other hand, it invokes the opposite or inverse idea of a 'fear-inspiring ... denial of the ordinary limits of human suffering',[9] embodied in the terrifying individual who rejects values and morality of the community, fearlessly defying the wrath of God. For Craig, this dialectic is epitomised by the antinomanist theme of Hogg's *Confessions of a Justified Sinner*, while remaining equally relevant to the various manifestations of absolutism and increasingly person-alised traumas that have marked the twentieth century. Moreover, for Craig, this fundamental conflict between the fearful and the fearless has served to negate any notion of history as a progressive force with humanity living 'under the curse of the unending repetition of the same inescapable dialectic'.[10] The metaphor of duality, of a split or fractured self, has of course been applied to Scotland in other pervasive ways. Gregory Smith's familiar term, Caledonian antisyzygy, was originally applied to the integration of realism and fantasy in the Scottish literary tradition (particularly central to the narrative strategies of Hogg and Stevenson).[11] But it has subsequently been extended to encompass the broader concept of a national culture irredeemably split and deformed along the fault line of British/Scottish identity that relates back to the 1707 Act of Union. This historical expression of duality is subsequently overlaid with further expressions of fundamental division: Highland and Lowland, Catholic and Protestant, Nationalist and Unionist. This schizophrenic impasse returns us to Craig's identification of the 'counter-historical' tradition in Scottish fiction. Drawing on the idea of history as a form of narrative practice or literary genre in which 'even the most balanced history is conjecture, is founded not on reason but on the imagination, however circumscribed by common sense',[12] Craig suggests that behind the order of historical events – those that can be composed or ordered into a narrative of progress – there are other events constituting 'a counter-historical flux'. Such events are 'out of history', yet remain potent and resistant to repression:

> History can only be written when there is a composed order in the world, and it is only the composed order of the world that can be narrated by the historian. All the rest is 'silence' and 'oblivion' to history, but the un-narratable, capricious world of the Barbarian remains there, outside the borders of narration, on the frontiers of historical order.[13]

This play of history and counter-history is central to the Scottish historical novel in the nineteenth century, from the Waverley novels of Sir Walter Scott to Hogg and Stevenson's cornerstones of Calvinist-inspired duality. Such a tradition serves to confront the limitations of both the prevailing historicist ideologies of both nineteenth-century history and the realist novel, the aesthetic justification of such assumptions. Indeed, what is buried by the historian returns to haunt, in much the same way as the Freudian notion of repression: 'the more insistently he exiles the evil, the more insistently he buries it, the more insistently will it return to take its revenge upon him'.[14] All of which suggests a deep-seated affinity between the Scottish cultural imagination and the Gothic, existing beyond the realm of folk-tales concerned with ghosts, witches and hauntings and of a tainted past soaked in the blood of the Covenanting 'killing-time' and the massacres of Glencoe and Culloden. Consequently, manifestations of Calvinist-inspired fear continue to have a significant presence in Scottish literary and cinematic fictions, including the works of James Kelman, Alasdair Gray, Janice Galloway, A. L. Kennedy, Irvine Welsh and Alan Warner discussed in the previous chapters of this book.

## IAIN BANKS AND CONTEMPORARY SCOTTISH GOTHIC

Another consistently successful and prolific Scottish novelist in this regard is Iain Banks, whose *œuvre* is distinguished by the integration of an engagement with the traditional concerns of literary fiction – contemporary subjectivity, politics and society – and a more self-conscious exploration of formal issues such as narrative technique, authorship and the conventions and limits of genre.[15] Consequently, he has been defined, like Alasdair Gray, as an exemplar of contemporary postmodernist writing[16] – a link acknowledged by Banks in the clear influence of *Lanark* over his 1986 novel *The Bridge*, which features a similar formal construction in its combination of realism and fantasy. The realist sections of *The Bridge* relate the life of Alexander Lennox, a modern-day 'lad o' pairts' who rises from his working-class Glaswegian origins to become a rich Edinburgh-dwelling engineer. But material success fails to bring contentment and Lennox finds himself trapped between two world-views: the Scottish socialist tradition of his father, on one hand, and a mix of Edinburgh bourgeois gentility and Thatcherite materialism, on the other. *The Bridge* begins with a car crash on the Forth Road Bridge and thereafter Lennox remains confined to a hospital bed, hovering between life and death in a coma. This motivates the fantastical sections of the novel in which Lennox's imaginary alter ego, John Orr, finds himself in the strange other world of the Bridge, comprising an entire community enclosed within a monstrous version of the Forth Railway Bridge – a high-tech version of Mervyn Peake's *Gormenghast*, itself described by David Punter as 'the final Gothic castle'.[17] Banks introduces a third narrative dimension into *The Bridge* through Orr's dreams, featuring the figure of a medieval barbarian accompanied by a familiar, in the shape of a monkey, who rides on his back. The warrior's dialogue is rendered in vernacular Scots, rendering him a Gothic manifestation of the Scottish hard man, while his RP-speaking companion symbolises the unshakeable presence of official 'civilised' culture in a new twist to the metaphor of Scottish duality.

Banks's affinity with the macabre was clearly signified in his 1984 debut novel, *The Wasp Factory*, a dark tale of adolescent alienation and violence that marked a new vitality in a specifically Scottish variant of the Gothic. Narrated in the first person, *The Wasp Factory* recounts the activities of Frank Cauldhame, an obsessive and sadistic 17-year-old living with his reclusive scientist father on a small island in the Moray Firth near Inverness linked to the mainland by a bridge. Frank spends much of his time engaged in bizarre rituals designed to protect his domain from the outside world. These include regular consultations with the wasp factory, a contraption based around the face of an old clock into which Frank places live wasps which in turn make their way randomly into one of twelve chambers, each of which contains a different kind of death trap. These rituals represent Frank's attempts to tap into certain supernatural and pagan powers:

> All our lives are symbols. Everything we do is part of a pattern we have at least some say in. The strong make their own patterns and influence other people's, the weak have their own courses marked out for them. The weak and the unlucky, and the stupid. The Wasp Factory is part of the pattern because it is part of life and – even more so – part of death. Like life it is complicated, so all the components are there. The reason it can answer questions is because every question is a start looking for an end, and the Factory is about the End – death, no less. Keep your entrails and sticks and dice and books and birds and voices and pendants and all that crap; I have the Factory, and it's about now and the future; not the past.[18]

The novel begins with the news that Frank's insane brother Eric has escaped from an asylum and the subsequent narrative is partly structured around Eric's impending return, punctuated by his phone calls to Frank. If Frank's mindset and behaviour represent Punter's Gothic concerns of paranoia and barbarism, the question of taboo is raised in relation to two separate revelations. The first of these concerns the fact that between the ages of six and nine, Frank was responsible for the deaths of three members of his family, including two cousins and his little brother. The second revelation relates more fundamentally to Frank's damaged self. We gradually ascertain that Frank suffered an accident at the age of three when he was apparently castrated by the family bulldog, which in turn appears to provide a motivation for his violent behaviour as an over-compensation for this sense of 'lack'. But the final shocking twist comes with the revelation that rather than being a castrated male, Frank is actually a biological female brought up as a boy and given regular doses of male hormones. He is the subject of a long-running scientific experiment carried out by his father, reminiscent of both Frankenstein's monster and the beast-men of H. G. Wells' *Island of Dr. Moreau*. Punter identifies child abuse as one of the major contemporary anxieties of concern to the modern Gothic, a theme Banks explores in *The Wasp Factory* by way of Frank's ultimate status as both perpetrator and victim of abuse. Moreover, the numerous acts of brutality towards animals – perpetrated by Frank, Eric and Blythe (the first of Frank's own victims) – can be read as a close approximation to child abuse, reinforcing the novel's engagement with this particular taboo.

*The Wasp Factory* also offers up a rich and thoughtful meditation on the question of contemporary masculine identity, giving the theme of duality a potent new expression in the guise of Frank/Frances. The link between violence and misogyny as inter-related symptoms of a fundamental identity crisis is articulated by Frank's admission that his

greatest enemies are women and the sea … Women because they are
weak and stupid and live in the shadow of men and are nothing
compared to them, and the Sea because it has always frustrated me,
destroying what I have built, washing away what I have left, wiping
clean the marks I have made.[19]

The essential fluidity of the sea and its elemental power to erase boundaries
represent the antithesis of Frank's obsessive need to control and micro-
manage his world. This is in turn something he has inherited from a father
obsessed with measuring and labelling and who is also metaphorically
castrated through his bad leg, which prevents him climbing the ladder into the
loft where Frank keeps the wasp factory. The expressions of ultra-violence on
the part of both Frank and Eric are contrasted with an alternative feminine
impulse towards caring and nurturing, which the latter had initially demonstrated in his choice of career as a doctor prior to his breakdown. Frank's
reincarnation as Frances on the other hand clearly embraces the potential
reorientation of his energies towards a more feminine expression, as suggested
by the final image of him cradling his brother's head in his lap as he contemplates his new 'self'.[20]

This fundamental reinvention of self can also be projected onto the Scottish
national psyche, with *The Wasp Factory* positioned as a fable about the need to
move beyond self-defeating myths rooted in masculine hardness and violence.
National specificity also arises through the trope of the island, a recurring
emblematic feature in representations of Scotland concerned to stress
Otherness through distance – geographical, social, moral – from metropolitan
certainties, conventions and rules.[21] Frank's self-imposed isolation on his
island is a fundamental part of his being; he is the undisputed (and despotic)
master of this domain and he draws upon all his pseudo-occult rituals
and resources to protect his 'kingdom' from the outside world. As such, he
appears to be living in a kind of self-imposed state of siege, giving justification
to his elaborate and obsessive rituals. In its isolation, Frank's island comes to
fulfil the function of the Gothic castle – the physical isolation mirroring his
psychic isolation from self-knowledge:

I like to get away from the island now and again. Not too far; I still
like to be able to see it if possible, but it is good to remove oneself
sometimes and get a sense of perspective from a little farther away.
Of course, I know how small a piece of land it is; I'm not a fool. I know
the size of the planet and just how minuscule is that part of it I know.
I've watched too much television and seen too many nature and travel
programmes not to appreciate how limited my own knowledge is in
terms of first hand experiences of other places; but I don't want to

go further afield, I don't need to travel or see foreign climes or know different people. I know who I am and know my limitations. I restrict my horizons for my own good reasons; fear – oh, yes, I admit it – and a need for reassurance and safety in a world which just so happened to treat me very cruelly at an age before I had any real chance of affecting it.[22]

What Banks presents here is an extreme form of the Calvinist 'fearful self' that has served to keep many Scots firmly in their allotted place, rather than seek adventure, experience and growth. In this way *The Wasp Factory* establishes what Craig identifies as a recurring theme in Banks's fictions: in which characters escape their fears precisely by transforming themselves into something fear-inspiring – 'effectively by taking upon themselves God's role in relation to the rest of humanity'.[23] Frank's fear of the outside world is sublimated by his becoming a fear-inspiring presence within his limited domain. But the conclusion of the novel suggests a reversal of this trajectory, with Frances constituted in stark contrast to Frank as an ordinary human being prepared to look positively towards a new beginning.

The concerns of the Gothic are appropriated and explored in many different ways in Banks's subsequent fiction, including his 1992 work, *The Crow Road*, a much more naturalistic novel than *The Wasp Factory*. However, the very first sentence immediately suggests the presence of altogether darker and more surreal undertones:

It was the day my grandmother exploded. I sat in the crematorium, listening to Uncle Hamish quietly snoring in harmony to Bach's Mass in B minor, and I reflected that it always seemed to be death that drew me back to Gallanach.[24]

Structured as a perceptive and sensitive *bildungsroman*, *The Crow Road* charts the experiences of Prentice McHoan, a 22-year-old university student who is confronted with the complexities and uncertainties of adulthood, a process that forces a reassessment of relationships with his family, friends and lovers. Banks also draws heavily on aspects of melodrama and detective fiction, with Prentice drawn into a search to discover the truth surrounding the mysterious disappearance of his favourite uncle, Rory, some eight years previously. Prentice's investigations lead him to unearth the dark secret that Rory had in fact been murdered by his own brother-in-law, Fergus Urvill, after discovering that Fergus had been directly responsible for the death of his wife, Rory's sister Fiona. Prentice reconstructs this sequence of events via clues scattered through Rory's work files – a project entitled 'the Crow Road', which in McHoan family parlance is also a euphemism for death. Like *The*

*Wasp Factory*, the narrative of *The Crow Road* ranges back and forward across time, elaborating and elucidating not only Prentice's formative experiences but also those of his father and uncles, providing the clues from the past that he must piece together to reach the understanding he seeks. It is this very burden of family secrecy, and in the ways in which the past returns to haunt the present, that give *The Crow Road* its Gothic affinities, in addition of course to the recurring spectre of death that claims six lives during the course of the novel. In retracing Rory's footsteps, Prentice also functions as a kind of double for his uncle, revealing then confronting the guilty Fergus and ultimately driving him to suicide.

The inter-relation between the various characters also raises important questions of class, heritage and place. The social tapestry of *The Crow Road* interweaves the lives of three families: the middle-class McHoans, the aristocratic Urvills and the working-class Watts. All three are linked through marriage and live in the community of Banks's fictionalised town of Gallanach and the surrounding area in rural Argyllshire – the centre of old Dalriada, the ancient kingdom of the Scots. This stable, if essentially hierarchical, community is continually reinforced through family ritual, most notably the numerous funerals, and the Hogmanay celebrations that invariably involve big parties at Gaineamh castle – the ancient seat of the Urvills, restored by Fergus to its former glory and the symbol of his power and status in the community. The castle is, of course, a significant figure in the annals of the Gothic, described by Victor Sage as 'a barbarian labyrinth of darkness that … holds up to ransom easy notions of secular humanism and progress'.[25] While Cairns Craig notes that in Banks's fictions the recurring motif of the castle serves to dramatise the relationship between culture and violence: 'Internally it represents a secure space within which culture can be protected, where personal relations and aesthetic appreciation can flourish but, externally, it is built as a strategic emplacement in the business of war and conquest.'[26]

It is therefore significant that the first hint of Fergus Urvill's 'dark side' is revealed in the ruins of the castle – prior to its renovation – during a childhhod game of hide and seek. On being teased by the other children, Kenneth McHoan notices how 'a blank emotionless expression gradually replaced the anger on Fergus's face. Kenneth had the fleeting, extraordinary impression of seeing something buried alive, and felt himself shake suddenly, almost spastically, shivering.'[27] This glimpse of an ancient residual barbarism motivates both Fergus's 'accidental' blinding of Lachy Watt and his later murders of Fiona and Rory. Yet Banks resists the temptation to portray Fergus as an ogre, rather, he is a successful, if rather ruthless, Tory businessman and landowner whose veneer of respectability and civilisation contains within it a kernel of something more ancient and destructive.

*The Crow Road* also provides Banks with an opportunity to interrogate questions of religious belief which, in the context of the present discussion, can be related to the conundrum at the heart of the legacy of Calvinism. Prentice's quarrel with his father over the very substance of faith and meaning results in a break in communication that, tragically, remains unresolved when Kenneth meets his own bizarre, and suitably Gothic, demise. In the attempt to prove the non-existence of God to his deeply religious brother Hamish during a drunken argument, Kenneth climbs a church tower and is struck by lightning. The schism between father and son relates to a number of issues already raised in the present discussion, particularly the centrality of fear. Prentice recalls their fatal final argument:

> He pointed one finger at me. 'You're too frightened to admit how big everything else is, what the scales of the universe are, compared to ours; distance and time. You can't accept that individually, we're microscopic; here for an eye-blink. Might be heading for better things, but no guarantees. Trouble is, people can't believe they're not the centre of things, so they come up with all these pathetic stories about God and life after death and life before birth, but that's cowardice. Sheer cowardice. And because it's the product of cowardice, it promotes it; "The Lord is my shepherd". Thanks a fucking lot.
> So we've to live like sheep. Cowardice and cruelty.'[28]

Similar questions of fear, responsibility and fate are also central to Banks's subsequent novel *Complicity*, a taut thriller which, despite its overt concerns with contemporary society and politics, signals a return to the familiar Gothic brew of paranoia, barbarism and taboo. The issue of duality is also central in this tale of a cynical Edinburgh hack, Cameron Colley, who may also be a brutal serial killer responsible for the complicated and gruesome murders of a number of high-profile establishment figures. Banks conveys this ambivalence by the technique of shifting back and forward between the 'I' of Colley's narrative and the 'You' of the serial killer episodes. Despite his fulminations against capitalism, imperialism, exploitation and greed, Colley is ultimately revealed to be complicit with the system he purportedly abhors, exemplifying a lifestyle totally dependent on its products. While his own propensity for exploitative fantasies and power trips is revealed through an addiction to computer games and in his illicit sexual liaisons with Yvonne, the wife of his friend William. After being arrested for the murders, Colley deduces that the real killer who has apparently framed him is none other that his best friend Andy Gould. The reasons are again buried in a past that gradually emerges to haunt the present, rooted in a double betrayal when, as boys, Cameron had twice run away at moments Andy most needed him. Emotionally scarred by his experiences in the Army, including active service in the Falklands, Andy seeks revenge on a society that has 'let him down'. Ironically it is Cameron who provides the direction through an angry but rather flippant article suggesting that various pillars of the establishment be 'taken out'.

Concerns with the negative consequences of the onward march of global capitalism and imperialism emerge in both *The Bridge* and *The Crow Road*, but *Complicity* takes the ramifications of the complacency and culpability shared by those who reap the benefits of the system to a new level of terrifying realisation. Once again fear lurks within this heart of darkness, but this fear has an aspect of novelty, the horror of which is contemplated in the short final chapter when Colley recalls an incident in Mary King's Close, the subterranean medieval plague street in Edinburgh buried under the High Street. Unknown to Colley and their female companions, Andy had arranged for the lights to go out as a practical joke:

> in those moments of blackness you stood there, as though yourself were made of stone like the stunted, buried buildings around you, and for all your educated cynicism, for all your late-twentieth-century materialist Western maleness and your fierce despisal of all things superstitious, you felt a touch of true and absolute terror, a consummately feral dread of the dark; a fear rooted back somewhere before your species had truly become human and came to know itself, and in that primaeval mirror of the soul, that shaft of self-conscious understanding which sounded both the depths of your collective history and your own individual being, you glimpsed – during that extended, petrified moment – something that was you and was not you, was a threat and not a threat, an enemy and not an enemy, but possessed of a final, expediently functional indifference more horrifying than evil.[29]

The chilling banality of this very indifference underpins Colley's complicity in the global system. In this way, Banks's Gothic sensibility confronts the horror of the modern world, a horror rooted not in the fear of the past but in the (barely concealed) barbarism of contemporary civilisation itself.

## GENDER, CLASS AND THE GOTHIC

Beyond the work of Banks, the Gothic mode has proven particularly influential in contemporary Scottish writing. Alan Bissett suggests that it can be discerned in the work of almost all of Scotland's great modern novelists from Ian Rankin to Janice Galloway, Irvine Welsh to A. L. Kennedy.[30] There have also been a number of self-reflexive re-workings of the tradition rooted in Hogg and Stevenson, most notably by Emma Tennant and John

Herdman.[31] Even more interesting and audacious is Alasdair Gray's re-working of Gothic sentiment and themes in his 1992 novel *Poor Things*, his most ambitious and important work since *Lanark*. On the face of it, this is a bizarre memoir of an upwardly mobile farmer worker's son who in the Victorian era rises to become a Glasgow public health officer. This tale is dominated by his relationship with a woman who, he discovers, apparently committed suicide before being subsequently reanimated by an eccentric surgeon – who transplanted the brain of her unborn child into her skull in the process. In addition to the obvious allusions to Frankenstein – the promethean surgeon is named Godwin Bysshe Baxter, invoking Mary Shelley's father and husband[32] – the dualistic structure of Gray's novel recalls both Hogg's *Confessions of a Justified Sinner* and Stevenson's *The Master of Ballantrae*. The primary narrative is the memoir of Archibald McCandless, but this is appended with a long letter written by his wife Victoria (who first appears as Godwin's 'creation' Bella Baxter) dismissing his florid version of events 'as sham-Gothic as the Scott monument, Glasgow University, St Pancras Station and the Houses of Parliament'.[33] These conflicting accounts are further framed by Gray's own 'editor's introduction' and the extensive endnotes that make a case for the veracity of McCandless's outlandish story.[34] When one considers that within McCandless's memoir there are also conflicting accounts of Bella/Victoria's elopement and travels with the rakish Duncan Wederburn from both parties, *Poor Things* is fundamentally a novel in which irrationality, uncertainty and doubt reign supreme. But as John C. Hawley notes, for all the 'pyrotechnic allusions to Gothic fiction, there are as many to books preoccupied with the social condition of Britain'.[35] In particular, Gray engages with the birth of the new woman, shifting the male focus of his previous major works *Lanark* and *1982 Janine* towards nationally inflected questions of fractured female identity – the predicament of Bella/Victoria echoing that of Thaw/Lanark in various significant ways.[36] Moreover, the temporal sweep of *Poor Things* ranges from the Victorian era of high imperialism to a consideration of social and political developments during the first half of the twentieth century – Victoria's letter is written in 1914 on the eve of war, while Gray's notes summarise a career that ended with her death in 1946, after the election of the Atlee Government. In this way the novel engages with a history of Glasgow up to the very point in history when *Lanark* begins.

But I want to consider two contrasting manifestations of a Gothic sensibility in Scottish writing that shed a different kind of light on the tensions and conflicts that continue to sustain a literature of duality and fear. Both narratives are also located in the under-represented north-east of Scotland, reinforcing the uneasy resonance of the rural at the heart of this explicitly anti-Kailyard thrust in contemporary Scottish fiction. Elspeth

Barker's 1991 novel, *O Caledonia*, is a feminist reworking of Scottish Gothic directly inspired by Walter Scott's poem 'The Lay of the Last Minstrel', which contains the lines, 'O Caledonia! stern and wild,/meet nurse for a poetic child'.[37] The novel opens with the suitably gothic image of the castle of Auchnasaugh with its stained glass window and stone staircase – at the foot of which the body of young Janet is found 'oddly attired in her mother's black lace evening dress, twisted and slumped in bloody, murderous death'.[38] *O Caledonia* subsequently charts Janet's short life from its beginning in war-time Edinburgh before her family's move to Auchnasaugh. The eldest of five children, Janet is a loner who prefers the company of books, her pet jackdaw and an eccentric elderly family cousin, Lila, a Russian refugee who also resides at the castle. Janet's imagination is fed by a love of classical myths, fairy tales and the ballads that inspired Scott, but in Elspeth Barker's Caledonia she finds anything but the sustenance suggested in 'The Lay of the Last Minstrel'. While suffused throughout with an ironic wry humour, the novel depicts yet another vision of Calvinist repression, uncompromisingly reflected in the community's response to her death – a tragic outcome that is ultimately blamed on the young girl herself. Janet counters this with the powers of her imagination, transforming the castle into a place of light and beauty: 'she had no fear of its lofty shadowed rooms, its dim stone passages, its towers and dark subterranean chambers, dripping with verdigris and a haven to rats'.[39]

As a child, Janet is horrified by the acts of cruelty and violence towards animals that she witnesses, particularly those perpetrated by Jim, the castle's hunchback gardener. This is gradually replaced by a different kind of threat that begins to emerge with the onset of puberty. The first serious manifestation occurs when, after discovering a room full of erotic books, Janet suffers an attempted sexual assault by Raymond Dibdin, a young family friend. She responds in robust fashion by pushing him into a patch of giant hogweed, resulting in his hospitalisation for burns caused by the plant's sap. At the age of 16 she again is forced to reject the advances of man who makes a pass at her at the Hunt Ball. But such experiences are overshadowed by the rather nastier encounter with a man while first-footing a local widower with her father and brother. Without any warning the man suddenly pinches her breast 'with a hand which had no fingers, only a row of wizened stumps. As suddenly, his hand dropped, he turned on his heel and walked away Janet stood there.'[40] Having no recourse to the kind of knowledge or experience that would help her to deal with this unpleasant and deeply confusing situation, Janet's response is to hold her breath and faint. Her next encounter with an older man is to have infinitely more serious consequences. Following a row, Janet refuses to accompany her family on a trip and is left in the castle alone. As the evening draws in she begins to feel vulnerable and to combat her new fears Janet drinks some whisky. The mild intoxication leads her to put on her mother's dress and high-heeled shoes, and chant a spell to the moon to call her lover to her side accompanied by 'Orpheus and Euridice' on the record player. On seeing a dark male figure appear in the hall she rushes down the stairs to embrace him, believing in her passionate euphoria that the gods have answered her prayer:

> There was a dreadful cry of outrage and disgust: she heard a voice hiss, 'You filthy wee whore', but she did not feel the knife as it stabbed down and down again. Only a great languor seemed to draw her downwards, slowly falling as Orpheus cried out for her, falling towards the roar of the waters of Avernus.
>
> Jim wiped his rabbit-skinning knife on his trouser leg. He had come in to turn off the music and the lights and so he turned them off. Then he went into the outer darkness. For a long time the castle was silent.[41]

The gardener had already been identified as potentially deviant – the young Janet having caught him looking at a pornographic magazine in the kitchen and later her mother observes him creeping out of Lila's room. Yet the cold savagery of Janet's murder evokes the shocking barbarity of a society where old men can molest young girls at will, while female expressions of desire are so threatening they are met with the cold steel of a knife.

The spectre of damaged masculinity pushed to the extreme is given one of its most horrifying manifestations in Duncan McLean's 1995 novel *Bunker Man*. His 1992 award-winning collection of short stories, *Bucket of Tongues*, contained a number of stories that begin an investigation into the darker side of masculine fear and the prevalence of (often undiagnosed) mental illness. McLean was to take this journey into a contemporary 'heart of darkness' much further in *Bunker Man*, which contrasted sharply with his 1994 debut novel, *Blackden*, an amiable and optimistic tale charting the experiences of an 18-year-old male in a parochial Scottish village in the north-east. *Bunker Man* begins in a largely naturalistic vein, introducing Rob and Karen Catto, a very ordinary and recently married young couple whose relationship is largely defined by an active and enthusiastic sex life. Rob is employed as a head janitor in a local secondary school while Karen works for an oil company, and on a night out with her colleagues the question of status, and Rob's insecurities about it, are gradually revealed. While the reader is initially sympathetic towards Rob, a sense of unease quickly emerges and then deepens as he begins to exhibit an irrational and rather nasty jealous streak. Before long, this has degenerated into a paranoid obsession with both Karen's fidelity and the 'bogey' figure, a burly hooded figure who has been seen prowling in the woods next to the school. The stranger is later revealed to be a mentally ill homeless man who is squatting in a wartime bunker. Rob also becomes embroiled in a sexual relationship with a precocious 14-year-old pupil, which gets increasingly abusive as his psychic state unravels.

Apart from one brief recollection of a humiliation at the hands of his father and brief hints of a lonely childhood, McLean provides little back story which might help to explain Rob's psychology. Rather, we are informed that his regular runs around the streets of Ferrybrae are not to allow him to think through issues but rather to allow him to clear his head of thoughts. This hint that all may not be well is later confirmed by the image of his head being like: 'a skip full of bees. Rob had the idea that if he opened his mouth a river of bees would come swarming out and terrorise the town. So he kept his mouth shut.'[42] Rob's deep-seated fears are forcefully linked to a sense of masculinity under siege, which in turn are projected outwards to a community terrorised by the threat of the bunker man. Central to Rob's mental degeneration is the link he makes between sex and power. This is demonstrated by the way in which the initial graphic descriptions of his and Karen's coupling begins to be replaced by increasingly violent and aggressive fantasies, characterised by countless graphic references to his 'hard cock' as the signifier of his potency but also of his hatred. As their domestic situation deteriorates, Karen claims to no longer know who or what Rob is and he responds with the exclamation 'I'm a man. I'm a man'.[43] But being a man for Rob means being under siege, regarding all other men as rivals

in the fight to keep on *living*. Every man is an enemy of every other man, a competitor, a rival. We all hate each other. You can't relax for a second for fear of getting stabbed in the back. That's what being a man's like ... me against the world, that's what it is. The whole fucking world against me! Not much wonder I'm fucking ... fucked up. Christ it's battle stations twenty-four hours a day when you're a man.[44]

This degree of macho paranoia is enacted on the Bunker Man, whom Rob befriends and manipulates in such a way as to fulfil his ultimate fantasy of watching him rape Karen before taking bloody revenge in the name of the entire community. A further displacement is enacted through Rob's affair with young Sandra Burnett who, unlike his wife, is emotionally vulnerable and gullible. Once their affair progresses from the initial frenzied grope in a storeroom, Rob begins to manipulate her in a predictable manner that reveals the depth of his misogynistic brutality, moving quickly from verbal to physical abuse. When she refuses to have sex with the Bunker Man, Rob threatens to beat her up: 'It's the same thing with you: punching and fucking, it's all you're good for in this life. That's why you were put on this earth: to be punched and fucked and like it.'[45]

In contrast to the other novels considered here, *Bunker Man* also presents an everyday proletarian manifestation of the Gothic, devoid of the sinister family seats, corrupt patriarchs, material wealth and power. Rob Catto can be regarded as a warped version of one of James Kelman's protagonists, pushed just that little bit further over the edge. Given the wider significance of the deep correspondence between Scottish culture and working-class experience, *Bunker Man* moves the Gothic beyond what Punter refers to as 'the vindication and substantiation of a middle-class world view',[46] through its projection of essentially bourgeois fears. The obvious risk run by McLean is that Rob Catto, like Barker's hunchback gardener, represents a confirmation of such fears, a working-class savage whose degeneracy is directly linked to his lowly social status. On the other hand, the barbarism he embodies is symptomatic of a society in which, as Marx predicted, ordinary human beings have become alienated from what it means to be human. Rob's visceral hatred and violent manipulation of others may be horrific, but unlike Banks's extreme and rather sophisticated killers, it is the familiarity of his symptoms that are most shocking, as witnessed by the expressions of misogyny, violence and fear that provide such titillating fodder for tabloid culture. And despite being written in the third person, the narrative point of view is clearly Rob's. This in turn forces the reader to share his increasingly warped and perverse viewpoint, a strategy also opens up the question of wider social complicity in the kind of pervasive forms of hatred – of women, of the mentally ill – that remain all too familiar in contemporary society.

## FEAR AND EXCESS IN 1990s' SCOTTISH CINEMA

The dark seam running through the contemporary Scottish novel has its corresponding expressions in television drama and cinema. While both *The Crow Road* and *Complicity* have been translated to the screen – as a four-part drama series and a feature film respectively – in each case the process of adaptation served to simplify and diminish the sophistication of Banks's original without adding anything novel or interesting.[47] More successful expressions of the Gothic can be identified which draw upon certain relevant traditions in the history of representations of Scotland in the cinema. There are two distinct strands of Scottish cinematic Gothic, both of which I have explored at length elsewhere.[48] On one hand we have a version of the trope of the island, discussed above in relation to Iain Banks, signifying isolation or remoteness and facilitating the exploration of a range of metropolitan desires and anxieties. Many island-located films involve an outsider arriving in a strange locale and result in some kind of romantic, comic, mystical or threatening confrontation – the darker side being represented by films such as *The Brothers* (David MacDonald, 1947) and *The Wicker Man* (Robin Hardy, 1973), both of which result in the death of the outsider at the hands of the locals. The other manifestation of the Gothic in Scottish cinema is primarily urban and located in a cycle of films inspired by the notorious activities of William Burke and William Hare who, in the late 1820s in Edinburgh turned to murder (rather than relying on grave robbing) to supply bodies for dissection in the city's medical school. The most interesting of the four screen versions of the Burke and Hare story being *The Flesh and the Fiends*, directed by John Gilling in 1959.

The rural Gothic tradition was rejuvenated in 1996 by the feature *Breaking the Waves*, a Scandinavian-French co-production directed by the iconoclastic Danish film-maker Lars von Trier. Set in an unspecified location on the north-west coast of Scotland in the early 1970s, the film tells the tragic story of Bess McNeil, a spirited but emotionally frail young woman who secretly communes with God in the austere Presbyterian church that serves this deeply religious community. Bess's insecurities are exposed by her marriage to Jan, an oil rig worker, who soon afterwards is paralysed in an accident. Having prayed to God to send him home, Bess blames herself for Jan's condition and when he encourages her to seek out other men for sex, she complies, believing it is a test of her faith and the only way he will make a recovery. Her promiscuity not only leads her to be shunned by her family and banished by the community, it also culminates in her inevitable tragic death at the hands of sadistic foreign sailors.

The Gothic elements of *Breaking the Waves* are similar to those of *The Brothers*. In both, the combination of repression (sexual and/or religious) and an impulsive and unashamed female sexuality results in the unleashing of the kind of communal fear and chastisement that Craig identifies in the Calvinist tradition. *Breaking the Waves* also directly ponders the link between religious fear and misogyny. The film's prologue has Bess informing the elders of her plans to marry, defying their attempts to discourage union with 'outsiders'. The fear of God is allied to a repressive patriarchal authority that dictates only men can speak in the church and attend the graveside at funerals, a belief system that mirrors the harsh, unforgiving nature of the environment itself. Beth's violation of the male prerogative on speaking in church provides the catalyst for her banishment by the elders. While the minister, who had previously praised her deep love of God, conspicuously fails to save Bess at her moment of need, turning away from her as she lies unconscious outside the church. Later at her funeral he is prepared to consign her, as a sinner, to the fires of hell. The fear of the community is also manifested in manner in which God talks through Bess, suggesting an intense psychological schism or doubling, although significantly what we have here is an insecure young girl's doppelgänger being a vengeful, jealous and very masculine deity. Such a reading is also supported by the knowledge that Bess is psychologically fragile and had previously suffered a breakdown following the death of her brother. Her conversations consequently become a struggle between the super-ego of the fearful Calvinist community – God accusing Bess of selfishness and urging her to learn to endure – and the id of Bess's own youthful vitality and spontaneity. These sequences are rendered very effectively by von Trier, the lingering close-ups of Emily Watson's child-like face invoking both the work of Ingmar Bergman, whose own obsessions with faith inform many of his films, and Carl Dryer's silent classic *Jeanne d'Arc*. But in contrast to Dreyer's still and contemplative visual style, the combination of wobbly hand-held camera and extreme widescreen frame in *Breaking the Waves* generates an ominous sense of unease on the part of the viewer, emphasising further Bess's profound instability and vulnerability.

The urban Gothic strain of Scottish cinema was also given a major rejuvenation in the mid-1990s by *Shallow Grave* (1995), the highly successful debut feature of the team of director Danny Boyle, writer John Hodge and producer Andrew MacDonald. The film tells the story of three obnoxious Edinburgh yuppies – Alex (Ewan McGregor), Juliet (Kerry Fox) and David (Christopher Eccleston) – who, on finding their mysterious flat mate Hugo dead in his room with a suitcase full of money, set about erasing all traces of him in order to keep the cash. But the emotional strain of dismembering and burying the body generates unbearable tension and mistrust among the three and order quickly begins to break down. David, the one who had to saw off Hugo's hands and smash his teeth, is particularly traumatised and takes to the attic with the suitcase. His increasingly deranged behaviour manifests itself in his spying on Alex and Juliet from a number of holes he drills in the ceiling, and in the eruption of violence including the slaying with a hammer of two thugs who turn up looking for the money. The film ends in a bloodbath with David pinning Alex to the kitchen floor with a knife, Juliet stabbing David through the back of the neck, killing him before making off with what she thinks is the money. The final twist is revealed by the close-up smile on Alex's face – he is saved from bleeding to death by the arrival of emergency services – and the revelation that he has hidden the cash beneath the floorboards.

In generic and aesthetic terms *Shallow Grave* has been discussed primarily in relation to the energetic and irreverent characteristics of American independent cinema and to the brooding qualities of *film noir*. But it can also been examined very productively in terms of the Gothic, particularly in relation to the Edinburgh setting and the symbolic function of the spacious Georgian flat where the bulk of the action takes place. The introduction to *Shallow Grave* features a high-octane ride through the streets of Edinburgh's new town, to the strains of pumping techno music and David's voice-over that notes, 'This could have been any city – they are all the same.' While the distinct architecture of the sequence questions such a bald assertion of universality, the images of the cobbled streets and buildings are contrasted with images of the camera prowling through a dark forest, in anticipation of the 'shallow grave' of the title. But this embodies a more profound contrast, or duality, between James Craig's eighteenth-century New Town, described by Tom Devine as one of 'the most compelling and enduring physical monuments to the Age of Reason in Scotland' – and the irrational, atavistic, and even pagan, associations of the forest. Such a contrast mirrors that at the heart of *Jeykll and Hyde*, although in *Shallow Grave* that drama is actually located in the city that provided Stevenson with his inspiration. The theme of the 'Shallow Grave' itself is also an inverted reworking of the Edinburgh ressurectionists, again partly immortalised by Stevenson in his chilling short story 'The Bodysnatcher'.

The New Town flat, a stylish environment characterised by spacious rooms, high ceilings and bright colourful decor, takes on many of the functions of the physical and symbolic functions of the Gothic, containing and constraining the action and reflecting the psychological states of the central protagonists. Once trust breaks down between Alex, Juliet and David, it is significant that it is David, a chartered accountant who most fully embodies Edinburgh's association with prudence, sobriety and conservatism, who experiences the most profound transformation. His retreat to the loft provides an interesting new twist on the 'madwoman in the attic' theme. From the beginning, David displays classic symptoms of insecurity: he is repressed and jealous of the rapport between Juliet and Alex and is subsequently the most unsettled, or fearful, of the three when Hugo is found dead. After the gory deed is done, the flatmates attend a party where David explodes with aggression at a former boyfriend of Juliet's in a foretaste of the violent psychotic he will subsequently become – prompting Alex to remark, 'You really explored your maleness to the full there. You were magnificent!' David's subsequent acts of voyeurism from the attic, combined with his recourse to violence – he almost drills a hole in Alex's forehead and he grips Juliet's face so hard that he leaves bruises in the shape of his finger marks – vividly demonstrate the extreme symptoms of his fractured psyche. But David also remains the character who motivates the film – from the initial close-up of his face (later revealed as the point when his mind has begun to unravel), to the final shot of his body being locked up in the morgue – give a suitably paranoid edge to the entire narrative.

The theme of masculinity in crisis is explored in a rather different way in *Orphans* (1999), the feature debut of actor Peter Mullan. In his acclaimed short films, Mullan had demonstrated a penchant for dark subject matter, but *Orphans* is primarily a sensitive meditation on the theme of loss, charting the different ways in which four Glasgow siblings respond to the death of their beloved mother. The film follows the bizarre and extreme events that befall them during the twenty-four hours before the funeral. As night falls over the city a storm begins to brew, providing an appropriately elemental backdrop to the proceedings. But the storm is also highly symbolic, the collective flashback to the night their mother looked after the 'Orphans' as children during a previous storm serves to highlight that this time they have to face their fears alone. While less overtly Gothic than *Breaking the Waves* or *Shallow Grave*, Mullan's film similarly engages with the idea of fear, in relation to broad questions of faith but also to the potentially destructive powers of damaged masculinity.[49] The uncertainty engendered by the death of their mother affects the orphans in different ways. While the grief of wheelchair-bound Sheila (Rosemarie Stevenson) is largely overshadowed by her physical disability, the others all manifest extreme psychological symptoms. The eldest brother, Thomas (Gary Lewis), aspires to hold the family together but his dogged fidelity to the promise he made his mother to remain with her during the night before her burial leads him to forsake the much more important needs of all three of his siblings. Thomas's fear of responsibility is repressed by a self-righteous adherence to his promise. Michael (Douglas Henshall) is separated from his wife and is confronted as much with his failures as a husband and father as with his role as a son and a brother. He is stabbed in the side during a pub brawl and spends the night wandering around with the life-blood slowly draining from him. Michael's attempts to make the injury look like an industrial accident, so allowing him to claim compensation, end up with him falling into the Clyde and floating down the river in a kind of mock crucifixion. Youngest brother John's (Stephen McCole) response to Michael's wounding is to obtain the means by which he can take revenge on the perpetrator. John calls on his cousin, Tanza, another unpleasant border-line psychotic who provides him with the necessary weapon and ammunition.

*Orphans* is given further force by Mullan's bravura use of images and his eclectic mix of aesthetic styles, blending naturalism, expressionism, surrealism and magic realism in a manner that is both internally coherent and appropriate to the particular scenes and sequences in which they are deployed. The centrality of Catholic symbolism provides a touch of religious allegory as motivation for much of the dark humour, but it also lends a suitably grandiose framework for some of the more disturbing Gothic moments and images that abound in the film. These include the shot of the pick-up truck containing John, an angel of vengeance, disappearing into the red-lit tunnel like some vision of hell; John subsequently taking practice shots from the vehicle like a frenzied gargoyle; the wind lifting the roof off the church, smashing the statue of the Virgin like some apocalyptic struggle between the forces of good and evil; the funeral service in the ruins of the church with the blood-drained Michael hiding at the back like a vampire waiting for the deadly embrace of the dawn; doughty Thomas collapsing under the weight of the coffin he has insisted on carrying to the grave alone. The cumulative effect of such excess is the palpable sense of characters driven by forces beyond their control to the very edge of destruction before the storm ends, mother is buried and some form of calm can be restored. The final scene reveals Thomas, still obsessed with his mother but now spending his time at her graveside, being reunited with Michael, just out of hospital, and seizing the courage to say goodbye to his parents and accept reintegration into the family unit. In contrast to the bulk of the action, which takes place at night, this scene is bathed in bright sunlight in a reaffirmation of reason and security over chaos, fear and uncertainty.

## CONCLUSION: THE NATIONAL RESONANCE OF THE GOTHIC

The Gothic influence on contemporary Scottish fictions remains a potent one, particularly within the domain of the novel and the cinema. The indigenous Gothic impulse is arguably most powerful in its imaginative engagement with the deep-seated cultural fears wrought by the Calvinist theology that retains such a formative influence on the collective Scottish psyche. Related to this is the familiar issue of a fundamental national identity crisis, expressed in the concept of the Caledonian antisyzygy and creatively enshrined in the writings of Hogg, Stevenson and others. Yet both the Calvinist legacy and the enduring concept of national schizophrenia embody a profound contradiction: serving to retard or deform Scottish cultural life, while at the same time providing it with rich and distinctive well of creative inspiration. The thematic and aesthetic resources of the Gothic, with its embracing of various indeterminate, complex and shifting relationships – natural and supernatural worlds, reality and fantasy, past and present, sanity and insanity, self and Other – are particularly appropriate to the interrogation and projection of such nationally-specific conundrums. The fictions examined in this chapter also provide significant contributions to the on-going debate about the role of class and gender within Scottish identity. In particular, the ways in which the over-investment in a working-class, masculine identity has entailed the repression of certain destructive and dark forces that return to haunt the contemporary Scottish subject. Consequently, there seems to be a greater emphasis on problematic forms of masculinity when compared to certain conceptions of the English Gothic tradition. The theme of femininity in peril is not entirely absent, as examples such as *O Caledonia* and *Breaking the Waves* demonstrate. But the most productive and influential aspect of contemporary Scottish Gothic remains the 'masculinity in crisis' theme that links such diverse fictions as *The Wasp Factory*, *Bunker Man* and *Orphans*. Given the fundamental economic and social shifts that have displaced traditional masculine roles, what many of the works examined here are extreme and particularly stylised versions of the male anxieties and struggles that are equally central to the fictions of McIlvanney, McDougall, Kelman, Gray, Byrne, Forsyth, Welsh, Warner, Ian Rankin and others. Perhaps it is the very Gothic sense of unease, coupled with a tendency towards the demonisation of the privileged that facilitates this broader social vision. Finally, the function of space and place within the contemporary Scottish Gothic, and in particular the visceral and metaphorical power of the rural landscape, not only challenges the hegemony of an urban west-coast representation of Scottishness, it also serves to counter the more regressive associations of the Kailyard and Jacobite Romanticism by reconnecting the contemporary imagination with a darker and more atavistic past.

## NOTES

1. Angus Calder, 'By the Water of Leith I Sat: Reflections on Scottish Identity', in Harry Ritchie (ed.), *New Scottish Writing* (London: Bloomsbury, 1996), p. 237.
2. David Punter, *The Literature of Terror*, Vol. 2: *The Modern Gothic* (London: Longman 1996), p. 184.
3. Kelly Hurley, *The Gothic Body: Sexuality, Materialism and Degeneration at the* Fin de Siècle (Cambridge: Cambridge University Press, 1996), p. 5.
4. Cannon Schmitt, *Alien Nation: Nineteenth-Century Gothic Fictions and English National Identity* (Philadelphia, PA: University of Pennsylvania Press, 1997), p. 2.
5. Ibid. p. 14.
6. Karl Miller, *Doubles: Studies in Literary History* (Oxford: Oxford University Press, 1985), p. viii.
7. Novelist Ian Rankin argues that *Jekyll and Hyde* is nothing less that 'the archetype of an Edinburgh novel', 'Why Crime Fiction Is Good For You', *Edinburgh Review*, No. 102, 1999, p. 14.
8. John Herdman, *The Double in Nineteenth Century Fiction* (Houndmills: Macmillan, 1990), p. 16.
9. Cairns Craig, *The Modern Scottish Novel: Narrative and the National Imagination* (Edinburgh: Edinburgh University Press, 1999), p. 37.
10. Ibid. p. 57.
11. G. Gregory Smith, *Scottish Literature: Character and Influence* (London: Macmillan, 1919).
12. Cairns Craig, *Out of History: Narrative Paradigms in Scottish and British Culture* (Edinburgh: Polygon, 1996), p. 67.
13. Ibid. pp. 68–9.
14. Ibid. p. 81.
15. Since 1984 Banks has published no less than twenty-one novels, eight of which are located within the genre of science fiction and bear the name Iain M. Banks.
16. See R. J. Lyall, 'Postmodernist Otherworld: Postcalvinist Purgatory: An Approach to *Lanark* and *The Bridge*', *Etudes Ecossaises*, Vol. 2, 1993; Tim Middleton, 'Constructing the Contemporary Self: The Works of Iain Banks', in Tracey Hill and William Hughes (eds), *Contemporary Writing and National Identity* (Bath: Sulis Press, 1995); Thom

Nairn, 'Iain Banks and the Fiction Factory', in Gavin Wallace and Randall Stevenson (eds), *Scottish Fiction Since the Seventies* (Edinburgh: Edinburgh University Press, 1993), and Victor Sage, 'The Politics of Petrifaction: Culture, Religion, History in the Fiction of Iain Banks and John Banville', in Victor Sage and Allan Lloyd Smith (eds), *Modern Gothic* (Manchester: Manchester University Press, 1996).

17. David Punter, *The Literature of Terror*, Vol. 2, *The Modern Gothic*, p. 122.

18. Iain Banks, *The Wasp Factory* (London: Macmillan, 1984), pp. 117–18.

19. Ibid. p. 43.

20. Ibid. p. 183.

21. For a discussion of this in relation to Scottish cinema, see Duncan Petrie, *Screening Scotland* (London: BFI, 2000), pp. 32–42.

22. Iain Banks, *The Wasp Factory*, p. 136.

23. Cairns Craig, *Iain Banks's Complicity* (New York: Compendium, 2002), p. 33.

24. Iain Banks, *The Crow Road* (London: Scribners, 1992), p. 3.

25. Victor Sage, 'The Politics of Petrifaction', in Sage and Lloyd Smith (eds), *Modern Gothic*, p. 36.

26. Cairns Craig, *Iain Banks's Complicity*, p. 13.

27. Iain Banks, *The Crow Road*, p. 89.

28. Ibid. pp. 337–8.

29. Ian Banks, *Complicity* (London: Abacus, 1993), p. 310.

30. Introduction to Alan Bissett (ed.), *Damage Land: New Scottish Gothic Fiction*, (Edinburgh: Polygon, 2001), p. 5.

31. See John Herdman, *Three Novellas* (1987), *Imelda and Other Stories* (1993) and *Ghostwriting* (1996), all published by Polygon in Edinburgh. Emma Tennant has reworked Hogg's *Confessions* and Stevenson's *Jekyll and Hyde* from a feminist perspective as *The Bad Sister* (London: Victor Gollancz, 1978) and *Two Women of London* (London: Faber & Faber, 1989) respectively.

32. Stephen Bernstein explores the various allusions to the creator of *Frankenstein* in great detail in his extended analysis of *Poor Things*. Stephen Bernstein, *Alasdair Gray* (Lewisburg: Bucknell University Press, 1999), pp. 111–14.

33. Alasdair Gray, *Poor Things* (London: Bloomsbury, 1992), p. 275.

34. This case is presented as a retort to his friend, the Glasgow social historian Michael Donnelly, who shares Victoria's assessment of McCandless's memoirs.

35. John C. Hawley, 'Bell, Book and Candle: *Poor Things* and the Exorcism of Victorian Sentiment', *The Review of Contemporary Fiction*, Vol. 15, No. 2, 1995, p. 177.

36. Donald P. Kaczvinsky explores the ways in which Gray's heroine is connected to issues of Scotland's national identity in '"Making Up for Lost Time": Scotland, Stories and the Self in Alasdair Gray's *Poor Things*', *Contemporary Literature*, Vol. 42, No. 4, Winter 2001.

37. Barker's novel is examined by Carol Anderson as an example of a self-conscious reworking of the Gothic from an explicitly feminist perspective, 'Emma Tennant, Elspeth Barker, Alice Thompson: Gothic Revisited', in Aileen Christianson and Alison Lumsden (eds), *Contemporary Scottish Women Writers* (Edinburgh: Edinburgh University Press, 2000).

38. Elspeth Barker, *O Caledonia* (London: Hamish Hamilton, 1991), p. 1.

39. Ibid. p. 35.

40. Ibid. p. 144.

41. Ibid. p. 152.

42. Duncan McLean, *Bunker Man* (London: Jonathan Cape, 1995), p. 168.

43. Ibid. p. 185.

44. Ibid. p. 231.

45. Ibid. p. 225.

46. David Punter, *The Literature of Terror*, Vol. 2, *The Modern Gothic*, p. 202.

47. Despite some atmospheric touches, the 1996 BBC version of *The Crow Road* opts towards a largely naturalistic rendition of the novel that downplays any Gothic potential, while the film version of *Complicity* (Gavin Millar, 2000) conspicuously fails to capture the mixture of suspense and horror afforded by the serial killer theme.

48. See Duncan Petrie, *Screening Scotland*, Chapters 2 and 4.

49. This is couched in a veneer of pitch-black comedy which as Angus Calder has noted also links the work of such major Scottish writers as James Kelman, Alasdair Gray, A. L. Kennedy, Janice Galloway, Irvine Welsh, Iain Banks and Duncan McLean. 'By the Water of Leith I Sat: Reflections on Scottish Identity', in Ritchie (ed.), *New Scottish Writing*, pp. 236–7.

# CHAPTER 6

# Urban Investigations

## INTRODUCTION

The prevalence of the themes of darkness and fear in contemporary Scottish fictions stretches far beyond what I have defined in the previous chapter as the domain of the Gothic. They are equally central to the crime or detective genre, which has provided two of the most popular and enduring creations of the Scottish imagination in the past twenty years. As a networked prime-time television drama, *Taggart* has consistently delivered audiences on the kind of scale that have made it one of the most enduring British police series of all time. Created by Glenn Chandler in 1983 and featuring the eponymous dour, wise-cracking Glaswegian Detective Chief Inspector Jim Taggart, the series is still being produced some twenty years later. A comparable level of success has been achieved by Ian Rankin's series of novels featuring the exploits of maverick Edinburgh policeman, Detective Inspector John Rebus, initiated in 1987 and currently comprising fourteen novels, a novella and a book of short stories. Despite a slow start, the breakthrough came in 1997 when *Black & Blue*, the eighth outing for Rebus, won the Crime Writers Association Gold Dagger for the year's best crime novel, placing Rankin alongside such giants of the genre as Ruth Rendell and Dick Francis and ensuring best-seller status for all of the subsequent Rebus novels.[1]

Among other things, the detective provides an appropriate formal device by which the contemporary city can be explored, as Rankin has noted:

I chose a policeman because they have access to all areas. He is the perfect figure because he can go to the Lord Provost's private residence and ask questions, he can go to a junkie-filled tenement ... and ask questions; no doors are going to be closed to him or, if they are closed, they won't be closed for very long.[2]

Consequently, the close association Taggart and Rebus have with their respective cities has had a significant impact on the contemporary representation of Scotland's two major urban cities, challenging in the process the stereotypical and reductive opposition between the conception of Glasgow as essentially proletarian, tough, masculine, gregarious and open, Edinburgh as bourgeois, genteel, feminine, refined and closed. Or, put another way, between the embodiment of authentic urban Scottish identity, on the one hand, and of Anglo-centric collusion and compromise, on the other. In addition to the dissection and analysis of Scottish urban life, the detective genre also provides a rich insight into the trials and tribulations of contemporary masculinity. Defined by their profession in much the same way as the mythical shipyard riveter or the miner, Jim Taggart and John Rebus are tough, dedicated and resourceful individuals who are extremely good at their job. But unlike Tam Docherty or Dan Scoular, they are no longer required to carry the burden of hopes for the wider community or class, but rather reflect a society that has become more fragmented and individualistic. Consequently, Taggart and Rebus are also versions of the 'hard-man in crisis' – troubled, lonely and isolated figures struggling to make sense of a world and a profession that is rapidly changing about them.

## JACK LAIDLAW AND THE COMPONENTS OF THE SCOTTISH DETECTIVE

The Scottish contribution to detective fiction can be traced back to one of the founding figures of the genre. Arthur Conan Doyle was born in Edinburgh and was subsequently a student at the city's famous medical school where one of his teachers, Dr Joseph Bell, is reputed to have been the inspiration behind the creation of supersleuth Sherlock Holmes. However, a more direct precursor to Taggart and Rebus is William McIlvanney's maverick policeman, Detective Inspector Jack Laidlaw, who made his first appearance in 1977. As a follow-up to the 1975 Whitbread prize-winning *Docherty*, *Laidlaw* appeared to represent a retreat into the less heavyweight concerns of genre fiction. However, McIlvanney's primary purpose in writing the novel, and its two sequels *The Papers of Tony Veitch* (1983) and *Strange Loyalties* (1991), was to engage in a more accessible way with the social realities of contemporary Scotland, and in particular with the city of Glasgow. His achievement was subsequently praised by critics, Ken Worpole regarding *Laidlaw* as 'the most radical attempt to use the detective genre as a way of writing about class and city life from a socialist critical perspective'[3] in British fiction. While Simon Dentith lauds McIlvanney's skilful appropriation of the conventions of American hard-boiled style to challenge the dominant, more genteel, tradition of British crime writing, epitomised by the likes of Agatha Christie and Dorothy L. Sayers.[4] But McIlvanney set out to challenge as well as affirm certain generic conventions. Consequently, *Laidlaw* avoids the kind of narrative trajectory that leads both detective and reader to a resolution involving the solving of the crime and the apprehension or death of the criminal. Rather, the central mystery of the novel is Jack Laidlaw himself and the narrative a means of investigating the complexities and ambiguities that define the figure of the detective:

> Laidlaw invites us to join him in a place where there is no them and us. There is only us. It is a place where murder may result from a still-born attempt to love, where in the ugliest moments we may catch a momentary reflection of part of ourselves, where protectiveness may be a mode of destructiveness, where we may feel a little lost among the shifting borders of good and bad, of right and wrong, of normal and abnormal.[5]

Following the 'hard-boiled' tradition, Laidlaw is an instinctive but obsessive detective, a disgruntled, hard-drinking loner whose marriage is unravelling and who frequently finds himself in conflict with his colleagues. In creating such a flawed protagonist, McIlvanney eschews any simple moral opposition between the 'straight' world and that of the criminal, while Laidlaw regards detective work as 'a delicate symbiosis with the criminal world, a balancing of subtle mutual respects'.[6] Like his creator, Laidlaw is also steeped in existential philosophy, lending intellectual weight to his gloomy introspection and compounding deep-seated feelings of ambiguity as he struggles to live his life in a moral and meaningful way.

The exploration of place is also central to the Laidlaw trilogy. Simon Dentith suggests that the novels establish Glasgow as a specific rather than a representative locale in much the same way as cities like Los Angeles, New York and Chicago feature in classic American crime writing, allowing the genre to provide a particular kind of knowledge by recycling and representing 'a shared set of attitudes, responses and scattered shards of knowledge; together constituting a way of negotiating city life'.[7] Consequently, the topography of Glasgow is a running feature in all three Laidlaw novels from the very opening passages of *Laidlaw*, which charts in some detail a murderer's flight from Kelvingrove Park to his hideout in a tenement by Glasgow Green. Dentith also highlights the importance of demotic speech as another convention of the genre which McIlvanney uses effectively, the combination of the direct honesty and black humour that pervades Glaswegian banter conveying the sense of a city formed by the harsh experience of industrialisation. The fact that Laidlaw is not a native to Glasgow helps to shed light on the way in which the city is represented in the trilogy. For, as we have seen, the novels are also fundamentally concerned with the uncovering of a sense of the city and the distinctive forces that animate it, stimulating a curiosity that could only originate from without. But at the heart of McIlvanney's vision of Glasgow lies a key contradiction. On one hand he conveys his admiration for the working-class virtues of ordinary Glaswegians, in particular their generosity, 'Socratic scepticism' and distinctive patter'.[8] While on the other, he also confirms the familiar reputation for hardness and violence associated with 'the city of the stare'.[9] This contradiction is directly acknowledged in *Laidlaw*, with Glasgow's essential nature conveyed in terms of 'the right hand knocking you down and the left hand picking you up, while the mouth alternated apology and threat'.[10]

But from the vantage point of the new millennium, what is particularly striking about the depiction of Glasgow in the Laidlaw trilogy is the fundamentally proletarian identity bestowed on it by McIlvanney. At one point in *The Papers of Tony Veitch*, Laidlaw surveys Glasgow from the vantage point of Ruchill Park:

> He could see so much of it from here and it still baffled him. 'What is this place?' he thought.
>
>     A small and great city, his mind answered. A city with its face against the wind. That made it grimace. But did it have to be so hard? Sometimes it felt so hard. Well, that was some wind and it had never stopped blowing. Even when this place was the second city of the British Empire, affluence had never softened it because the wealth of the few had become the poverty of the many. The many had survived, however harshly, and made the spirit of the place theirs. Having survived affluence, they could survive anything. Now that the money was tight, they hardly noticed the difference. If you had it, all you did was spend it. The money had always been tight. Tell us something we don't know. That was Glasgow. It was a place so kind it would batter cruelty into the ground. And what circumstances kept giving it cruelty. No wonder he loved it. It danced among its own debris. When Glasgow gave up the world would call it a day.[11]

This virtue has also shaped the criminal fraternity and it is significant that gang-boss John Rhodes' implied integrity is based on his association with his family and the East End community he continues to live in. This is in sharp contrast with Matt Mason's inauthentic, self-serving, *nouveau riche* aspirations, epitomised by his large house in the exclusively bourgeois suburb of Bearsden. As Ray Ryan puts it, 'Rhodes is authentically Glaswegian ... whereas Mason is a simulacrum of an alien identity, and so it is he, Mason, that Laidlaw will finally prosecute in *Strange Loyalties*.'[12] The refusal of any viable alternative construction of Glasgow is also apparent in the description of Tony Veitch's cramped student flat, its wall adorned with an array of posters and images depicting radical political heroes and ideals, art and cinema. These images, together with the books in the flat 'were a denial not just of the room but of the city beyond it, a refusal to have vision circumscribed by circumstances'.[13] Yet this flat is located in the city's fashionable West End, an area boasting the University and the BBC and traditionally populated by professionals, intellectuals and writers and constituting a more cerebral culture of ideas that is just as real, legitimate and relevant as Laidlaw's world of 'authentic' Glaswegians. All of which renders McIlvanney's detective as trapped in a bygone era and dependent on an increasingly obsolete image of an old Glasgow that would be eclipsed by a fundamentally new vision of the city in the 1980s.

## A MAN OF THE PEOPLE: THE LIFE AND DEATH OF JIM TAGGART

> To be judged a success on ITV at peak time series should get over nine million viewers ... By this criteria of popular appeal, Scotland has produced only one big hit over the past ten years, *Taggart*.[14]

These remarks by Gus MacDonald, written when he was Managing Director of Scottish Television PLC and therefore one of the most powerful figures in the television industry in Scotland, attest to the highly significant position *Taggart* occupies in the history of Scottish television drama. Such consistently high audience ratings have ensured the longevity of a series that began with a three-part pilot in 1983 and in the following twenty years has had to survive in an increasingly competitive market-driven environment.[15] In addition to its domestic popularity, reinforced by the appearance of an extensive collection of vintage *Taggart* stories on video and DVD, the series has also been a major international success story with sales to more than forty countries. The series has proved to be highly resilient and adaptable to major changes in the regular cast, allowing it to survive the tragic death in 1994 of principal actor, Mark McManus, robbing the series of its central character, and the subsequent on-screen demise of Taggart's colleague and successor DCI Michael Jardine (James Macpherson) in January 2002.[16]

When *Taggart* first appeared it seemed suspiciously similar to *Laidlaw*, which, despite obvious dramatic potential, had failed to be adapted for the screen. Whatever its provenance, the idea for a drama series featuring a Glasgow detective was that of producer Robert Love who commissioned a three-part pilot from Glenn Chandler, a promising writer who had emerged from a series of half-hour studio plays, *Preview*. However, the impact of the subsequent series depended greatly on the inspired casting of Mark McManus as the detective at the heart of the drama. A former schoolboy boxer, McManus became a familiar face on British television with a succession of tough guy roles including a coal miner who turns to boxing as a way out of poverty in the 1930s in *Sam* (1974–75), and as the tragic Scottish fighter Benny Lynch in Bill Bryden's 1976 TV adaptation of his own stage play. McManus subsequently appeared as Detective Chief Superintendent Lambie in the popular series *Strangers* (1980–82), which gave him the kind of profile necessary for Love and Chandler's new drama to have any chance of being commissioned by the ITV network. While primarily a 'whodunit' investigation of a serial killer responsible for raping and strangling three women, *Killer* effectively establishes the character of Chief Inspector Jim Taggart of Maryhill CID, linking him inextricably with the city of Glasgow in the process.

The significance of place is central from the start of the first episode which opens with a sequence of aerial tracking shots that transport the viewer from open countryside to suburbia and then on to the centre of Glasgow itself with the River Clyde a distinctive feature. We are then transported to Kelvingrove Park and the diminutive figure of a jogger who is about to discover a body, thus initiating the investigation.[17] Taggart's own close identification with his city is established through a series of oppositions between him and his new partner, Detective Sergeant Peter Livingstone (Neil Duncan), a high-flying university graduate from Edinburgh.[18] In contrast, Taggart is the son of a Glasgow tram driver who has come up through the ranks and whose approach to detective work depends on instinct, experience and bluff pragmatism rather than on the application of theories learned in the classroom. He immediately establishes his authority over the younger man through verbal means, ridiculing Livingstone's middle-class accent, his use of language and his university scarf – 'What football team is that?' The gulf between them is further reinforced by their respective drinking habits, Taggart's neat whisky contrasting with Livingstone's half-pint of lager and blackcurrant. But Taggart's jibes also contain an important hint of insecurity. Livingstone's presence renders him acutely conscious of the contradictions of Glasgow and in particular the narrow association of his 'dear green city'[19] with 'tenements, alcohol and punch-ups'.[20]

Taggart's problematic home life also confirms another dominant convention of the genre. His wife Jean (Harriet Buchan) is disabled and confined to a wheelchair but is possessed with an independent spirit that exacerbates the emotional and social distance from her husband. Like Livingstone, she has a degree and an active interest in the arts and other leisure pursuits and is occasionally asked to give public lectures and seminars. In *Killer*, these domestic tensions provide an edge to Taggart's dealings with the staunchly bourgeois Mrs Patterson, whose husband is a respectable businessman with social links to Taggart's boss. While clearly intimidated by her world – she offers him 'lapsang' when all he wants is 'tea' – Taggart's regular visits, coupled with hints he makes about his sterile marriage, suggest more than a hint of desire for Mrs Patterson. And when Charlie Patterson is ultimately identified as the serial killer, Taggart's responds with such ferocity and hatred that he has to be restrained by Livingstone from beating the murderer to a pulp. This loss of control reveals the degree of repression inherent in Taggart's psyche, a consequence of his own deep insecurities relating to both sexuality and class and the final image of the sodden and shivering detective stranded in the River Kelvin conveys his desperation and bewilderment in a powerful and tantalising manner.

*Killer* successfully laid the foundations for the subsequent series, now entitled *Taggart*, which began to appear regularly from 1985.[21] The early episodes saw the development of the character broadly in line with the elements introduced in *Killer*, including Jim Taggart's professional recklessness and vulnerability and his half-hearted inclinations towards infidelity. The question of class also continued to provide an edge to Taggart's relationship with his own boss, Superintendent Jack McVittie, who belongs to a kind of 'old boy' golf-playing establishment far removed from the back streets of working-class Glasgow. But having opened up these interesting areas of conflict, the series began to settle down into a rather more reassuring and predictable narrative format dominated by the particular investigations being pursued by Taggart and his colleagues. The contradictions and complexities glimpsed in *Killer* and some of the other early episodes subsequently tend to be reduced to Mark McManus's trademark craggy deadpan scowl and abrasive verbal put-downs, with any physical action being delegated to his younger sidekick. These characteristics may signify his old-fashioned and weary disdain for anything perceived as too politically correct, trendy or modern, but they are also clearly presented as a kind of endearing front behind which there lies an essentially stable, dedicated and supportive detective and husband. Taggart may be frequently confused or even exasperated by the way the world is changing but he is rarely threatened by such changes in any fundamental way. And while allowing the odd moment when he is forced to reconsider his attitudes – such as his perceived insensitivity towards a rape victim in 'The Killing Philosophy' (1987) – Taggart's scepticism is presented as essentially sound and commonsensical. Consequently, McManus's taciturn detective comes to enshrine a familiar archetypal Glaswegian, embodying the same virtues and values identifiable in the 'Laidlaw' novels. Moreover, his characteristic 'patter' corresponds closely to William McIlvanney's identification of the distinctive properties of Glasgow speech, namely the 'deflation of pomposity and humour'.[22]

The investigation of criminal activity, primarily murder, has remained the central driving force of the individual *Taggart* stories. The plots might involve a broad range of scenarios and character types but are usually structured around various unexpected twists and red herrings as the narrative – and the investigation – progress towards inevitable resolution and closure. The killer is rarely revealed to the audience until the case is solved, reinforcing identification with the detectives. Occasionally a degree of complexity is introduced to the plot in terms of subsequent murders and the revelation that more than one perpetrator is involved, but it is rare that Taggart and his team will be working on more than one case at any particular moment. This reliance on discrete investigations also precludes any attempt to construct a wider perspective on the nature and extent of criminal activity on Taggart's patch. Unlike the 'Laidlaw' novels, there are no recurring villains, linked plots or revelations of structures of organised crime or institutional corruption. In *Taggart* crimes tend to be perpetrated by deviant individuals, often respectable middle-class professionals, who kill for predictable reasons be it psychopathology, personal material gain, revenge or self-protection. This necessarily reductive perspective not only removes these crimes from any wider social or political context, it also allows each crime to be solved, bringing each story to a satisfactory conclusion.

McManus's dominant presence was balanced with other elements as the series has progressed. In 1987 DC Michael Jardine was introduced as a new foil for Livingstone, but with the latter's departure he quickly became Taggart's new 'neighbour'. Being the son of a former colleague whose premature death was partly a result of his heavy drinking, Taggart is consequently warmer towards Jardine than he had been to Livingstone. But this is tempered by the discovery that the newcomer is a tea-totaller and a practising Christian. However, no attempt is made to make Jardine's faith a serious issue, a further indication of the disinclination to explore potential tension and conflict within the characters in relation to the central narrative focus on the investigation at hand. And while single, Jardine is not averse to pursuing women, which reconfirms Taggart's own increasing sense of marital fidelity and lack of interest in other romantic possibilities. The overtly male bias of the series was tempered in 1990 with the arrival of DC Jackie Reid (Blythe Duff), initially introduced as a community WPC before being seconded to CID. A more instinctive and knowing character than Jardine, Reid soon came to display her own brand of bluff pragmatism that suggested certain similarities with Taggart himself. She has also proved to be more durable than her male colleagues, and thirteen years on is still a leading character in the series.

One element that has continued to distinguish the series, however, has been the city of Glasgow, described by Robert Love as 'the hidden star of *Taggart*',[23] the centrality of which subsequently became enshrined in the recurring title sequence first introduced in the second story 'Dead Ringer' in 1985. This sequence incorporates a montage of panoramic cityscapes and emblematic images followed by a line drawing of Jim Taggart's unmistakable countenance superimposed onto the city. As Ian Spring notes, 'we are invited to associate Taggart metonymically with the city of his birth. Taggart is Glasgow'.[24] The other elements in the sequence, namely the series logo, rendered in appropriately masculine metallic lettering, and the accompanying soundtrack – 'No Mean City' featuring the guttural vocal of Maggie Bell, power chords and wailing guitar – further serve to signify the hard and uncompromising attributes of both protagonist and environment. Yet this familiar association with toughness is only one possibility offered by the rich environmental and social contrasts distinguishing Glasgow and the series consequently makes use of a wide range and variety of locations both within the city and the surrounding countryside. While exterior locations have always been an important element in *Taggart*, this was enhanced considerably by the move towards all film production, beginning in 1987 with 'The Killing Philosophy'. The production had previously used a mix of filmed exteriors and studio sequences originated on video and while this was common practice in drama production at the time, the emphasis on locations in the series had already minimised the number of video interiors being used.

The establishment of *Taggart* as a successful networked drama series coincided with a number of initiatives that contributed to the re-branding of a city hitherto associated with poverty, violence and alcohol. These included the 'Glasgow's Miles Better' campaign launched in 1982, the announcement in 1986 that Glasgow had been designated European City of Culture for 1990 – the moment identified by Ian Spring as the birth of the idea of the 'New Glasgow'[25] – and the Garden Festival of 1988. *Taggart* played its own part in this process of popular re-imagination through its representation of the city as a socially and architecturally diverse entity boasting well-tended parks, impressive Victorian architecture and fashionable shopping centres, bars and restaurants. While the more traditional images of crumbling tenements, gap sites and seedy pubs are not entirely absent, the emphasis tended increasingly towards the depiction of a more bourgeois milieu of conspicuous con- sumption and leisure. Consequently, the series contributed significantly to establishing the motifs of 'the new Glasgow' – from the red sandstone tenements of the West End to the converted lofts of the Merchant city, the modern shopping environment of Princes Square to the Victorian splendour of Kelvingrove Park – that have re-inscribed the city in the popular imagin- ation as successful, confident and welcoming. Within this new typography, the ubiquitous River Clyde has been transformed from a site of production into one of consumption – the industrial shipyards replaced by picturesque waterside developments featuring modern offices, conference centres and luxury flats.[26] The centrality of the new Glasgow to *Taggart* may also explain why the series was able to survive the loss of its nominal star, whose closer associations with the city's past than its future risked rendering him an anachronism.

## INTO THE DARK HEART OF AULD REEKIE: THE STRANGE CASE OF JOHN REBUS

In *Strange Loyalties*, Jack Laidlaw's investigations of his brother's death lead him to Edinburgh's New Town, a place that represents the antithesis of his beloved Glasgow:

> This was in its origins the most English place in Scotland, built to be a Hanoverian clearing-house of the Scottish identity. The very street names declare what's happening, like an announcement of government policy in stone: you have Princes Street and George Street and Queen Street with, in among them, Hanover Street and Rose Street and Thistle Street. Any way you count it, the result is the defeat of Scottishness. This was an English identity superimposed on the capital of Scotland, an attempted psyche-transplant: 'Scottishness may have been a way of life but Britishness can be a career. You are not where you come from but where you can go.'[27]

The charge of bourgeois in-authenticity levelled at Edinburgh in McIlvanney's novel – echoed by Jim Taggart's description of the Edinburgh Festival as 'Scottish as Salami' – is a reminder of the antagonism between Scotland's two main urban centres. But just as *Taggart* had helped to challenge certain reductive and stereotypical conceptions of Glasgow, so the fictional exploits of John Rebus have imaginatively reinscribed Edinburgh as a dark and fractured entity, and consequently a rich and highly appropriate terrain for the genre of detective fiction. Ian Rankin began writing fiction while a graduate student at Edinburgh University researching a doctoral thesis on Muriel Spark and his first published book, *The Flood* (1986), is a *Bildungsroman* featuring a young man growing up in Fife who dreams of moving to the Scottish capital. But like McIlvanney before him, Rankin aspired to write for a larger audience without compromising his desire to tackle serious issues and, partly inspired by the example of *Laidlaw*, he subsequently turned to the vehicle of the crime thriller. Fascinated at the time by semiotics, Rankin derived his hero's name from a puzzle feature from the pages of *The Sunday Post* and consequently it is the enigma of Detective Sergeant John Rebus of the Lothian and Borders Police force that becomes the central investigative focus of *Knots & Crosses*. Aged forty-one, Rebus is already in mid-career. He lives alone in an untidy and rather bare flat in the predominantly middle-class Marchmont area of Edinburgh, a home he bought with his ex-wife and so is a constant reminder of happier times. Rebus is a maudlin obsessive with an unhealthy lifestyle to match, seeking solace in alcohol, tobacco and the obscure annals of progressive rock. He believes in God but distrusts organised religion, although in a later novel he develops a close bond with a street-wise Catholic priest. While regularly rubbing colleagues up the wrong way, Rebus does inspire loyalty from those who can understand him, such as Jack Morton, his partner on the serial killer case he is investigating. He is also clearly attractive to women and begins a brief and ill-advised relationship with Detective Inspector Gill Templer.

The plot of *Knots & Crosses* quickly becomes personal. While involved in a desperate attempt to identify and catch a serial killer responsible for kidnapping and strangling a number of young girls, Rebus has also received certain anonymous letters containing pieces of knotted string and cryptic messages. And when his own 11-year-old daughter Sammy is kidnapped, it becomes obvious that these are clues relating to the case sent by the killer, subsequently identified as Graham Reeve, a former colleague from Rebus's days in the SAS. The two had formed a close bond during an excessively brutal training programme that involved various forms of torture, including simulated capture and imprisonment. When Reeve failed to pass the gruelling ordeal, he blamed Rebus for betraying his trust and for the next sixteen years has harboured an obsessive grudge against his former colleague, planning his revenge in the form of an elaborate game that will culminate in the ultimate destruction of Rebus himself. For his own part, Rebus is revealed as having been seriously damaged by his experiences in the SAS, manifesting in periodic and extremely intense anxiety attacks. One of these occurs during a drunken session of casual sex with a stranger, transforming his lust to overwhelming and violent feelings of fear and revulsion. It is only when the details of what happened to him and Reeve during SAS training are revealed under hypnotism – courtesy of his younger brother Michael – that Rebus is able to come to terms with his trauma.

Despite having a close identification with Edinburgh, Rebus is, like his creator, essentially an outsider, having been brought up across the Firth of Forth in Fife in the dead-end town of Cardenden. This mirrors the relationship between Ayrshire-born William McIlvanney and Glasgow, which similarly motivates the element of curiosity as motivating the creative interrogation of his adopted home city. Rankin has expressed his own interest in Edinburgh in the following way:

[I]t's got a very dark history. It's a very repressed city, a very Calvinist, Presbyterian place. As opposed to Glasgow, which seems to be very

Celtic and open and brash and loud. Even the crime in Edinburgh is different from what you see in Glasgow. Glasgow crime tends to be easily identified and solved. Maybe you're wearing the wrong football colours and you get stabbed to death – that's a typical Glasgow crime. But in Edinburgh, the typical crime is grave robbing. Things happen under cloak of darkness. It's a place of conspiracies, a city with a village mentality, where everybody knows everybody else.[28]

If McIlvanney successfully fuses hard-boiled detective fiction with European existentialism, it is Rankin's fascination with the theme of duality and its elaboration in the Scottish literary tradition of Hogg and Stevenson that gives his own contribution much of its distinctive force.[29] The following contemporary articulation of the city in *Knots & Crosses* provides just one example of this guiding perspective:

Edinburgh's an easy beat, his colleagues from the West Coast would say. Try Partick for a night and tell me it's not. But Rebus knew different. He knew that Edinburgh was all appearances, which made crime less easy to spot, but no less evident. Edinburgh was a schizophrenic city, the place of Jekyll & Hyde sure enough, the city of Deacon Brodie ...[30]

The homage to Stevenson, which Rankin had acknowledged in *Knots & Crosses*,[31] is more overt in the second 'Rebus' outing, *Hide & Seek*,[32] with Rebus even reading *Jekyll and Hyde* as relevant to an investigation that uncovers the taint of corruption and criminality at the very heart of Edinburgh's professional establishment itself. Now promoted to Detective Inspector, Rebus's tenacious investigation into the suspicious death of a young drug addict in one of the city's slums reveals a web of extortion, prostitution and illegal prize fighting centred on a secret club, called appropriately 'Hydes', hidden beneath a respectable casino and drinking club. Edinburgh is conspicuously absent from Rebus's third outing, *Wolfman* – subsequently re-titled *Tooth & Nail* – which sees him seconded to assist on another serial killer case in London, this time involving the gruesome mutilation of the female victims. While affording an interesting opportunity to re-acquaint Rebus with his estranged wife and daughter, the novel is weakened by the rather easy and small-minded antagonism displayed towards London and its inhabitants.[33]

Having successfully established a new level of ambition for the series, Rankin began to use Rebus to explore even weightier issues that also broadened the focus beyond Edinburgh to consider certain 'state of the nation' questions relevant to Scotland. But in widening the perspective, Rankin also reconfirmed Edinburgh's place within a wider national and international network of political, economic and social forces and their relationship to criminality, reclaiming the city once and for all from any simplistic identification with the preservation of the British state. *Mortal Causes* tackles the ugly side of Scottish sectarianism via an investigation into a gun-running operation involving a shady militant Scottish nationalist organisation, the Sword and Shield, who are supplying weapons to loyalist paramilitaries in Northern Ireland. *Let it Bleed* sees Rebus uncover a murky web of corruption involving local politicians, civil servants and big business that reaches right into the heart of the establishment itself, including the collusion of the Permanent Secretary at the Scottish office and the Deputy Chief Constable of Lothian and Borders Police. While the award-winning *Black & Blue* links the organised running of drugs from Glasgow to Aberdeen, police corruption and the power of the oil industry in Scotland with a nation-wide investigation into a murderer whose crimes are a direct homage to the notorious Bible John, the serial killer who terrorised Glasgow in the late 1960s. Rankin even has the real Bible John, now a successful businessman, pursuing his own attempt to track down the copycat killer.

Much of the action in *Dead Souls* – published in 1999, the year a devolved parliament returned to Edinburgh – is set near the site of major new construction developments by Holyrood Palace. At the end of the novel Rebus returns to the location and ponders the advent of a new era:

> The sun had set, but it wasn't quite dark. The twilight could last an age at this time of year. Demolition work had stopped for the day. He couldn't be sure where everything would go, but he knew there'd be a newspaper building, a theme park and the Parliament building. They'd all be ready for the twenty-first century, or so the predictions went. Taking Scotland into a new Millennium. Rebus tried to raise within himself a tiny cheer of hope, but found it stifled by his old cynicism.[34]

The theme of devolution is subsequently central to Rebus's next outing, *Set in Darkness*, which begins with a corpse being discovered in Queensbury House, a grand old building constructed by the architect of the 1707 Act of Union that will now be linked to the new parliament complex. Rankin had initially planned to write a trilogy of novels around the re-establishment of a Scottish Parliament, but he subsequently changed tack and *The Falls* reprises the theme of individual criminal obsession, involving both the resonance of the past, when a retired pathologist is revealed as a serial killer inspired by a macabre episode in Edinburgh history,[35] and the sinister potential of contemporary interactive computer games, recalling the deadly riddles of *Knots & Crosses*.

By utilising the framework of the detective genre, Rankin has created a vast canvas upon which broad and challenging themes and ideas have been subsequently elaborated and developed to great effect. The series as a whole has tended to rely on the by now familiar device of the tenacious, instinctive detective refusing to be distracted from the scent. But while some of the early novels featured lone killers and psychopaths, the more ambitious additions have Rebus uncovering entrenched structures of organised criminal activity or institutional corruption. This in turn raises fundamental social, psychological, political and economic questions pertinent to the state of contemporary Scotland, and arguably Rankin's real motivation as a writer. In the only serious study of the Rebus phenomenon, Gill Plain argues that 'Rankin is less interested in whodunit, or even particularly in why they did it, than in what it means to live in a society in which such crimes are possible'.[36] Moreover, for Plain, the novels also fundamentally reject any Manichaean concept of the world. Rather, like McIlvanney before him, Rankin is more concerned with breaking down boundaries and simplistic understandings:

> Past and present, public and private, innocence and guilt, certainty and doubt – all are destabilised as Rebus's investigations expose not their difference but their proximity. The detective yearns for a world in which black and white are clearly demarcated, but is faced instead by the almost unbearable knowledge of his own complicity.[37]

The character of John Rebus consequently comes to carry a great deal of weight, rendering him a more complex and contradictory figure than Jim Taggart, or even Jack Laidlaw – although this is perhaps more a consequence of the size and scope of the 'Rebus' series compared to McIlvanney's more modest trilogy. Superficially he shares many similarities with his fellow 'hard-boiled' counterparts, Scottish and otherwise – the maverick and rather obsessive approach to the job, the wisecracking abrasiveness and hard drinking, the abject failure as a husband and father. Rebus is memorably described at one point as 'an irregular regular, a loner even in company, his brain and heart only fully engaged when he was working a case'.[38] But while ostensibly abiding by the rules of the genre, Rankin also provides a resonance that is particularly Scottish:

> police routine gave his daily life its only shape and substance; it gave him a schedule to work to, a reason to get up in the morning. He loathed his free time, dreaded Sunday's off. He lived to work, and in a very real sense he worked to live, too: the much-maligned Protestant work-ethic. Subtract work from the equation and the day became flabby, like releasing jelly from its mould.[39]

Yet Rebus remains far removed from the kind of entrepreneurial, self-sacrificing subject elaborated by Max Weber. Denied the intellectual refuge available to the philosophy-reading Jack Laidlaw, Rebus is a contemporary study of Calvinist angst – with its curious and contradictory mix of fearless initiative and fearful, self-limiting doubt – a deeply troubled individual, painfully aware of his own irrevocable flaws despite his undoubted skills as a detective:

> Rebus uncovered his chair and dragged it over to the bay window.
> He sat down and pulled his blanket over him, felt himself relax.
> There were lights on across the way and he concentrated on them.
> I'm a peeper, he thought, a voyeur. All cops are. But he knew he was
> more than that: he liked to get involved in the lives around him. He
> had a need to *know* which went beyond voyeurism. It was a drug. And
> the thing was, when he had all this knowledge, he then had to use booze
> to blank it out. He saw his reflection in the window, two-dimensional,
> ghostly.[40]

This returns us to the fundamental question of psychic and moral duality that directly inspired the genesis of Rankin's hero. Despite an apparent obsession with justice, Rebus, like Laidlaw, often appears to have more in common with the villains he is pursuing. His inclination towards insubordination and the flouting of authority frequently distances him from the official police line and he regularly finds himself suspended from duties, often the result of having been set up or framed by his adversaries. Inevitably, Rebus also finds himself the subject of investigations, most seriously in *Black & Blue* where he is implicated in the alleged framing of Lennie Spaven by his former mentor Lawson Geddes, in a case dating back to his early years as a policeman. At the same time Rebus is also unknowingly under surveillance by Bible John, who fears that the investigation into the copycat killings of Johnny Bible will ultimately lead the police back to him – the fact that both Bible John and Rebus are involved in a race to catch the 'upstart' also links them in a very intriguing way. This theme of Rebus as simultaneous hunter and hunted, initially established in *Knots & Crosses*, recurs frequently throughout the series which serves to intensify his feelings of vulnerability.

But it is Rebus's relationship with gangster Maurice Gerald Cafferty – first introduced in *Tooth & Nail* and subsequently a major presence in *The Black Book* – that provides the most sustained focus of his complex position in relation to criminality and justice. Rankin has asserted that one major difference between Rebus from Laidlaw is the latter's adherence to an old-fashioned moral code that no longer exists.[41] Yet the Rebus/Cafferty relationship increasingly comes to bear more than a passing resemblance to that between

Laidlaw and John Rhodes. Having triumphantly put Cafferty away at the end of *The Black Book*, Rebus subsequently gets locked into a complex psychological power struggle with his adversity that results in a kind of unacknowledged mutual dependency. Despite being incarcerated in Barlinnie Prison, in *Mortal Causes* Cafferty puts pressure on Rebus to find those responsible for killing his son. He is even able to engineer a temporary break-out to take his revenge, but in the process ends up saving Rebus's life in a highly significant action that would be repeated in *Set in Darkness*. Thereafter, Rebus displays an apparent compulsion to return to Cafferty in prison to seek his help in return for disrupting the activities of rival villains. This takes on a more dangerous and personal edge in *The Hanging Garden* when, in a reversal of the situation in *Mortal Causes*, Rebus asks for Cafferty's help in tracking down the person responsible for the hit and run incident that has left Sammy Rebus fighting for her life. The stakes are raised when Rebus agrees to be 'Cafferty's man' an action symbolically akin to making a pact with the devil. While never subsequently requesting that the debt be repaid, this 'agreement' nevertheless hangs over Rebus's subsequent dealings with Cafferty in *Set in Darkness* and *Resurrection Men*.

Further insight into John Rebus is provided by his relationships with colleagues. There are those, primarily superiors and rival DIs, who despise Rebus and regard him as a threat. In contrast, there are friends and protégés on the force like Jack Morton, Brian Holmes and Siobhan Clarke who admire Rebus and understand what makes him tick. A third group comprises those who appreciate Rebus while regretting his maverick tendencies, yet who ultimately prove supportive when the chips are down. This includes DCS 'Farmer' Watson, Rebus's boss for the bulk of the series, and Gill Templer, a rising star in the force whose dalliance with Rebus in *Knots & Crosses* continues to inflect their relationship with a residual mixture of tension and affection. All of these relationships are determined by the kind of character Rebus is. For Gill Plain he comes to embody the familiar image of the Scottish hard man in crisis, struggling to hold on to his masculine ideals against the encroachment of feminisation. His persona automatically places him outside the forces of modernisation that have seen the emergence of a very different kind of policeman typified by the well-groomed, media-friendly corporate man exemplified by the likes of Charles Ancram (the Glasgow detective called in to investigate the Spaven case in *Black & Blue*), Assistant Chief Constable Colin Carswell and Detective Inspector Derek Linford. In true Rankin style, this clash between competing modes of masculinity is not presented in any simplistic framework of right and wrong, good and bad. Rather, Rebus is painfully aware of his self-destructive tendencies and the price he has paid in emotional terms including the failure of both his first marriage and his subsequent relationship with (the aptly named) Patience Aitken. Even the return of daughter Sammy from London in *Let it Bleed* conspicuously fails to change Rebus and, despite isolated moments, the two remain at best casual acquaintances rather than close friends. The inadequacy of the situation is brought home in *The Hanging Garden* as Rebus anxiously waits to see if his daughter will regain consciousness after her accident:

> Sammy had brought home these essential truths: that he was not only a failed father but a failed human being; that police work kept him sane, yet was a substitute for the life he could have had, the kind of life everyone else seemed to lead. And if he became obsessed with his case-work, well, that was no different from being obsessed with train numbers, or cigarette cards or rock albums. Obsession came easy – especially to men – because it was a cheap way of achieving *control*, albeit over something practically worthless.[42]

Rebus is not the only character confronting this kind of struggle with priorities and serious life choices, however. His initial protégé, Brian Holmes, demonstrates the same positive and negative qualities as Rebus, being introduced in *Hide & Seek* as an up-and-coming, efficient detective who is subsequently promoted to DS. But just as he starts to make a name for himself so the inevitable cracks begin to show in terms of an unhealthy obsession with cases, straining both his health and his marriage. The crunch comes in *Black & Blue* when after savagely beating a suspect in custody, Holmes finally decides to follow the advice of his wife and resign from the force. *Black & Blue* is also the novel that sees Rebus reunited with his old friend Jack Morton who is assigned to mind him during the internal investigation into the Spaven case. Initially presented in *Knots & Crosses* as yet another version of the self-destructive hard man, Morton is now well dressed and in good health, having given up both alcohol and tobacco – while Rebus in contrast is drinking to excess. For Gill Plain, Morton comes to function as 'a curious combination of mother and lover',[43] a nurturing feminised presence cooking him meals and helping him redecorate his increasingly shabby flat. Rebus both appreciates and resents this intrusion, and the confusion generated results in a public brawl between the two men that culminates in Rebus bursting into tears. While Rebus's body takes a great deal of punishment throughout the series – he is beaten up on numerous occasions and even faces death in more than one denouement – these experiences usually serve to reaffirm his masculine, and rather masochistic, toughness rather than exposing an emotional Achilles' heel. This particular 'breakthrough', however, renders the subsequent death of Jack Morton, during an undercover operation in *The Hanging Garden*, almost unbearable for Rebus, coming on top of the hospitalising of Sammy Rebus. These cumulative blows find Rebus at his lowest ebb at the beginning of *Dead Souls*:

> [O]nce again Rebus's speech had gone unspoken, the one about how
> he'd lost any sense of vocation, any feeling of optimism about the role –
> the very existence – of policing. About how these thoughts scared him,
> left him either sleepless or scarred by bad dreams. About the ghosts
> which had come to haunt him, even in daytime.[44]

Having hit rock bottom, the Rebus presented in the subsequent novels is a
considerably lighter and more balanced individual. But more significantly
these also mark the emergence of DC Siobhan Clarke as major figure in
the series, providing Rebus with a potential successor able to cope with the
encroaching feminisation without running the risk of symbolic castration.
The irony of this is not lost on Gill Plain who notes that 'the hero's legacy
must be handed to a daughter rather than a son',[45] ending in the process a
'masochistic paternal lineage' running from Rebus's mentor Lawson Geddes
to Brian Holmes. Clarke was initially introduced as a young DC in *The Black
Book*, marked out not only by her gender but also by being English – albeit
with a childhood connection to Edinburgh where her parents taught at the
university. A graduate herself, Clarke has ambitions to make a successful
career for herself in the police. She is single, fiercely independent and is fond
of both music and football, being a loyal supporter of Hibernian FC. But
despite her desires to do the right thing, Clarke is fascinated by Rebus's
maverick methods:

> She had accused her superior of not exactly motivating those who
> worked for him, but this was a lie. He could draw you in to a case,
> and into his way of thinking about a case, merely by being so narrow-
> minded about the investigation. He was secretive – and that drew you
> in. He was tenacious – and that drew you in. Above all, though, he had
> the air of knowing exactly where he was going.[46]

Clarke quickly proves herself a very astute and perceptive detective and by *Set
in Darkness* she is assuming more active responsibility for cases. But she also
increasingly finds herself caught between two very different role models in
Rebus and Gill Templer, who in *The Falls* has reached the rank of Detective
Chief Superintendent following the retirement of 'Farmer' Watson. Templer
clearly regards Clarke as her own protégé, inviting her to meet her closest
friends and indicating how a woman should play the game to further her
career in what is still, despite the process on feminisation, a male-dominated
institution. But the younger woman is already beginning to show signs of the
kind of maverick tendencies characteristic of Rebus:

> She wasn't a born outsider in the way she sensed John Rebus was, but
> she'd learned that she liked it on his side of the fence ... At one time,

she'd thought she could learn from Gill Templer, but Gill had become just like the others. She had had her own interests to protect, whatever that took ... If rising through the ranks meant losing a part of herself Siobhan didn't want it.[47]

In the process of making a name for herself as a detective, Siobhan Clarke has inevitably to negotiate other difficult relationships, including the unwanted advances of male colleagues. She reluctantly dates Derek Linford a couple of times in *Set in Darkness*, much to Rebus's chagrin. While in *The Falls* Clarke finds herself in a clinch with her partner Grant Hood, but the problem disappears when Hood is promoted to the post of media liaison officer. And by *Resurrection Men* Clarke has formed a platonic friendship with Eric Bain, a young computer nerd from police headquarters. Having realised the difficulty of sustaining relationships, Clarke has decided to avoid complications by remaining single. However, this also seems to confirm Rebus's existential predicament, and *Resurrection Men* even ends with her admitting to the police councillor that the only significant relationship she has is with the job.

Inevitably, the 'Rebus' novels proved irresistible for adaptation and feature-length versions of *Black & Blue*, *The Hanging Garden*, *Dead Souls* and *Mortal Causes* were produced by Scottish Television and Clerkenwell Films and broadcast in 2000 and 2001.[48] The character of John Rebus was assumed by actor John Hannah, also credited as executive producer on the four films. As contemporary television drama, the films are slick and glossy, featuring strong casts, high production values and an appropriately 'moody' sense of visual style. Some of the resulting *Rebus* films are more successful than others, but in general terms as adaptations they do tend to suffer from the inevitable compression and streamlining of 400–500 pages into the limitations of a two-hour drama.[49] It is not that Rankin's work is unsuited to the process of adaptation, but its ambition would be better served by the space afforded by the four-hour mini-series format. Moreover, despite a close attention to character detail and performance, John Hannah's demeanour ultimately lacks the kind of tarnished world-weariness that defines Rebus in the novels and gives him his defining substance.

## CONCLUSION: A VERY SCOTTISH GENRE?

Ray Ryan suggests that the apparently random death of Scott Laidlaw in *Strange Loyalties*, the third and final Laidlaw novel, 'generates an allegorical quest for what constitutes Scotland'[50] – part of McIlvanney's on-going commitment to authentic indigenous expressions of Scottish humanism that had been systematically undermined by the Thatcherite revolution. Unlike its predecessors, *Strange Loyalties* confronts the consequences of the triumph of the very values of self-serving individualism that Laidlaw associates with Matt Mason, in contrast to the idealism of his dead brother Scott, who functions as a metaphor for Scotland itself. But Ryan argues that this quest is ultimately reductive: 'In responding to Scotland's disenfranchisement under Thatcherism, McIlvanney here comes dangerously close to endorsing an essentialist, unapologetically masculinist, ethnically tinged foundational myth as their replacement.'[51] The attempt to define a viable communitarian Scottish identity in an era of post-industrialisation and global capitalism entails the exclusion of all who fail to embody those values imputed as authentic and virtuous. Among the characters found wanting are Scott's widow Anna, now residing in the dubious environs of Edinburgh's New Town and refusing to provide Laidlaw with any insight or understanding into Scott's death. In the perpetuation of crass stereotype, the self-serving and spiteful Anna is aligned with the inauthentic identity of bourgeois Edinburgh, and consequently finds herself 'epistemologically removed from the idea of the nation, the category from which all value in the novel derives, and condemned to be a mere object of history'.[52] Moreover, Ryan suggests that *Strange Loyalties* ends on a note of disabling pessimism, Laidlaw alone with a bottle of whisky having ultimately failed to find any adequate answers to his questions.

The Rebus novels, on the other hand, provide a more positive trajectory, despite the various fluctuations in the personal fortunes of central character himself. The series plays out a kind of family saga in which Rebus's failure as a father to Sammy is ultimately compensated by the emergence of his surrogate daughter Siobhan Clarke. The fact that Siobhan is also a professional, who understands and shares her mentor's identification with the job, erases the gulf between the professional and domestic spheres that Rebus, like many other fictional policeman, has conspicuously failed to reconcile. The symbolic succession of the daughter in the more recent additions to the series also provides a viable answer to the erosion of the traditional Scottish hard man by the forces of feminism and advanced capitalism. Moreover, this process is located alongside the recovery of a political identity for Scotland, which, despite Rankin's guarded scepticism, is a positive outcome arguably anticipated by the series as a whole. Throughout the Rebus novels Scotland is consistently presented as a distinct, viable and thoroughly contemporary social entity, finding its own ways to deal with the various problems afflicting the modern world. Moreover, Rebus isn't forced to carry the burden of anxiety for a vanishing way of life in the way Laidlaw is, his problems being of a distinctly more personal nature. He is motivated primarily by the desire to penetrate and uncover the hidden worlds of criminality and corruption that exist beneath the surface of the city – to confront and give substance to the

'Mr Hyde' components of contemporary Edinburgh (and Scotland) – rather than by some existential quest for meaning.

Collectively, Jack Laidlaw, Jim Taggart and John Rebus confirm a distinctively Scottish contribution to the detective genre over the past twenty-five years. While Scottish crime writing may have been a somewhat limited field prior to the emergence of 'Laidlaw', it subsequently burgeoned in the 1980s and 1990s with key contributions made by Frederic Lindsay, Quintin Jardine, Paul Johnson and Christopher Brookmyre. At the same time, the impact of feminism has also given rise to an equally important group of Scottish women crime writers including Val McDermid, Denise Mina and Manda Scott. Prior to *Taggart*, the major Scottish contributions to the genre on television included Edward Boyd's series *The View from Daniel Pike* (1971–72), featuring the adventures of a debt collector, and *Sutherland's Law* (1972–76), concerning the exploits of a procurator fiscal in a picturesque highland fishing town. More recent examples include a three-part adaptation of Frederic Lindsay's *Brond* (1987), *The Justice Game* (1989), and David Kane's *Jute City* (1991). High-profile Scottish characters have also featured in a number of crime dramas set in England including *Cracker* (1993–96), distinguished by Robbie Coltrane's sensitive portrayal of the alcoholic, gambling-obsessed forensic psychologist. While *The Vice* (1999–2002) and *Messiah* (2001–2) both feature Ken Stott playing versions of the familiar hard-bitten, brittle Scottish detective. Stott also appeared as a psychotic policeman in Anthony Nielson's 1998 feature film, *The Debt Collector*. Interestingly cinema is one arena in which the Scottish detective has failed to make a significant impact. Bill Forsyth provided a refreshing twist on the theme of investigation in *Comfort and Joy* (1984), and the aesthetics of neo-noir were reworked to stylish effect in *Shallow Grave* (Danny Boyle, 1995). But the only *bona fide* contribution to the urban detective thriller during the 1990s was *The Near Room* (David Hayman, 1996), a dark and disturbing tale of paedophilia, corruption and murder featuring a burned-out hack searching for his illegitimate daughter. Such an impressive range of contributions to detective fiction may primarily be a consequence of the genre's general popularity, regardless of questions of national specificity. However, as the close consideration of Laidlaw, Taggart and Rebus demonstrates, the genre does provide an accessible format through which relevant issues can be interrogated. The centrality of class, gender, national identity and the modern city, alongside considerations of the meaning of morality, justice and criminality in modern society, provides a clear indication of the more weighty dimensions that are contained within contemporary Scottish crime fiction, and equally central to the reimagination of the nation itself.

# NOTES

1. Gill Plain notes that this award led Orion to reissue Rankin's back-list, and by 1998 Rankin had set a new record by occupying six of the top ten places in the Scottish Book Marketing Group's annual survey, with *Black & Blue* top of the list. *Ian Rankin's Black and Blue* (New York: Continuum, 2002), p. 19.
2. Gill Plain, 'An Interview with Ian Rankin', *Scotlands*, 5.2, 1998, p. 106.
3. Ken Warpole, *Dockers and Detectives: Popular Reading, Popular Writing* (London: Verso, 1983), p. 46.
4. Simon Dentith, 'This Shitty Urban Machine Humanised: The Urban Crime Novel and the Novels of William McIlvanney', in Ian A. Bell and Graham Daldry (eds), *Watching the Detectives: Essays on Crime Fiction* (Basingstoke: Macmillan, 1990).
5. William McIlvanney, 'The Courage of Our Doubts', *Surviving the Shipwreck* (Edinburgh: Mainstream, 1991), p. 162.
6. William McIlvanney, *The Papers of Tony Veitch* (London: Hodder & Stoughton, 1983), p. 254.
7. Simon Dentith, 'This Shitty Urban Machine Humanised', p. 31.
8. William McIlvanney, 'The Courage of Our Doubts', *Surviving the Shipwreck*, p. 157.
9. William McIlvanney, *The Papers of Tony Veitch*, p. 1.
10. William McIlvanney, *Laidlaw* (London: Hodder & Stoughton, 1977), p. 72.
11. William McIlvanney, *The Papers of Tony Veitch*, pp. 261–2.
12. Ray Ryan, *Ireland and Scotland: Literature and Culture, State and Nation, 1966–2000* (Oxford: Oxford University Press, 2002), p. 70.
13. William McIlvanney, *The Papers of Tony Veitch*, p. 118.
14. Gus MacDonald, 'Fiction Friction', in Eddie Dick (ed.), *From Limelight to Satellite: A Scottish Film Book* (London: BFI/SFC, 1990), p. 197.
15. During its peak, *Taggart* was drawing an average audience of around 12 million viewers, with a record 18.3 million recorded for the 1992 New Year special 'Violent Delights'.
16. McManus featured in a total of thirty-one *Taggart* stories, including twenty-four three-episode stories and seven New Year specials.
17. This location is yet another parallel between the first Taggart drama and the original *Laidlaw* novel.
18. This is a common device in British crime fiction and is examined by Merja Makinen in her essay 'Feminism and the "Crisis of Masculinity" in Contemporary British Detective Fiction', in Anne Mullen and Emer O'Beirne (eds), *Crime Scenes: Detective Narratives in European Culture since 1945* (Amsterdam: Rodopi, 2000).
19. One of the possible origins of the name Glasgow is the term *glas cu*, meaning 'dear green place'. Mark McManus and Glenn Chandler, *Taggart's Glasgow* (Oxford: Lennard Publishing, 1989), p. 128.
20. David Mckie suggests that *Killer* ends up reaffirming the stereotypical identification between the city and violence. See Mckie, 'Networking Scottish TV: Popular and Classic', *Cencrastus*, No. 16, Spring 1984.
21. On the production side, Glenn Chandler continued to be the principal writer, providing the scripts for all but nine of the thirty-one stories featuring McManus.
22. William McIlvanney, 'Where Greta Garbo Wouldn't Have Been Alone', *Surviving the Shipwreck*, p. 182.
23. Quoted in Geoff Tibballs, *Taggart Casebook* (London: Boxtree, 1994), p. 12.
24. Ian Spring, *Phantom Village: The Myth of the New Glasgow* (Edinburgh: Polygon, 1990), p. 81.

25. Ibid. pp. 39–42.
26. This kind of touristic gaze, incorporating aspects of the old as well as the new Glasgow, was itself the focus of Mark McManus and Glenn Chandler, *Taggart's Glasgow* (Oxford: Lennard Publishing, 1989).
27. William McIlvanney, *Strange Loyalties* (London: Hodder & Stoughton, 1991), p. 151.
28. J. Kingston Pierce, 'Ian Rankin: The Accidental Crime Writer', www.januarymagazine.co/profiles/ianrankin.html
29. Rankin has described his own influence as 'a dark Gothic tradition of Scottish writers such as Robert Louis Stevenson and James Hogg filtered through a love of American cinema and fiction', *Edinburgh Review*, No. 102, 1999, p. 14.
30. Ian Rankin, *Knots & Crosses* (London: The Bodley Head, 1987). Quotation from the edition published as part of *Rebus: The Early Years*, p. 157.
31. Ian Rankin, 'Exile on Princes Street' Preface to *Rebus: The Early Years* (London: Orion, 1999), an Omnibus edition containing the first three 'Rebus' novels, *Knots & Crosses, Hide & Seek* and *Tooth & Nail*.
32. Ian Rankin, *Hide & Seek* (London: Barrie & Jenkins, 1990).
33. Consequently Rankin returned Rebus to 'Auld Reekie' for *Strip Jack* (London: Orion, 1992).
34. Ian Rankin, *Dead Souls* (London: Orion, 1999), p. 481.
35. The plot of *Set in Darkness* (London: Orion, 2000) also features the new National Museum of Scotland, another new institution that served to reinforce the reinvigorated sense of national identity ushered in by devolution.
36. Gill Plain, *Ian Rankin's Black and Blue*, p. 29.
37. Ibid. p. 30.
38. Ian Rankin, *Black & Blue* (London: Orion, 1997), p. 372.
39. Ian Rankin, *Let It Bleed* (London: Orion, 1995), pp. 121–2.
40. Ian Rankin, *Black & Blue*, p. 329.
41. See Gill Plain, 'An Interview with Ian Rankin', *Scotlands*, 5.2, 1998.
42. Ian Rankin, *The Hanging Garden* (London: Orion, 1998), p. 372.
43. Gill Plain, *Ian Rankin's Black and Blue*, p. 58.
44. Ian Rankin, *Dead Souls*, p. 17.
45. Gill Plain, *Ian Rankin's Black and Blue*, p. 57.
46. Ian Rankin, *The Black Book* (London: Orion, 1993), p. 110.
47. Ian Rankin, *The Falls* (London: Orion, 2001), p. 443.
48. *Black & Blue* was broadcast on 26 April 2000 with *The Hanging Garden* and *Dead Souls* following on 6 and 13 September of the following year. *Mortal Causes* was scheduled for 20 September but was pulled following the attack on the World Trade Center in New York two weeks earlier.
49. This 'attempt to fit a quart into a pint pot', as Gill Plain aptly puts it, entailing a process of simplification and omission when compared to sophistication and complexity of the original novels, *Ian Rankin's Black and Blue*, p. 74.
50. Ray Ryan, *Ireland and Scotland*, p. 80.
51. Ibid. p. 86.
52. Ibid. p. 83.

# CHAPTER 7

# Narratives of Childhood

## INTRODUCTION

A significant recurring figure in Scottish fictions is that of the child. While Scotland clearly has no necessary cultural affinity with such a universal concept as childhood, the problematic relationship between the identities of 'child' and 'adult' in films and novels inevitably assume a particular resonance in the context of Scotland's own uncertain status as a nation. Alan Riach suggests that while forms of indigenous culture have flourished in the late twentieth century, Scotland effectively remained 'an absent political entity in search of its own statehood, an heroic ideal, orphaned from itself and travelling in a world without closure'.[1] The figure of the orphan consequently remains a common one in contemporary Scottish culture, the roll call of examples including *Morvern Callar*, *Tutti Frutti*'s Danny McGlone, Eddie McKenna of *Takin' Over the Asylum* and Inspector John Rebus. The focus on childhood also comes to provide a new variant of the familiar motif of the Caledonian antisygyny, with the schizophrenic national subject reconfigured in the split between child and adult. The child represents a Scottish identity that is essentially immature and which has only two options available to it: to remain in a perpetual state of (rebellious) retardation or to take its place in the rational, mature and adult realm of British identity. But the Scottish child who has put away childish things is effectively orphaned, detached from its familial roots and ties and unable to fully recognise itself as an adult subject without adopting an alternative identity.

Beyond the symbolic and figurative resonance, there are certain historical and sociological factors that may also help to explain the fascination with childhood in recent Scottish fictions. The resolutely proletarian emphasis of Scottish novels and films has had implications for the kinds of images of children and childhood presented. While Scottish working-class families tended to be tightly knit and historically larger than their English counterparts,[2] they were also vulnerable to a variety of inter-related economic and social problems, including unemployment, poverty, bad housing, poor health and delinquency, particularly in urban areas. And while the worst horror stories of Scottish inner-city slum living tend to relate to the first half of the twentieth century, the political impact of Thatcherism and the New Right ushered in a new era of multiple social deprivation and with it increased strains on the domestic family unit. Alongside the dramatic rise in unemployment, the 1980s witnessed a significant increase in matrimonial break-up and divorce and in the number of children born out of wedlock. The result was that by the end of the century one in five Scottish families were headed by a single parent – in the vast majority of cases the mother. This gives an added significance to contemporary Scottish fictional representations of children and childhood, particularly in terms of the kind of social and domestic problems their protagonists tend to encounter.

Despite a shared concern with the figure of the child, none of the films and novels considered below were made for an audience or readership of children or young people, raising the problematic issue of what is essentially an adult film-maker or writer communicating with his or her (adult) audience through the point of view of the child. While this is frequently motivated by an autobiographical impulse, it does not simplify the complex narrative and thematic issues at sake. This very question is insightfully explored by Marina Warner, who identifies a central contradiction or tension embodied by the figure of the child.[3] On one hand, we have the familiar association of the child with purity and innocence, a prelapsarian ideal from which adults have necessarily become estranged. On the other, children are also believed to have a closer relation to fantasy. This split is further intensified around the contradictory ideas of the innocent child as a *tabula rasa* on which experience leaves its, usually corrupting, mark, and of the imaginative child as – in certain puritan scenarios such as the 'God-fearing' tradition of Calvinism – corrupted by original sin and therefore to be subject to discipline and punishment.[4] While Warner doesn't engage directly with questions of national identity, her feminist perspective does raise a salient point for the subsequent discussion of Scottish fictions. Through a consideration of the influential myth of *Cupid and Psyche*, Warner suggests that childhood innocence tends to be coded as female:

> one of the reasons why so many films (and, indeed, literature) about
> initiation focus on girls, and are often made or written by women:
> I think that they are feeling somehow this undertow of symbolism,
> that the soul, the seeker, the psyche, has a feminine physical
> constitution before entering into adult differentiation.[5]

Yet paradoxically, in the Scottish context the vast majority of child-centred narratives are 'authored' by male film-makers and writers and are fundamentally concerned with questions of masculinity. While the failure of Alasdair Gray's tragic alter-ego Duncan Thaw to achieve a satisfactory adult identity precipitates his descent into hell, Bill Forsyth's adolescent Gregory seeks recourse in childish fantasies as a response to his libidinal urges and is subsequently instructed in the art of seduction by his 9-year-old sister. But it is the figure of the damaged child who subsequently becomes a damaged adult – central to both *Lanark* and *1982 Janine* – that more frequently haunts the highways and byways of contemporary Scottish fictions, most notably in the work of Iain Banks (*The Wasp Factory*, *The Bridge*, *Complicity*) and Irvine Welsh (*Marabou Stork Nightmares*, *Filth*). This recurring sense of pathology returns us to the problem of the overt masculinisation of Scottish culture and its over-emphasis on physical and emotional hardness, brutality and aggression.

## THE CENTRALITY OF THE CHILD IN SCOTTISH CINEMA

The figure of the child has proven particularly resonant in cinema. When Scottish film-makers first began to move into the realms of fiction after years of being restricted to documentary production, one of the few sources of finance they could approach was the Children's Film Foundation. Consequently this modest but significant watershed was characterised by the kind of plucky kids that featured in films like *Flash the Sheepdog* (1967), *The Big Catch* (1968) and *Mauro the Gypsy* (1972). This close association with youth was embellished further with the appearance of Bill Forsyth's *That Sinking Feeling* in 1979, the first truly indigenous Scottish feature of the sound era. However, the real watershed in cinematic representations of the child is undoubtedly Bill Douglas's acclaimed autobiographical trilogy, *My Childhood* (1972), *My Ain Folk* (1973) and *My Way Home* (1978). Writing in 1992, John Caughie suggested that while one could discern a school of Scottish comedy bearing the influence of Bill Forsyth, 'the "school" of Douglas has not been copied, far less developed'.[6] A decade on it is now possible to posit Douglas as ultimately a more influential figure than Forsyth, as the father of a new Scottish art cinema and its apparent obsession with issues of autobiography, memory and the figure of the child. Douglas's *Trilogy* recounts the harrowing experiences of a grim childhood in the mining village of Newcraighall in the 1940s and early 1950s. *My Childhood* depicts young Jamie's life with his cousin Tommy and their maternal grandmother towards the end of the war, the harsh material and emotional impoverishment being alleviated only by a friendship with a German prisoner-of-war working on a nearby farm. After grandmother's death, Tommy is incarcerated in a children's home and Jamie is taken in by his father's family. The harsh privations endured at the hands of his cold and vindictive paternal grandmother becomes the primary focus of *My Ain Folk*, the most harrowing film of the three, which culminates in Jamie being carted off to the same children's home. *My Way Home* moves the story on a few years with Jamie about to leave the home. After an ill-fated attempt to live first with his father and then with a foster mother, Jamie spends a period in a hostel before being called up for national service. It is during his posting in Egypt that he finally finds redemption through his friendship with Robert, a young middle-class Englishman who introduces him to books and the possibility of a more optimistic and fulfilling future.

Douglas's austere black-and-white images embody an intimate stillness and intensity recalling the world of silent cinema and reinvesting in the medium what Andrew Noble memorably describes as 'that pristine capacity to see the objects of the world as if for the first time'.[7] The unblinking gaze of the camera reveals the pain and world-weariness palpably etched on the face of young Jamie (as embodied by Stephen Archibald) while simultaneously reflecting the material privations of his world. In addition, Douglas's use of contrapunctal imagery, narrative ellipses and visual symbolism combine to prise open the interior subjective realm of retarded emotion, empathy and understanding, forcing the viewer to share Jamie's restricted and often confused perspective on the world around him. In this sense the *Trilogy* adheres to the conception of the child as an innocent abroad, intensifying the heart-breaking cold brutality, injustice and neglect that he suffers throughout. *My Childhood* concentrates primarily on Jamie's loneliness and isolation and with the stark poverty within which circumscribes his life with Tommy and their grandmother. His father absent and his mother incarcerated in an asylum, Jamie is effectively an orphan. *My Ain Folk* depicts the brutality of Jamie's paternal household, the total abdication of responsibility by a weak and feckless father, the cruelty of his bitter and frigid alcoholic grandmother and the brutality of a violent uncle, recently returned from the war. While *My Way Home* charts a new phase of institutional (as opposed to domestic) suffering with Jamie's experiences in the children's home and then as homeless dosser seeking refuge in a Salvation Army hostel.

Jamie's ill-fated attempt to reintegrate himself into his paternal family in the third part of the *Trilogy* results in his being scorned when he professes his ambitions to become an artist rather than a miner. His father's hard-bitten wife berates him in a manner that reveals a poverty of the imagination to match any material privations the boy has endured:

> An artist? Don't come here with your high-falootin' ideas. You go and
> do an honest day's work and get some dirt on your hands … If you
> were meant to be different you would have been born different …
> This is your place in life.[8]

This crushing of ambition serves to undermine the romantic and enduring myth of the 'lad 'o' pairts'. It becomes increasingly obvious that Jamie's only hope of salvation lies beyond the confines of Scotland and, as Andrew O'Hagan notes, 'Jamie, at last, like many of us, had to leave home to home in on himself.'[9] Douglas's condemnation of his native land and its cultural failings could hardly have been more virulent and his *Trilogy* stands in opposition to certain cosy traditions of Scottish cinematic representation in the same way that the anti-Kailyard novels of John MacDougall Hay and George Douglas Brown constitute a response to the literary movement associated with Barrie, Crockett and McLaren. Moreover, Douglas's Jamie – as a repository of unremitting and unbearable suffering – can also be posited as a potent iconographic repost to J. M. Barrie's eternal child, *Peter Pan*.

The films of childhood that have come in the wake of Bill Douglas share certain key elements, tending to be narratives about male children in working-class families who are unsettled in some way due to the literal or figurative absence of fathers. This is such a recurring element that it assumes a particular potency as a symptom of the national identity crisis, which within such a traditional patriarchal culture confirms the Scottish fictional child as orphaned. As a means of reflecting on a national predicament, Tony McKibbin also links this to that other fundamental touchstone of Scottish identity, class:

> There's a strong sense that Scotland defining itself as working class is
> perhaps concomitant with our interest in films so focussed on youth
> and childhood, as if in each instance there's a carapace of power
> stronger than any decision made by the protagonists.[10]

One might also bring in the masculine bias of many Scottish fictions here. McKibbin is critical of the way in which this association promotes a certain 'victim culture' with Scots unwilling or unable to take responsibility for their own destinies. For example, Jamie's redemption requiring the intervention of a middle-class Englishman who functions as a big brother figure, raising his younger sibling's horizons in a way that the kindly superintendent of the children's home in Edinburgh is unable to do. This in turn confirms the necessity of external intervention for the Scottish child to achieve a fulfilling adult status, effectively to 'find himself'.

The films most closely related to Douglas's tone in terms of their engagement with childhood suffering are Michael Radford's *The White Bird Passes* and Lynne Ramsay's *Ratcatcher*. The former is a 1980 BBC adaptation of Jessie Kesson's autobiographical novel, which prompted the 'rediscovery' of Kesson as a significant creative figure and the republication of a novel that had first appeared in 1958. *The White Bird Passes* recalls the emotional intensity of Douglas while recounting a strikingly similar tale of childhood poverty, parental neglect, enforced institutionalisation and the subsequent struggle for meaning, liberation and fulfilment. Set in the mid-1920s, it charts the experiences of 8-year-old Janie (Vicki Masson), the daughter of an Elgin prostitute who is taken into care after her mother is declared unfit to raise her. Despite her dire circumstances, Janie is a bright and imaginative young girl who is able to draw a certain comfort from her relationship with her mother Eliza (Isobel Black) despite having to continually vie for her attentions with various rough and insensitive 'gentlemen callers'. Radford affords his child protagonist a certain control over the narrative that Douglas denies his fictional alter ego, by structuring his film as a series of impressionistic recollections from the point of view of an older Janie, on the verge of leaving the orphanage and making her own way in the world. Another echo of Douglas comes in the manner that Radford confronts the shortcomings of a fearful culture of stifling acquiescence, that denies creative ambition as wholly inappropriate. Janie's proclamation to the trustees of the orphanage of her desire to 'write great poetry, as great as Shakespeare', instantly recalls the ambition of Jamie to be an artist. But despite the fact that Janie has achieved the best marks for English in Aberdeenshire, the trustees of the orphanage regard her 'a disintegrated personality' more suited to service than higher learning – let alone creative expression. If Douglas gives lie to the egalitarian myth of the 'lad o' pairts', the life chances of a talented but ultimately illegitimate and orphaned country girl appears even more circumscribed by cultural and social expectation.

While Radford's aesthetic approach in *The White Bird Passes* owes more to the influence of Italian neo-realism and its successors than to the more precise formalism that inspired Douglas, Lynne Ramsay's *Ratcatcher* (1999) provided Scottish cinema with its most obvious homage to its most revered cine-poet. Initially trained as a cinematographer, Ramsay had generated a great deal of critical interest with her award-winning short films, *Kill the Day* and *Gasman*, distinguished by, as Lizze Francke has put it, their examination of 'the fragility of evolving into a human being'.[11] Set in the early 1970s against the backdrop of the Glasgow refuse collector's strike, *Ratcatcher* concerns the experiences of James Gillespie (William Eadie), a boy haunted by his involvement in the accidental drowning of his friend Ryan Quinn. James's inability to repress the feelings of guilt motivate a compulsion to return to the site of the incident, the dark and stagnant waters of the canal that runs through the rundown and rat-infested housing scheme where he lives with a long-suffering mother, feckless father and two sisters. James dreams of escape, a yearning given material substance in the scene when he come across a building site on the edge of town and amuses himself by exploring the empty houses. The joyful abandon is enhanced further when through one of the windows he sees a glorious field of golden corn golden wheat set off by a blue sky. This vision, framed by the window, is like a cinematic dreamscape recalling the opening of *My Ain Folk*, in which an enchanted Tommy watches the Technicolor images of *Lassie Come Home* at the local cinema with tears in his eyes. James climbs through the window and cavorts joyously through the wheat. But just as the movie ends and Tommy is carted off to a children's home in Douglas's film, so too James's reverie is revealed as little more than shadows on a wall – he returns to the building site on a grey rainy day to find that glass has now been placed in the window, imprisoning him in a house that feels restrictive, dark and claustrophobic, the spirit-crushing slum of the future.

While *Ratcatcher* ostensibly conveys a familiar vision of the deprivations of proletarian Glasgow life, the focus on James's interiority renders the film as more of an impressionistic accretion of fragments – of moments, emotions, sensations, experiences – than a unified rendering of time, place and social relations. Central to this is the predicament of the child, caught at a moment of transition in which he attempts to resist succumbing to environmental pressures to become a particular kind of adult. Ramsay has described her own perception of childhood as 'a blank canvas, in terms of the direction you can take for good or bad'.[12] This is given force in James's culpability and moral turmoil over the death of Ryan and the struggle between his fantasy of a better life marked by space, freedom and sunshine and the grim realities of his Glasgow slum. As Emma Wilson suggests:

> Survival and optimism are intermittent in the film, rising and
> subsiding, with no sure basis. In this sense *Ratcatcher* is not
> prescriptive but patient, attentive to its child survivor, inflected by
> his disturbed perceptions, hesitant about whether his trauma can be
> adequately witnessed, remembered, represented or survived.[13]

Throughout, James remains a lonely outsider, a status particularly marked in relation to the other male characters. He fails to share his drunken and feckless father's obsession with football, almost a prerequisite in itself for being a proper working-class Scottish male, and his sensitivity and introspection distance him from the brutal and exploitative world of the local teenage gang led by Matt Monroe. Indeed, James's feelings of empathy tend to be directed towards the most marginalised members of the neighbourhood including the slow-witted animal lover Kenny, who as Emma Wilson points out also functions as a double for Ryan Quinn, and the forlorn and myopic figure of Margaret Ann (Leanne Mullen), whose own emotional damage is conveyed in the way in which she allows herself to be routinely abused by Monroe's gang. Motivated by tenderness rather than hate, James (temporarily) redeems her innocence as a young girl – rather than the debased slag she has become in the eyes of her contemporaries. In their first encounter he unsuccessfully tries to retrieve her glasses from the canal, then in a later incident, when he is coaxed by the gang to take his turn with her, James covers Margaret Ann's body with his, hiding and protecting her from further abuse. While Margaret Ann had initially flirted with James in an overtly sexual manner, this is eclipsed by their subsequent interaction including a very tender scene in which the two play in the bath together after James has attempted to rid his friend's hair of nits. However, the redemptive force of this uninhibited and joyful moment is undercut by its juxtaposition with shots of an unconscious Kenny being pulled out of the canal by James's father – a stark reminder of the burden of James's guilt over Ryan and ultimately of his inability to escape it. When Margaret Anne returns to her former ways with the local boys and Kenny reveals that he had witnessed the earlier drowning, James is compelled to return to the canal where he allows himself to sink into the dark murky depths.[14]

A starkly contrasting contemplation of childhood is offered by Ian Sellar's 1989 film *Venus Peter*, an affectionate depiction of a young boy growing up in a rural Orcadian fishing community in the late 1940s, adapted from Christopher Rush's autobiographical memoir *A Twelvemonth and a Day*.[15] From the moment Peter (played by 9-year-old Gordon R. Strachan) is baptised with salt water, his world is dominated by the sea, a close identification almost resulting in tragedy when he attempts to hold his breath indefinitely under water. Despite his longing to be reunited with an absent father whom he has been told is serving in the navy, Peter at least has the benefit of a loving and supportive family network facilitating greater opportunity for him to indulge his powers of imagination. He is aided and abetted in this by his grandfather (Ray McInally), a fisherman who spins poetic yarns about the sea and gives the boy a telescope through which he can observe the world about him. More importantly it is through this looking glass that Peter projects the fantasy images of his father as a handsome captain of a boat decked out in brightly coloured sails. The child's love of poetry is fuelled by the formidable old landlady Epp (Sheila Keith), who simultaneously terrifies him with her tales of hellfire and damnation, and subsequently by his teacher, Miss Balsilbie (Sinead Cusack), an irrepressible romantic with whom he becomes temporarily infatuated. Peter also identifies with the child-like Princess Paloma (Juliet Cadzow), a wild, silent and mentally unstable woman rumoured to be the offspring of Tahitian royalty who lives alone in a big house and who also seeks refuge in imaginary worlds. In equating the death of the fishing industry with the inevitable loss of childhood innocence, *Venus Peter* is essentially an elegiac tale in the mythopoeic tradition of rural Scotland associated with the literary works of Edwin Muir, Neil Gunn and George Mackay Brown.[16] But at the same time, Sellar creates an interesting tension between Peter's immersion in a world of the imagination that inures him against the worst aspects and the emotional and economic stresses of a community confronting the immanent demise of its primary industry. This is conveyed not as elegy but rather as a reminder that imagination and fantasy can provide a psychological defence against the harsher aspects of material existence and parental absence.

The powers of the child's imagination are explored in a rather different way by writer David Kane and director Chris Bernard in their 1988 BBC television film *Shadow on the Earth*. Set in a west Lothian mining village at the time of the first manned space flight in 1961 the film uses childhood fantasy to comment on the insidious problem of Scottish sectarian conflict and bigotry. Obsessed with the space race and science fiction films, young Billy Wilson, his older brother Alex and their friend Sammy become convinced that their reclusive white-haired neighbour is an alien from outer space, a suspicion apparently confirmed when they break into his house and find a room full of star maps and a telescope pointed at the heavens. When the boys attempt to burn him out of his house on Guy Fawkes night, Mr Morris subsequently reveals that his strange appearance is the result of being an albino. While this fails to have any effect on the older boys who are driven by their hatred and fear to smash the telescope Morris had saved for two years to buy, Billy, the most imaginative of the three, finds an empathy with the strange old man and his passion for space. This preserves the possibility of dispelling 'the shadow on the earth' cast by bigotry and hatred and fuelled in the community by the local Orange Lodge of which Billy's grandfather is a proud member. In addition to the direct link between aliens and Catholics, *Shadow on the Earth* also explores the ways in which Scottish working-class patriarchal culture serves to construct girls and women as 'other'. Despite his anti-sectarian and socialist beliefs, Billy's father is unsympathetic to his talented wife's ambitions to study art at night school in a manner that directly echoes similar moments of thwarted ambition in *My Way Home* and *The White Bird Passes*.

This interest in the relationship between the imagination of the child and the often harsher realities of the world around him is also played out in *Small Faces* (1996). A collaboration between director Gillies Mackinnon and his screenwriter/producer brother Billy, this is another highly personal film inspired in part by the McKinnons' childhood experiences in late 1960s' Glasgow. *Small Faces* consequently takes the form of an intimate portrait of the relationships between three brothers growing up against a backdrop of conflict between the notorious Glasgow gangs of the period. At the centre of this narrative is Lex McLean (Iain Robertson), a precocious 13-year-old living in a cramped flat in Govanhill with his brothers Alan (Joe McFadden) and Bobby (J. S. Duffy) and their long-suffering mother (Claire Higgins). Lex and Alan are both talented artists, a skill that distances them from the emotionally disturbed and educationally subnormal Bobby who seeks belonging as a member of the local gang led by the spivish Charlie Sloan (Garry Sweeney). But while Alan is a gentle and mature individual, Lex displays a edge of unpredictability that echoes Bobby's erratic behaviour, while his imaginary gang map of Glasgow suggests a view of the world that has already been forged in relation to violence and territoriality. Moreover, it is Lex who unwittingly ignites hostilities with a rival gang when he shoots its psychotic leader Malky Johnson (Kevin McKidd) in the face with an air gun. This conflict becomes progressively serious, culminating in the horrific murder of Bobby on an ice rink. The construction of Lex as a psychologically complex central character – the film's narrative begins and ends with his voice-over – eschews the distanciation that characterise Douglas, Ramsay and even Sellar's depiction of the child, fixing Lex more as a mini-adult than as a child. And while *Small Faces* raises a number of interesting and complex moral issues – the relationships within the McLean family, the choice between creativity and violence, the transformation from childhood innocence to adult responsibility – the film ultimately fails to develop or explore these issues in a wholly satisfactory way. Lex's final decision to remain a child – and the manner in which he (and by extension the film) seems to dispense with Bobby's death, and Lex's own responsibility for that death – suggests McKinnon's over-reliance on finding a conventional narrative resolution rather than challenging confrontation with loss, guilt and childhood suffering that distinguishes a more complex and challenging film like *Ratcatcher*.

If *Small Faces* appears ultimately too glib, then *Sweet Sixteen* (2002) returns us to the vexed issue of whether the human spirit can overcome the weight of adversity piled upon it by modern life. Written by Paul Laverty and directed by Ken Loach, this film – the only example considered here that is not set in the past – concentrates on the experiences of a boy on the threshold of adult responsibility. Liam (Martin Compson) is a 15-year-old from Greenock waiting for his mother to be released from prison where she has been serving a drug-related sentence. A permanent truant, Liam has already fallen into a life of petty crime, selling black market cigarettes in pubs with his friend Pinball (William Ruane) who is also a compulsive joyrider. Liam resists helping his mother's latest violent boyfriend, Stan (Gary McCormack), in his attempts to smuggle heroin into the women's prison, but decides to start dealing himself in order to buy a caravan for his mother when she gets out.

This in turn brings him to the attention of a big-time dealer who, impressed with his entrepreneurial skills and spirit, employs Liam to run a service using a pizza delivery business as a front. Significantly, Liam's faith in his mother is not shared by his sister Chantelle (Annmarie Fulton), who is also a young single mother trying to make a life for herself and her young son Callum. Chantelle provides Liam with the love, support and stability he craves from his mother, but as he becomes more and more drawn into the world of drug dealing so his chances of having a 'normal' life rapidly disappear. The film culminates tragically with Liam having threatened his sister with violence after their mother has returned to her boyfriend, stabs Stan in the stomach and leaves him for dead. In an echo of Truffaut's *Quatre Cent Coups*, the final scene places Liam on a deserted beach, facing the sea with nowhere to run – the added poignancy being that it is the day of his sixteenth birthday and his life, rather than at a new beginning, seems to be prematurely over.

Despite his problems, Liam is presented as a bright and resourceful individual, generous to those he cares about, who ultimately craves a sense of normality but is caught between his responsibilities towards his sister, his hopes for a brighter future with his mother and his involvement in the local drug scene. But Liam also harbours a dark side, his unstable background having already made him fearless to the point of recklessness. This is evinced when, having been robbed of his drugs by three thugs, Liam relentlessly keeps on coming back at them, taking savage beatings in the process, until his drugs are returned. As Chantelle bathes his wounds, she reminds him of the way he behaved in the face of aggression at the children's home the two had once spend time in: 'You didnae fight them because you were brave. You fought them because you didnae care what happened to you. That's what broke ma heart … How can you really care for us when you don't care about yourself?'

Two scenes marking in different ways his 'coming of age' also highlight the fundamental dilemma Liam faces in growing up. In the first he is caught shaving by his sister and her friend Susanne who tease him in a good-hearted way about it. This is directly followed by Liam being tested by his new associates who ask him to kill someone in a pub with a knife. While it transpires this is a trick, it is nevertheless clear that Liam was prepared to go through with it and his reward is to be allowed to join the other 'hard men' for a drink in the bar, marking his own acceptance as a bona fide member of the gang. Liam's subsequent outbursts of violence confirm a sadly predicable mode of behaviour, marking him out as ultimately little more than another tragic study in Scottish male self-destructiveness.

Such cinematic narratives of childhood – particularly those with clear auto-biographical associations – inevitably pose the question of what becomes of the child when he or she grows up. In the case of Douglas and Kesson, we are aware that a childhood marked by crushing poverty has been superseded by adult creative fulfilment and even bourgeois respectability. Yet such transcendence is rarely confronted as a central issue by film-makers who tend instead to restrict their vision to a past circumscribed by material and psychological adversity. As Tony McKibbin argues, 'We have still to see a cinema develop out of the psychic conflict of the bourgeois adult with the memory of a poverty-stricken child.'[17] The problem of moving beyond the impasse of suffering is also interrogated by Jonathan Murray who questions the trope of childhood in Scottish cinema as potentially regressive, suggesting that 'its associated qualities of innocence, immaturity and lack of power seem disturbingly easy to map onto discourses of national identity in an elegiac and politically self-defeating way'.[18] Murray then identifies what he considers to be the beginning of an alternative possibility by reference to Peter Mullan's feature *Orphans*, which deals with the familiar problem of loss in a refreshingly different manner. The decline of the Clyde shipyards may provide a direct context for Michael's predicament, his self-pitying response to both his mother's death and to his own failure as a father being to turn the knife-wound he suffered in a pub brawl into a faked accident at work that will allow him to claim bogus compensation. Yet, as Murray suggests, the subsequent launching of Michael into the Clyde constitutes not a symbol of his powerlessness but rather as a kind of surreal re-baptism, the renewal of a man who has finally acknowledged the emotional truth of his love for his mother rather than repressing and externalising this through aggression and self pity. In this way, *Orphans* 'reconceives the model of childhood experience as national-allegorical trope as a nascent state, characterised to a degree by possibility and fluidity, not by a retrospective and elegiac acknowledgement of inevitable closure and trauma'.[19] The symbolic use of the river as a source of renewal also counters the devastating watery death of James Gillespie in *Ratcatcher*, or the sea as a metaphorical dead end that marks *Sweet Sixteen*, while the climactic reunion of the Flynn family by their mother's grave intimates a positive way forward that does not ignore moral, emotional or intellectual complexity in the way *Small Faces* does.

## THE CHILD AND THE ADULT IN SCOTTISH LITERATURE

Children also feature as a significant presence in contemporary Scottish literature. However, the greater scope of the novel as a form has provided a different kind of latitude in which childhood becomes recast as a phase in the broader canvas of a person's life cycle. The scope of the life narrative also affords writers the opportunity to reflect on wider issues in a more concerted way, including the relationship between the fortunes of the central protagonist to some kind of wider national predicament. A more recent example of a Scottish writer who not only shares this kind of ambitious perspective but has also engaged with questions of childhood, memory and autobiography in innovative and challenging ways is Andrew O'Hagan, who first caught the imagination with a highly provocative journalistic analysis of the murder of the Liverpool toddler James Bulger in 1992 by two 10-year-old boys.[20] O'Hagan had also written a critical appreciation of Bill Douglas, inspired in part by his own memories of childhood trauma:

> I was already biting my nails at the age of five, chewing into them till they bled. My earliest memory is of me crouched below the kitchen sink watching my father, an AA veteran, scoop handfuls of green and yellow capsules into his mouth from a clear plastic tub he hid in the top cupboard. Often, panting milky breath, I'd peer through a button-hole in my mother's maroon raincoat, watching her slapping him over the breakfast table. Like most kids I knew, I spent my formative days under coats, within dens and in the long grass – hiding from my dad.[21]

O'Hagan's first novel, *Our Fathers*, begins with the childhood recollections of a character called, significantly, Jamie, who at the age of six travels with his parents from the town of his birth, Berwick on Tweed, to Saltcoats in Ayrshire. Jamie Bawn's immediate family is a study in dysfunction, presided over by a violent, alcoholic father and a mother who, while attentive and loving, plays a masochistic and destructive role in encouraging, rather than attempting to diffuse, the hatred between her husband and son.[22] Rather than responding to his father Robert's cold brutality by becoming a delinquent like his friend Berry, Jamie finds refuge in the world of books and the imagination. His education also helps to forge the poetic sensibility that colours his narration, marked by a sensitivity to the life-enhancing properties of the landscape and nature, as well as to the psychic disorders that shape and warp relationships. O'Hagan relates the negative force that Robert Bawn represents to his son to a devastating assessment of Scotland's own (self-imposed) limitations:

> In my father's anger there was something of the nation. Everything torn from the ground; his mind like a rotten field. His was a country of fearful men: proud in the talking, paltry in the living, and every promise another lie. My father bore all the dread that came with the soil – unable to rise, or rise again, and slow to see the power in his own hands. Our fathers were made for grief. They were broken-backed. They were sick at heart, weak in the bones. All they wanted was the peace of defeat. They couldn't live in this world. They couldn't stand

who they were. Robert's madness was nothing new: he was one of his own kind, bred with long songs of courage, never to show a courageous hand.[23]

But childhood is only one element of a novel that is primarily concerned with reconciliation and understanding. The narrative pivots on the adult Jamie's return to the home of the grandparents who had brought him up after his father's violence had finally driven him away from home. Jamie's paternal grandfather, Hugh Bawn, had been an idealistic Socialist pioneer of the municipal housing boom on Clydeside in the 1960s. But he is now an old man, dying in a small flat on the eighteenth floor of a dilapidated tower block he had been responsible for building – the utopian housing dream of the future transformed into the crime-ridden new slum of the present. Despite their formerly close relationship, Jamie has been estranged from his grandfather for many years, partly due to his job as a demolition expert responsible for literally raising Hugh's lifework to the ground. The latter, for his part, is a stubborn and foul-mouthed curmudgeon, who, despite his ill health, still summons up the energy to be aggressive and abusive towards the prodigal grandson. This masculine relationship is itself enclosed within a broader sweep of Scottish history. Hugh's own mother, Euphemia Bawn, was a firebrand who played a major role in the Glasgow rent strikes of 1915, helping to forge a particular Scottish attitude to public housing that was to be her son's own calling in life. The ultimate failure of this utopian dream is the poignant legacy that *Our Fathers* confronts, linking the personal, the social and the political in a skilful and insightful analysis of Scotland's shortcomings as a nation. Significantly, this engagement is also aware of events beyond Clydeside. Jamie's grandmother Margaret is from Highland stock, her own links to social 'improvement' brought about by the clearances giving added resonance to Hugh's great project as Glasgow's 'Mr Housing'.

After Hugh's death, Jamie confronts his own ghosts by going in search of his father – briefly glimpsed at the back of the church during the funeral service. The subsequent reunion with Robert, now sober and living in a caravan in Dumfries, brings about the glimmer of an understanding between father and son. While the AA meetings that Robert attends provides a sense of personal recovery linked to the potential for a national healing:

Recovery was the story of the moment, and they all told these stories, and listened to the stories of one another, and they brought the old stuff of wars and ideals, of history and dreaming, of enlightenment and love and deliverance and progress, and they made it swell the narrative of their own improvement. They believed in the unity of needs; they had made a nationhood of self-rescue. Our fathers were dead and gone;

here were the living, and every wind of tradition came about them, every breath of the past came in whispers to make them new, and here they were, a gloaming of faces in a tartan séance, a calling-down of ghosts from the greenwood side.[24]

*Our Fathers* concludes with Jamie's discovery of his handwriting as a child on the back of a picture found among Hugh's personal items. On it Jamie had written, 'There are ruined buildings in the world ... but no ruined stones',[25] a prophetic reminder of the limited and fragile legacy that human beings leave in the vaster scheme of things and a vindication of Jamie the child's own connection to awe-inspiring forces of nature. But this is no elegiac hymn to landscape and we are left with the adult Jamie ready and willing to assume his own responsibilities to a neglected partner in Liverpool who had elected to terminate a pregnancy because of his inability to deal with the idea, let alone the reality, of starting a family. In this way Jamie's narrative is about confronting the past in order to face the future. And while the rendering of this narrative may share much with Bill Douglas's or even Lynne Ramsay's examinations of damaged childhood, the resolution of *Our Fathers* has more in common with *Orphans* in its search for meaningful and restorative closure. O'Hagan's figurative Scottish orphan learns not only to find his own way in the world by acknowledging his father, this also may remove the barriers to him becoming a father some time in the future.

A rather different kind of life-narrative is provided by Alan Spence and Irvine Welsh in their respective novels, *The Magic Flute* (1990) and *Glue* (2001), which both follow the unfolding relationships between a group of friends from childhood to adulthood. Such an inter-subjective developmental form also provides interesting and fertile terrain on which wider 'state of the nation' issues can be explored. Spence's *The Magic Flute* charts the fortunes of four working-class Glaswegians over a period of eighteen years from 1962, when at the age of 12 they are on the verge of moving from primary to secondary school, to 1980.[26] Welsh presents an almost identical scenario in *Glue*, but his protagonists are from Edinburgh and the time period covered ranges from a prologue set in 1970 to an epilogue set in 2002. Consequently between them these two novels engage with some forty years of social, political and economic change in Scotland and the world beyond, from the utopian promise of the 1960s, through the chill winds of Thatcherism, to the post-industrial realities of the present day. In addition to their similar narrative construction, *The Magic Flute* and *Glue* share a number of thematic concerns, the most defining of which is the emotional significance of peer group friendships that the Scottish films of childhood, with their emphasis on the isolated individual, largely ignore.

In recalling the Glasgow of the 1960s and 1970s, *The Magic Flute*[27] initially constructs a rather traditional image of a working-class urban community in Glasgow's Govan, a district primarily associated with shipbuilding and the football team Glasgow Rangers. The novel begins with the four young protagonists – Tam Rae, Brian Ritchie, Eddie Logan and George Wilson – going along to join a Flute band, fixing them with a particular sectarian identity as Scottish Protestants. But while the power of the music is initially aligned to regressive sectarian identities, Spence depicts the Protestant community of Govan with subtlety and sensitivity, recognising the positive as well as the negative aspects of this close-knit working-class Glasgow neighbourhood. The theme of music as a profound, spiritual and redemptive force is continually returned to throughout the novel, but Spence also engages with more material issues in the various life-narratives of his four central characters. A combination of domestic and educational factors plays a major part in determining the four boys' subsequent experiences and opportunities. Brian and Tam are fortunate in having broadly supportive and nurturing families. Brian's mother has aspirations for her son beyond divisive tribal associations and is adamant that he will have nothing to do with an Orange flute band; while despite their poverty, Tam's family encourage him in his passion and even club together to buy him a second-hand flute. In contrast, George's father is a staunch Orangeman and self-serving hypocrite who thinks nothing of using his Masonic connections to pull strings for himself and his son. But it is Eddie who suffers the greatest domestic hardship, his father is a drunk and a gambler, his mother hard and embittered and his elder brother a bully, and by the age of 12 he is already showing the signs of delinquency and violence that will restrict his life chances.

These various inclinations are exacerbated by a segregated education system defined by the tyranny of the eleven-plus examination that decided future opportunities for children at a ridiculously young age prior to the gradual introduction of comprehensive secondary education in the 1960s.[28] Such institutionalised discrimination splits up the group with Brian and Tam, having successfully passed the exams, attending the local grammar school. In contrast, George's failure condemns him to follow the already underachieving Eddie at the junior secondary. While stopping short of rubbishing the myth of Scottish egalitarianism, Spence vividly demonstrates the ways in which opportunities for social mobility are already largely predetermined and when they do allow for advancement can be socially and domestically divisive. Consequently, it is Brian and Tam whose lives diverge most radically from that of their parents, the subsequent bohemian and creative existence of these grammar school boys, in line with the hippy ideals of the late 1960s/early 1970s, also contrasting starkly with the respective fates of their less privileged contemporaries. Rather predictably, George follows his allotted path in life, becoming a rather confused and disenchanted younger version of his father, while the increasingly disaffected Eddie establishes himself as 'mental' hard man, leading off a Glasgow gang like those depicted in *Small Faces*, before drifting into more serious criminality, thieving and enforcing for a loan shark. His only way out of criminality is to join the Army and Eddie finds himself on a tour of duty in Ulster

The different trajectories that come to define the individuality of the four characters are defined in a key montage sequence that cuts back and forward between the four as a series of life-changing events unfold one Friday night in 1969. George's conformity is confirmed when he is initiated into the Masonic lodge that his father is a member of, an experience that moves from confusion, fear and trepidation to a sense for the first time of belonging to something. Meanwhile Eddie is tragically killed after being lured into an IRA trap while out drinking with another off-duty soldier in Belfast. But Brian and Tam experience more positive and life-affirming transitions. After a fraught evening alone in his digs, revising for an important exam, the former channels his energy into the creation of a cut-up poem. While Tam embarks on an acid trip which, echoing Brian's emotional trajectory, takes him from black paranoia to a life-affirming epiphany, culminating a blissful physical and spiritual union with Ruby, the woman he has become infatuated with. It is significant that these more creative characters are the two bearing the most direct autobiographical relationship to Spence:

> I'm the writer Brian would have liked to be, and Tam's the musician I would have liked to be. I invented these characters and was consciously putting them in situations that I'd been in, and allowing the fictional side of it to develop, rather than straight autobiography.[29]

And while the surviving protagonists become even more isolated from one another, Spence conspires to reunite Tam and Brian as a means of finding a resolution to his saga. The narrative device here is the death of John Lennon in 1980, the consequence of which prompts Tam to return to Scotland from New York where he has been living for some time and Brian to summon up the courage to quit his teaching job to become a writer. *The Magic Flute* ends with Tam looking through the package he has received from Brian. This includes a short story entitled 'Flute Music', a first-person version of the beginning of the novel and a life-affirming testimony to the bond between the two. Tam's return to Scotland also provides another perspective on the theme of finding one's way home, in this case to a nation at the start of a decade that was to mark a fundamental cultural transformation.

In a similar fashion, Irvine Welsh's *Glue* depicts the enduring friendship between Carl Ewart, 'Juice' Terry Lawson, Billy Birrell and Andrew 'Gally' Galloway, over a period of three decades from the boys' early school years to their mid-thirties. Once again, the distinction between relatively stable and dysfunctional families proves to be an important one. As self-consciously nurturing fathers, Duncan Ewart and Wullie Birrell are keen to instil certain moral values into their sons, while in sharp contrast, Terry Lawson and Andrew Galloway are forced to deal with the implications of paternal absence. Terry's narrative begins with the traumatic moment when his father walks out on his mother, while Andrew finds himself 'the man ay the house' at the tender age of five when his father is sent to prison. The boys' teenage years are subsequently marked by their formative sexual exploits and the lure of the local gang, headed by somewhat familiar psychotic hard men. But while Billy, the physically toughest of the friends, distances himself through his interest in sport, Gally, the smallest and most emotionally immature of the quartet, becomes involved with a gang of football casuals as a means of proving himself. Gally's reckless habit of carrying a knife leads to him taking the blame for a stabbing outside a night-club for which, in a tragic echo of his father's fate, he is sent to prison. By the time they have reached their mid-twenties the characters paths have, like those of *The Magic Flute*, begun to diverge. Having established himself first as a boxer, Billy is now a businessman running his own trendy city centre club, while Carl is a successful DJ working the clubs in Edinburgh, London and abroad. Significantly both have moved out of the scheme in Stenhouse and into the city, marking their transition from dependent sons into economically independent adults. In contrast, Terry remains in a rut, permanently unemployed and living with his mother. But the real tragedy is Gally who has now served a second prison sentence, a result of an accidental injury caused to his young daughter during a fight with her mother. To make matters worse, he has also tested HIV positive after a brief flirtation with heroin. Gally's situation leads him to commit suicide by throwing himself off Edinburgh's George IV Bridge in front of his three friends. This proves the shock that finally dissolves the glue that had bound them together for so long. As Carl Ewart reflects:

> That was the last time it was special. After that we kept away from each other. It was if we learned about loss too young and wanted to take ourselves away from each other before the others did it first. Even though we wirnae really that far fae each other; me, Billy, Terry and I suppose Gally became the four corners ay the globe after that night.[30]

The three remain estranged for almost a decade with Terry scamming on the estate, Billy running his city centre bar and Carl working abroad away from family, friends and Scotland. Carl is in Australia when he gets the news that his father has had a stroke and is dying. He manages to get back in time to say goodbye before being confronted by Billy and Terry in a reunion that allows confessions to made about their various feelings of guilt and responsibility for Gally's suicide. In this way second tragedy serves to repair the effects of the first:

> Carl looked up at the dull sky and started to convulse in tearless heavy sobs that shook his thin frame. Billy and Terry glanced at each other. They were embarrassed, not so much of Carl, but for him. He was still a gadge after all.
>
> But through Duncan's death something hung in the air between them. There was just *something*, some kind of second chance, and even Carl seemed to sense it through his grief.[31]

As Matthew Hart points out, Duncan Ewart 'was the symbolic father of the group, an apologist for youth and the author of their childhood code of silence and loyalty and by closing with this death, *Glue* takes on a generational and patrilineal shape'.[32] But the novel also provides a corrective to one of the central problems of Welsh's *Trainspotting*, where the narrative trajectory had confirmed the unsustainability of the social group, predicated in part on Mark Renton's unresolved oedipal conflict with his father. In contrast, *Glue* sets up a sense of a sustainable communality, founded initially on the unselfish and nurturing rock represented by Carl Ewart's parents. His father is a committed socialist from Kilmarnock, a shop steward at the machine shop where he works. But significantly Duncan is also a Protestant and a freemason who served his apprenticeship in Glasgow before moving to Edinburgh, while his wife, Maria, on the other hand is from an Edinburgh Catholic family. In this way the Ewarts provide a corrective to the Rentons, a positive evocation of religious and cultural hybridity that refuses the tensions and antagonism of sectarianism.

Welsh also engages more forcefully than Spence with the broader social, economic and political changes affecting Scotland. *The Magic Flute* may touch on questions of social deprivation in the form of poverty, alcoholism and loan sharking – and even the beginning of drugs as a growing problem in Scotland's housing estates – but by this point in the saga the perspective is very much that of the appalled observer than a report from the coal-face. In dealing directly with a more brutal and destructive period in recent history, Welsh conveys an altogether rawer picture, primarily through the life and times of the west-side scheme of Stenhouse. Unlike the boys of Protestant Govan, the protagonists of *Glue* are at odds with their cultural environment in that (with the exception of Carl) they are die-hard supporters of Hibernian, the east-end Catholic football team, rather than the Protestant local club, Hearts, prompting Terry to muse that this shared commitment in adversity is the reason for their 'devil may care' hedonistic approach to life – 'we've no hud it easy like aw they cunts doon Leith. They dinnae ken whit being *real* Hibs is like'.[33] In 1970 the scheme is new and the novel begins with the Galloway family moving into their modern bright centrally-heated flat with large windows, signifying optimism and hope and the end of slum life. Twenty-four pages later this vision is already being dashed: 'as winter set in and the first bills came through the post, the central-heating systems in the scheme clicked off; synchronised to such a degree it was almost like they were operated by one master switch'.[34] In an echo of the death of Hugh Bawn's utopian dream in *Our Fathers*, by 1980 the scheme is already beginning to deteriorate. A further decade on, both the Birrells and the Ewarts homes have been 'fitted out with optimistic redundancy cash'[35] – the former family having purchased their council house while the latter have moved out to the suburbs. Things are tight for both as the reality of long-term unemployment begins to bite and it is subsequently revealed that Carl has had to help his parents out financially, saving them from the humiliation of having their house repossessed. Meanwhile by 2000, Andrew's father, feckless ex-con Davie Galloway, has been hired to work as a security guard watching the CCTV monitors in his control centre, the bright new hope for the future now a crime-ridden slum requiring round-the-clock surveillance. Yet despite this palpable sense of decay, Welsh ultimately forges a vibrant, new and progressive sense of Scottishness with Carl Ewart's return and his reunion with Billy and Terry. The novel ends with a coda in 2002, conveying a new kind of utopian national allegory that Matthew Hart aptly describes as ending 'happily in New Caledonia, friends gather round the big multi cultural mixing desk of devolutionary Scotland'.[36]

## CONCLUSION: ABSENT FATHERS AND THE FORGING OF A NEW SCOTLAND

The coda to *Glue* would appear to endorse the idea raised at the beginning of this chapter that the metaphorical problem posed by the recurring figure of the child, or of the Orphan, in Scottish fiction has been the absence of an independent nation–state. And if the restoration of a devolved Scottish Parliament in 1999 signifies the return of at least some degree of self-determination and responsibility to Scotland, then perhaps this can in turn be linked to the more optimistic resolutions of novels like *Glue* and *Our Fathers* and films like *Orphans*. In all of these the process of maturation from child to adult is successfully achieved, festering issues of family conflict are resolved, responsibilities are faced with courage, and the future is presented as one of potential opportunity. The figure of the child as a literal or metaphorical Orphan has proved to be a particularly interesting and suggestive in that the majority of the films and novels examined here tend to confirm the conception of the child as an innocent abroad who is led down or neglected in various ways by the family, the community and the society into which he or she is born. The child's progress is consequently a process of struggle – for understanding of the world and for the means of making things better. As we have also seen, the absence of fathers is perhaps an even more frequently recurring figure, this paternal lack a key source of the sense of dysfunction that permeates the representation of the Scottish working-class family, wreaking its ill-effects on the well-being of the child in the process. In some cases this can be related directly to material circumstances such as the economic and psychological damage wrought on men by the consequences of Thatcherite policies and the changes in global capitalism.

But the proliferation of absent fathers in Scottish fiction has an even more profound symbolic resonance in that the lack of strong parental guidance is another way of arguing that Scotland has been historically orphaned from its own past. In such a traditionally patriarchal society it is no surprise that this should be equated almost exclusively with the father. The various fictions explored above subsequently focus on the struggle of children to deal with the consequences of the missing or deficient father. In some instances the mother comes to play a more significant role, in others it is grandparents who assume this surrogate position, but rarely is the problem fully or satisfactorily dispelled. Indeed, it could be argued that the failure of the Scottish nation to fully realise its potential is bound up in some way with these collective representations of the failure of men to take responsibility for themselves, their partners and, most of all, their children. The overwhelming focus in fictions of childhood on boys also poses the question of whether or not the sins of the fathers will be visited on the children, ensuring that the cycle continues into the next generation. The struggle faced by the child to somehow become a secure, viable and content adult is consequently echoed on a broader level of Scotland's desire to become a secure, viable and content nation. The potential solution implied by the various films and novels explored here lies not in the externalising of blame (towards the English in particular) but in accepting the responsibility of putting the national household or community in order. In this way the child comes to function less of a misfit but rather as a future citizen of the new Scotland who has certain expectations and rights but also responsibilities in the forging of that new future.

## NOTES

1. Alan Riach, 'Nobody's Children: Orphans and their Ancestors in Popular Scottish Fiction', in Susanne Hagemann (ed.), *Studies in Scottish Fiction: 1945 to the Present* (Frankfurt: Peter Lang, 1996), p. 80.

2. Arthur McIvor notes that this was in part due to the smaller middle class in Scotland and in part to the regressive attitude taken towards birth control by the Scottish labour movement during the inter-war period, McIvor, 'Gender Apartheid? Women in Scottish Society', in T. M. Devine and R. J. Finlay (eds), *Scotland in the 20th Century* (Edinburgh: Edinburgh University Press, 1996).

3. Marina Warner, 'Through a Child's Eyes', in Duncan Petrie (ed.), *Cinema and the Realms of Enchantment* (London: BFI, 1993), pp. 38–9.

4. The respective tragic fates of the young female protagonists in Elspeth Barker's novel *Oh Caledonia* and Lars von Trier's film *Breaking the Waves* explored within the context of a Scottish Gothic tradition in Chapter 5 are instructive here.

5. Marina Warner, 'Through a Child's Eyes', in Petrie (ed.), p. 49.

6. John Caughie, 'Don't Mourn – Analyse: Reviewing the Trilogy', in Eddie Dick, Andrew Noble and Duncan Petrie (eds), *Bill Douglas: A Lanternist's Account* (London: BFI, 1993), p. 198.

7. Andrew Noble, 'Bill Douglas's Trilogy', in Eddie Dick (ed.), *From Limelight to Satellite: A Scottish Film Book* (London: BFI/SFC, 1990). p. 136.

8. Bill Douglas, 'My Way Home', in Dick *et al.* (eds), p. 94.

9. Andrew O'Hagan, 'Homing', in Dick *et al.* (eds), p. 213.

10. Tony McKibbin, 'Scottish Cinema: A Victim Culture?', *Cencrastus*, No. 73, 2002, p. 25.

11. Lizzie Francke in conversation with Lynne Ramsay, 'Childhood is a Black Canvas', the introduction to Lynne Ramsay, *Ratcatcher* (London: Faber & Faber, 1999), p. vii.

12. Lynne Ramsay, *Ratcatcher*, p. viii.

13. Emma Wilson, *Cinema's Missing Children* (London: Wallflower, 2003), p. 119.

14. This ending is deliberately ambiguous being inter-cut with images of James's family carrying their belongings through the golden field to the new house, yet the final image returns us to James under the water suggesting that the promise of a better life is nothing more than the dying boy's fantasy.

15. Rush's original novel, published in 1985, is set in the village of St Monans in the East Neuk of Fife.

16. Sellar avoids some of the more sentimentalised conservatism of Rush's original novel which bemoans the destruction of the community, their story telling and affinity with the sea: '(t)he faces in the firelight have faded into the garish light of the TV screen and of what is sometimes called progress'. Christopher Rush, *A Twelvemonth and a Day* (Aberdeen: Aberdeen University Press, 1985), p. 306.

17. Tony McKibbin, 'Scottish Cinema: A Victim Culture?', *Cencrastus*, No. 73, p. 28.

18. Jonathan Murray, 'Contemporary Scottish Film', *Irish Review*, 28, Winter 2001, p. 82.

19. Ibid. p. 84.

20. He later wrote, 'there were things about them which were recognisable, things about their lives, their ways of walking and inclining their heads towards each other. Their stances ignited memories that I'd never had reason to think about, and my editor suggested I write them down.', Andrew O'Hagan, *The Missing* (London: Picador, 1995), p. 94.

21. Andrew O'Hagan, 'Homing', in Dick *et al.* (eds), p. 205.

22. Aspects of this narrative have autobiographical resonance with O'Hagan's own childhood in Ayrshire as glimpsed in his essay 'Homing'.

23. Andrew O'Hagan, *Our Fathers* (London: Faber & Faber, 1999), p. 8.

24. Ibid. p. 277.

25. Ibid. p. 282.

26. Spence's previous collection of short stories, *Its Colours They are Fine* (Edinburgh: Canongate, 1987) also follows the lives of particular characters within a similar time

frame from childhood, through the confusions of their teenage years and into the world of work, relationships and the ubiquitous Glasgow gangs.

27. Alan Spence, *The Magic Flute* (Edinburgh: Canongate, 1990).

28. By 1974 98 per cent of secondary school pupils in Scotland attended comprehensive Schools compared to less than 50 per cent south of the Border. T. M. Devine, *The Scottish Nation, 1700–2000* (London: Allen Lane, 1999), p. 580.

29. Alan Spence, in Isobel Murray (ed.), *Scottish Writers Talking 2* (East Linton: Tuckwell Press, 2002), p. 187.

30. Irvine Welsh, *Glue* (London: Jonathan Cape, 2001), p. 492.

31. Ibid. p. 539.

32. Matthew Hart, 'Solvent Abuse: Irvine Welsh and Scotland', *Postmodern Culture*, Vol. 12, No. 2, 2002, p. 5.

33. Irvine Welsh, *Glue*, p. 326.

34. Ibid. p. 27.

35. Ibid. p. 183.

36. Matthew Hart, 'Solvent Abuse: Irvine Welsh and Scotland', p. 6.

# CHAPTER 8

# International Cross-Currents

## INTRODUCTION

The Introduction to this book proposed an essentially polysemic conception of national identity as a means of capturing the complexity and diversity of contemporary cultural formations. This inevitably includes the web of tangled relationships between a geographically limited nation and the international world outside it. In the case of Scotland, much of the new-found cultural confidence and vibrancy has had important consequences in relation to this international dimension, challenging the idea of the 'Scottish predicament' of cultural self-obsession in the process. International relations have provided an array of cross-cultural affinities, interactions and influences which have been mobilised to re-imagine Scotland and its place in the world – for example, the emphasis on historical or ideological connections with alternatively America and continental Europe as a strategy of resisting or bypassing English metropolitan culture. Such attempts to reposition the nation reminds us that national identity has an important relational component in the sense that it is partly defined in opposition to that what it is not. Moreover, national identities are always hybrid, pluralistic and dynamic, involving a myriad of real and imaginary connections to other national and cultural formations, something rendered all the more significant by the intensification of global cultural exchange facilitated by late capitalism. Scotland's status as a comparatively small nation is also a key issue, the cultural consequences of which are considered by Cairns Craig via the concept of core and periphery derived from the work of the American sociologist Michael Hechter.[1] Within this perspective, peripheral nations are frequently seen as possessing no meaningful or influential indigenous cultural traditions, which in turn allows any significant works that have been produced to be incorporated into the traditions of a larger core nation. In this way, Scottish literature and film can and has been annexed to broader English or

British traditions or histories. Against such hegemonic incorporation, Craig proposes an idea of alternative non-centrist traditions that develop through a cluster of marginal or peripheral nations:

> This does not mean that in peripheral countries there is no native tradition, but that the relationship between what is 'integral' to those cultures and what is 'dependent' on outside forces has a different balance than it has in countries which have the political integrity and cultural power of the core. The relationship of 'dependence' on outside forces through which peripheral cultures develop is, however, all too often seen as *only* a function of their relationship with the core, when by virtue of the very fact that they feel threatened and repressed by the core culture, their true relationships are not centripetal but centrifugal, not towards the core but towards the other marginal cultures who share a similar relation to the core.[2]

Craig also draws an important distinction between the production of official histories of culture, usually written by and in the interests of the core, and the actual histories of such production which often suggest a rather different perspective on the contribution of peripheral or small nations. In this respect he cites the example of Yeats, Joyce and Beckett, three Irish writers who collectively 'have provided the key discourses by which we have tried to make literary sense of the Twentieth Century'.[3] Consequently, Craig calls for a 'peripheral perspective' that 'allows us to draw our own lines of filiation, within our own culture, between ourselves and the core cultures, but most important of all between ourselves and other peripheral cultures'.[4] The subsequent invigoration of Scottish cultural production in the two decades since this essay first appeared has provided an abundance of material relevant to such a re-imagination of both indigenous national traditions and inter-national cultural relations.

Such debates are inevitably dominated by Scotland's historical relationship with England, and the incorporation of both nations into the British State through the 1707 Act of Union. But while Scotland may have given up its political independence, it certainly did not relinquish its own national identity. Not only did Scotland retain many of its key economic, legal and religious institutions, it also held onto a crucial sense of difference or semi-independence as a 'stateless nation'[5] within the Union. Moreover, the Scottish contribution to Britain's development as an imperial power during the eighteenth and nineteenth centuries in both an administrative and a military capacity has been widely acknowledged by historians. For Linda Colley, the Empire 'enabled Scots to feel themselves peers of the English in a way still denied to them in an island kingdom'[6] and consequently their 'disproportionate contribution to the Great Game persisted throughout the nineteenth century and on until the end of the Empire'.[7] This international involvement has deeper roots and prior to 1707 Scots had already established a formidable overseas presence – as clerics, scholars, mercenaries, merchants, tenant farmers and peddlers – particularly within the countries of northern Europe from Scandinavia and the Netherlands to Poland and Russia. Consequently, as Angus Calder notes, 'the wandering Scot – soldier, farmer, trader – was a well-established prototype by the seventeenth century'.[8] This tradition of mobility combined with Scottish involvement in the Empire to feed waves of emigration from the eighteenth century onwards, creating in the process a sizeable and significant Scottish diaspora in the new colonies of North America, Australasia and South Africa.[9]

Scotland also experienced waves of immigration during the nineteenth and twentieth centuries and, while on a much smaller scale, this was nevertheless significant in terms of the development of a culturally diverse Scottish population. By far the largest ethnic grouping to come to arrive were the Irish, who by 1851 already made up 7.2 per cent of the Scottish population. The vast majority of Irish immigrants were Catholic and they tended to settle in Glasgow, Motherwell, Paisley, the Lothians and Dundee where they developed distinct and often introverted communities with their own religious, educational, social and political institutions. The smaller Protestant Irish community in Scotland did not suffer the same discrimination as their Catholic counterparts and tended to integrate more successfully, a process further enabled by the fact they had access to higher skilled jobs. Irish Protestants also formed the backbone of the Orange Order in Scotland, fuelling the sectarianism that continues as a presence in lowland Scotland today – particularly at football matches featuring the Glasgow 'Old Firm' of Celtic and Rangers and in Orange parades that take place during the July marching season. But despite the continuing symbolic presence of a sectarian divide, it is significant that the West of Scotland has not been engulfed by the violence that has characterised the 'Troubles' in Northern Ireland. Other immigrant groups who have made their presence felt in Scotland in various ways include the Italians, who arrived in the late nineteenth and early twentieth centuries and became strongly associated with the catering trade, the ice cream parlours, chip shops and cafés that sprang up throughout the country. A similar association exists in relation to the Indians and Pakistanis who were initially encouraged to come to Scotland in the 1960s to work on the busses, but who subsequently opened grocery stores and curry houses. The Asian influx was followed by Chinese migrants from Hong Kong, many of whom also were linked to the restaurant trade.[10]

The international connections forged by these various waves of migration continued to influence the development of Scottish cultural identity. For some, the exodus of Scots during the nineteenth century led many members of the intelligentsia to gravitate south and apply their talents to nurturing and benefiting a British rather than a Scottish intellectual culture.[11] However, the renaissance of the past twenty years has helped to redress this process of marginalisation or inferiorisation. Moreover, the upsurge of intellectual engagement that has developed in tandem with cultural production has generated a productive re-evaluation of indigenous Scottish tradition, including its external links. In this way Scottish philosophy and literature come to be linked with an array of key European thinkers and writers including Marx, Kierkegaard, Gramsci, Kafka, Camus and Sartre. During the 1990s Europe also began to play a significant role in Scottish politics. For Christopher Harvie, it 'became as magic a word as community'[12] particularly among those members of the political classes increasingly alienated from the little England nationalism of the Conservative Government. During the 1990s even the Scottish National Party began to campaign on a slogan of an independent 'Scotland in Europe'. At the same time the continuing lure of the United States as a symbol of freedom and opportunity in opposition to the restrictive, class-ridden and patrician vestiges of Anglocentric hegemony remains a potent one, dovetailing as we have seen with the equally mythic notion of Scottish egalitarianism.

## SCOTLAND AND THE PROBLEM OF SOUTH BRITAIN

The most significant international relationship to preoccupy contemporary Scottish writers and film-makers is that between Scotland and the 'auld enemy', England. More often than not, if a sense of Scottishness is being defined, it is in opposition to ideas of Englishness, with overarching institutions and belief systems sometimes invoked as tangible evidence of such a fundamental opposition – from the contrast between Presbyterian and Episcopalian theology to divergent political allegiances and voting patters north and south of the border. The structuring opposition of the respective Scottish and English national character has also been explored by Carol Craig via the use of Jungian psychological archetypes.[13] Rather than return to the common analysis of the Scottish character as somehow essentially schizo-phrenic (split between Scottish/British, Highland/Lowland, head/heart, etc.), Craig attempts to define the key distinctive components of the Scottish psyche by drawing some interesting and provocative contrasts with its English counterpart in the process. She suggests that the Scots are an extravert culture, principled, energetic and outward-looking, sociable and collectivist, guided by a strong oral tradition and a plainness and simplicity in matters of taste and interaction. In contrast, the English are an introvert culture, pragmatic, reflective and insular with a predisposition towards privacy, individualism, a love of the written word and refinement in the domain of manners.[14] While providing considerable evidence to support the use of particular categories, Craig is careful not to over-state her case and she also incorporates a space for contradictory or countervailing tendencies. But however insightful such a schema may be, the relationship between Scotland and England cannot simply be understood only in terms of an essential opposition. Despite the resurgence of a stronger sense of a distinct and separate Scottish identity, given institutional form by political devolution, the concept of Britishness still holds sway as social surveys concerning identity continue to demonstrate. As David McCrone demonstrates with reference to a range of statistical data, while 61 per cent of people living in Scotland give a higher priority to being Scottish than British (according to the 1997 Scottish Election Survey), 69 per cent claim some kind of dual identity. Despite devolution, Scots significantly retain a sense of Britishness that is mobilised in particular circumstances.[15]

The relationship between Scotland and England is dramatised in contemporary Scottish fictions in a variety of ways. One recurring narrative strategy involves the central protagonist travelling from Scotland to England (or vice versa), a journey in which the physical and symbolic crossing of the border is paralleled by a psychological, intellectual or moral transformation. In A. L. Kennedy's novel *Looking for the Possible Dance*, for example, Margaret Hamilton travels by train from Glasgow to London and reflects back over her life, experiences and relationships, particularly with her late father. While initially conceived as an escape from the double blow of losing both job and boyfriend in quick succession, Margaret is forced to reassess her situation as the passing landscape becomes more and more unfamiliar and foreign. Consequently on arriving at Euston she resolves to return home in order to repair a relationship with a man whose emotional needs she now understands are greater than her own. Reversing the trajectory, Jamie Bawn, the protagonist of Andrew O'Hagan's *Our Fathers*, travels to Scotland from England not once but twice in the course of the novel. The first time as a 6-year-old moving to the land of his parents for the first time, and then subsequently as an adult returning to confront the ghosts of his past. Mirroring Margaret Hamilton's epiphany, Jamie is able to both recognise the needs of others and summon the courage to face up to his own responsibilities with a renewed sense of hope and purpose.

Another recurring trope is the figure of the Scot in London. In some cases – such as in Ian Rankin's third 'Rebus' novel, *Tooth & Nail* – the protagonist remains essentially a stranger abroad, unable to fully comprehend metropolitan life and culture and desperate to return to the familiar and comforting certainties, while elsewhere Scots are presented as a fully integrated part of the Capital's diverse social fabric, as in David Kane's Camden Town romantic comedy *This Year's Love* (1999). The lure of London's economic opportunities also looms large, as is evinced by the film version of *Trainspotting* in which Mark Renton temporarily escapes his junkie life in Edinburgh by becoming an estate agent enthusiastically flogging overpriced London properties to aspirant yuppies. The metropolis is also conveyed by way of a playful and explicitly touristic gaze featuring stereotypical images of red busses, pearly queens, punks in the Kings Road, and various famous landmarks, contrasting markedly with the non-stereotypical representation of Edinburgh in the film. Murray Smith regards this as part of a key opposition between notions of heritage culture and its flip side – which he terms garbage culture – conveyed via the images of degradation, decay, destitution and poverty elsewhere in the film.[16] The montage also contrasts with the London depicted in Irvine Welsh's original novel, a seedy place of shooting galleries, bed sits, squats and all-night porn cinemas that resembles an extension of the similarly twilight world inhabited by Mark Renton and his associates in Edinburgh. London recurs as a significant location in other Welsh fictions including the novella 'A Smart Cunt', whose transient protagonist Brian is a very similar character to Renton, and in *Porno*, the sequel to *Trainspotting*, which begins with Sick Boy working in a Soho sex club. This reiterates a sense of the perpetual movement characterising the margins of post-industrial society inhabited by Welsh's protagonists and necessitated by their involvement in scamming and drug dealing. But crucially it also locks Edinburgh into a wider set of geographical locations including London and Amsterdam, bound together in the new leisure economy that brings together the club music scene with the drug trade and sex tourism.

One of the most unusual fictional depictions of the ambitious Scot in London is undoubtedly Alasdair Gray's 1985 novel *The Fall of Kelvin Walker*. Set in the 1960s,[17] it charts the adventures of a gauche young Scotsman inspired by the philosophy of Friedrich Nietzsche who arrives in the capital with the express purpose of becoming successful as quickly as possible. Through a combination of deception, gall and luck, Kelvin becomes an overnight sensation as a hard-hitting television interviewer. Having reached the top, Kelvin's subsequent fall is even more rapid, when he is confronted live in the studio by his God-fearing father, a Session Clerk of the fictitious Free Seceders Presbyterian Church of Scotland, who reveals that his son had stolen money and pawned his mother's jewellery in order to leave his home town of Glaik. This public humiliation not only destroys Kelvin's television career, it also brings him back into the fold and he returns to Scotland with his father where he follows his brothers into the Kirk. In this way Gray uses this devastating satire of the 'lad o' pairts', to ponder the question of cultural power between Scotland and England in provocative ways. Kelvin's self-reliance, demotic directness and moral clarity – qualities consistent with Carol Craig's description of the Scottish national character – make him the perfect political interviewer, challenging smug authority and hypocrisy on behalf of the people. But after rediscovering his faith in God, manifest in a subsequent advocacy of a strict Presbyterian morality in his interviews, Kelvin quickly becomes a liability. And once deemed to no longer be serving the interest of the establishment (in this instance, the BBC and its role in giving the political process a veneer of accountability), he is effectively destroyed. Gray replays many of the same thematic concerns in his later novella *McGrotty and Ludmilla* (1990),[18] which as Stephen Bernstein notes, similarly depicts 'the limited but schizoid options of selfhood available to the Londonized Scot'.[19] In contrast to Walker's narrative of failure, this time an unlikely lowly Scottish civil servant, Mungo McGrotty, accidentally acquires knowledge (contained in a top secret report) that provides him with the power to outwit some of the most machiavellian players in Whitehall and ultimately to become Prime Minister. While it is the patrician arrogance of the ruling elite that provides the unwitting McGrotty with his opportunity, his rise to power inevitably involves co-option into the establishment. In this way Gray counters the idea that the Scots' mindset is necessarily inclined towards a progressive, communitarian view of the world by demonstrating how Calvinist 'Victorian values' lend themselves to the maintenance of reactionary authoritarianism and the preservation of class privilege. Just as Kelvin Walker's later religious career in Scotland positions him as 'a counterbalance to a succession of not very radical socialists'[20] so Mungo McGrotty becomes a Conservative Prime Minister successfully preaching a version of Margaret Thatcher's doctrine of embattled reactionary neo-liberalism.

The link between power and sex is a recurring theme within Gray's fiction. Both Walker and McGrotty become obsessed with ostensibly unobtainable English women and despite his political success, the latter is primarily motivated by his desire for Ludmilla, the cold, heartless and manipulative upper-class daughter of the Minister for Social Stability. Their sado-masochistic relationship suggests a different kind of metaphor of the union between Scotland and England which Gray develops further in his novel *Something Leather*. Ostensibly a response to a challenge by the American author Kathy Acker to write about female experience and emotions – rather mischievously couched within a tale of lesbian sado-masochism – *Something Leather* is actually concerned with the post-war development of Glasgow and in particular its transformation from seamy proletarian backwater to the European city of culture. And while unsparing in his depiction of the restricted and dowdy lives of his working-class protagonists Senga and Donalda and their fellow Glaswegians, Gray's main concern is to reveal the re-branding of Glasgow as a shallow and cynical marketing ploy. At the centre of this stands Harry (Harriet), a striking and statuesque artist and distant cousin of the queen who is invited to stage an exhibition of her work as part of the 'Year of Culture' celebrations by a former friend from her exclusive boarding school. The speech of these upper-class English characters is rendered in phonetic speech in a strategy that makes the voice of the Establishment alien in a manner usually adopted for Scottish vernacular in numerous novels:

> '... wha does the *cultcha* come from?'
> 'From the Thatcha govament,' says Linda promptly, 'and from Glasgow District Council. Glasgow once had the strongest local govament tha was, outside London. It owned a huge public transport system, housing schemes, docklands and lots of otha things Thatcha is allowing it to sell. Like local govaments everywha it is being steadily abolished, but since the people's elected representatives usually draw salaries until they die and get all sawts of perks *they* don't complain. Maybe they don't notice! Howeva, they want to show they can do moa than just sell public propaty to private speculatas, so they have gone in for Cultcha with a capital C – and tourism. Commercially speaking cultcha and tourism a the same thing.'[21]

Harry becomes involved in a bizarre S/M game involving Senga, Donalda and a younger Glaswegian called June. The older women have learned the fundamental relationship between power and sex the hard way and are now exploiting it for their own ends, while Harry's acquiescence derives from her upper-class upbringing, and her mother's total disinterest in her allowing a sadistic Scottish nanny to abuse her as a child. Her subsequent experiences at boarding school entailed the use of similar power games to reinforce the pecking order among the girls. So in this way, *Something Leather* suggests that structures of domination/subordination lie at the heart of both Scottish and English culture and consequently the relationship between the two.

## TRAVELLING SCOTS

The figure of the travelling Scot is also a recurring feature in contemporary fictions that focus more on Scotland's relationship to the world beyond the confines of the United Kingdom. In this context, the historian Christopher Harvie has described himself in the context of the new Europe as 'a sort of surrogate Jew'[22] – a restless wanderer yet at the same time predisposed to integrate in the kind of full and positive sense that had nurtured the great European intellectual tradition synonymous with Marx, Freud and Einstein.

As we have already seen, travel is a common theme in the fiction of Irvine Welsh, the junkie protagonists of *Trainspotting* clearly established as part of a wider community of 'Eurotrash', the casualties of the global forces of late capitalism. Travel is equally significant in the work of other contemporary novelists such as Alan Warner, Janice Galloway and A. L. Kennedy. The respective protagonists of *Morvern Callar*, *Foreign Parts* and *So I am Glad* all find a positive solution to their problems through experiences in Europe, the wider Continental cultural context providing in different ways an antidote to the limited horizons and claustrophobia imposed by an inward-looking Scottish existence. Other fictions confront the question of travel and its relationship to identity in more ambitious and fundamental ways. For example, in *Poor Things*,[23] Alasdair Gray's brilliant satire on Victorian morality and the emergence of the 'new woman', the worldly education of Bella Baxter takes the form of two extended vacations. The first of these is under the supervision of Godwin Baxter, the Glasgow surgeon who claims to have 'created' Bella in a bizzare Frankenstenian manner by reviving the body of a suicide and transplanting into her skull the brain of her unborn child. The subsequent grand tour is conceived of as an appropriate means of educating his protégé. More formative and profound, however, is Bella's second journey which begins with her elopement with Duncan Wedderburn and takes in various adventures in Italy, the Crimea, Egypt, Gibraltar before culminating in a Parisian brothel. As Stephen Bernstein puts it, these travels 'amount to a crash course in cynicism, optimism, dissolution, sexuality and responsibility'[24] and effectively pave the way for the future career of Victoria McCandless, as Bella Baxter is subsequently to become, as a pioneering doctor, suffragette and social reformer. This transformation also involves the subtle remaking of Bella's identity as Scottish and the eclipse of her English origins – the suicide whose body Baxter claims to have 'revived' having been revealed as the daughter of a rich Yorkshire industrialist.

The travelling Scot has also appeared in the work of writers like William Boyd and Candia McWilliam, who, by virtue of being boarding school-educated Scots, have lived for the majority of their lives outside Scotland and as such are often excluded from the mainstream of contemporary Scottish fiction. Boyd's 1987 novel *The New Confessions* is a sprawling tale of the life of John James Todd, the son of an eminent Edinburgh professor of anatomy who becomes a film-maker in an erratic international career that begins with a posting to the War Office film unit during the First World War. Todd works in the emerging British film industry in London in the early 1920s before moving to Berlin where he becomes a celebrated artist. Following the rise of Hitler, he returns to London before moving on to Hollywood where his fluctuating professional and personal fortunes involve an enforced sojourn in Mexico and finally he is driven into exile by the McCarthyite witch hunts of the 1950s. Throughout Todd remains an iconoclastic maverick in the style of Orson Welles, driven primarily by an obsessional desire to film his namesake Jean Jacques Rousseau's celebrated autobiographical work *The Confessions*. Born in 1899, Todd's life is also the story of the twentieth century up to early 1970s and the narrative is recounted retrospectively in the first person with Todd now an old man in exile on an unidentified Mediterranean island. The question of identity is central for the very first line of the novel – 'My first act on entering this world was to kill my mother.'[25] Todd's guilt colours his subsequent relationship with his rather distant and patrician father, but it also creates a large void that will haunt him throughout his life. During the latter stages of the Great War, Todd joins an English public school regiment and is sent to the Western Front where his identity is called into question in some very interesting ways. On one hand, he is marked out by virtue of his Scottish accent, yet he is also dismissed as an 'English Bastard' by a vicious and diminutive Scottish soldier, a spiteful member of a bantam regiment of the Grampian Highlanders he encounters at the third battle of Ypres. In this way, Todd is caught between cultures, distanced from both his sadistic fellow Scotsmen and his pompous and duplicitous English comrades alike. When he subsequently becomes a film-maker, he continues to be mistaken as English, but on moving to America in 1937 he is given a job as a writer at Fox alongside a number of other illustrious German émigrés and his office door bears the name 'J.J. Todt'. But while he may be mis-recognised, Todd resists any attempt to change his identity in the way that his Armenian producer Aram Lodokian does when, on emigrating to the United States, he transforms himself into the thoroughly Anglicised Eddie Simonette.

Douglas Dunn is correct in his assertion that ultimately James John Todd 'is pursued by his own life, by its similarities with Rousseau's, and it is a life in which a homecoming solves nothing'.[26] Yet Todd's connections with his father, his city and his country remain a constant in his life matched perhaps only by his life-long friendships with Karl Heinz Kornfeld, Eddie Simonette and former lover Doon Bogan. The nature of his problematic relationship with his father and his uncertain sense of his own self may very well be a consequence of his mother's death in childbirth. Yet in other ways the relationship between Innes and his son bear the hallmarks of Calvinist patriarchy, Todd's transgression being to break the bounds of what his father could imagine for him. His subsequent career as a wayward, romantic and self-indulgent film-maker is also in total contrast to that of his brother Thompson, a solid, respectable and highly conventional Edinburgh banker. Despite a life of exile, Todd's various returns to the city of his birth are highly significant. Edinburgh not only provides the main locations for his first film, the pot boiler *Wee MacGregor Wins the Sweepstake*, but it also continues to invoke Todd's unresolved relationship with his own father, whose love and acceptance he increasingly craves. During one visit for Thompson's wedding, having achieved fame with his German film *Julie*, Todd ponders the Edinburgh cityscape from his opulent suite in the North British Hotel. His feelings of personal triumph rapidly begin to evaporate:

> Here I was now, twenty-eight years old, wealthy, celebrated, large family, servants ... I should have been pleased with myself, smug, full of I-told-you-so superiority. But the longer I stood there looking at that uncompromising view the harder self-satisfaction was to achieve. I knew my father would be unimpressed.[27]

Todd's final return to Edinburgh comes in 1946, the poignancy of which is underlined by the fact that it is during this visit that the only affectionate physical contact with his father occurs when Innes touches his son's knee, while continuing to chide him for his failures.

While Boyd's Scots adventurer seems to inherit the roving spirit of Robert Louis Stevenson, in *Debatable Land*, published in 1994, Candia McWilliam evokes a more direct relationship with its axis of Edinburgh and the South Pacific. The central protagonist is Alexander Dundas, an Edinburgh painter approaching middle age, who signs up to crew a small boat on a voyage from Tahiti to New Zealand. His motivation is the familiar one of getting far away in order to make sense of his life and his identity, or as McWilliam puts it – 'He had come so far from home in order to see it clearly.'[28] He is voyaging with fellow Scot Elspeth Urquhart and her husband Logan, a rich Scots-American who is captain and owner of *Ardent Spirit*, the yacht they are sailing on. The journey presents Alec with an opportunity to reflect back on his life – his early friendship with an eccentric old blind commander and his sister, his later inability to grieve for his mother who died in her late forties, the on-going tensions with his father and his destructive relationship with partner Lorna who he admits to having treated very harshly and cheated on. Alec tells his fellow crew member Nick that Lorna has a child called Sorley, who he claims has been fathered by another man despite that fact that it is clear he is simply denying both his paternity and his responsibilities to the boy. Helped by Nick's urging to accept his son, Alec gradually regains a sense identity and purpose – 'It took the clear sight of an outsider to show him his own future'[29] – a transformation given added elemental force by the storm encountered on the last leg of the voyage which gives all of the protagonists a palpable sense of their own mortality

While Edinburgh holds a key significance for John James Todd in *The New Confessions*, McWilliam's evocations of the city are more fundamental to Alec's struggle to find a sense of himself. One of the first key discoveries of the city comes when he visits the camera obscura by the Castle and gazes on the silent city laid out in front of him. This experience leads Alec to explore Edinburgh at street level, which in turn begins to loosen his close domestic ties to his mother. It also gives him an attachment to sight over sound – something that may explain both his later decision to become a painter – and a voyeur – and also his inability to communicate fully with Lorna. The second time Alec contemplates Edinburgh comes during a picnic on Arthur's Seat with Lorna and his father after the latter has lost his second wife to the same cancer that claimed Alec's mother. At this moment a fear grips him, conveying both his own close identification with the city and his growing pessimism:

> He had made himself sad. He remembered what had gone in his shortish life. He wondered as he often did what had made a child love a city in this way, a child who had turned into an adult positively unconservative, yet so anxious, in this case to conserve. For more than two hundred summers the new Town and for more summers than could be counted the Old Town had been growing at a human pace. Now they were being lit from below like great rockets of stone, these buildings, and launched into the future and annihilation. The town that had been drained of a loch two centuries before was being drained of its own nature now.[30]

Scotland has a more contingent relationship to Elspeth and Logan Urquhart, whose own marriage is clearly in difficulty, forming a secondary and related focus to Alec's predicament in the novel. Logan is clearly more in love with his boat than his wife and before long Elspeth has intuited that he has begun an affair with the ship's cook, Gabriel. Elspeth is Anglo-Scots, but with a sensitivity to landscape, tradition and history inherited from her father – at one point she recalls a childhood visit to Culloden where she could feel the ground trembling. Yet her accent distances her from Scotland and she remarks to Alec that the Scottish yearnings for independence means there is less place for Anglo-Scots than there once had been:

> 'Things are bad. There could be a split. People want it. They sing about it. There was the fish, there is the oil. The stupidity of the South has hurt, the tactlessness that has looked like pillage, the willingness to treat the place like a plaid, to throw it on for ancient glamour and to throw it over puddles to save them getting their feet dirty. I fear for the border, I really do.'
>   He laughed at her.
>   'Here we are,' he said, 'on debatable lands.'[31]

For Aileen Christianson, the concept of 'debatable land' has a variety of connections – geographical, political, social and personal – including 'those areas of dispute, continuing ambiguity and exploitation, the space between classes, and, in the South seas, the exploited and the exploiters, whether the old colonisers or the new tourists. But it is also McWilliam's gap between people.'[32] Logan Urquhart, for his part, is caught between the two poles of his dual identity, a schizoid sense of self that lies at the root of his misanthropic loneliness and his self-centred restlessness: 'He had a great urge to patriotism, yet what was his country, Scotland or America? – the one too small, the other too large, in his view. He escaped from them; his urge to romantic patriotism attached itself to the sea.'[33] Yet just as the final storm forces Alec to face up to his life, so too it brokers the chance of a reunion between Elspeth and Logan as she glimpses some residual love for her husband. He reciprocates and in a quiet and apparently casual way that masks its deep sincerity, invites her to stay with him for a time.

The figure of the travelling Scot is less common in cinema and those films that have tackled the theme in recent years have been regarded as minor works. One film-maker who has engaged with Scotland's relationship with Europe from a particularly interesting, and highly personal, perspective however is the writer/director Ian Sellar. His 1983 film *Over Germany* is an autobiographical account of a young Scottish boy – the son of a bomber pilot and a Jewish refugee – who visits his German grandmother for the first time in the late 1950s. In Hamburg, a city his father bombed, the boy is confronted with the limitations of his comic-book preconceptions of Germany and crucially of his own relationship to her history. Sellar returned to the question of cultural identity with his later feature, *Prague* (1992), which is similarly concerned with a young Scotsman attempting to reconnect with Continental roots that were similarly a consequence of the disruptions of war. Alexander Novak (Alan Cumming) travels to the Czech capital in search of a fragment of old newsreel from 1941 apparently showing members of his family attempting to evade arrest and transportation to the Nazi death camps shortly before they disappeared. His progress is hampered by the Byzantine procedures of the national film archive, which has only recently become accessible with the collapse of the Communist regime in 1989, and when Alexander does eventually find the film, it is destroyed in a freak accident before he can view it. On the point of returning to Scotland in despair, Alexander is informed by Elena (Sandrine Bonnaire), the enigmatic archivist with whom he has a brief relationship, that the film depicted a little girl floating away in the river. That little girl was Alexander's mother and the fragment of film tangible proof of her escape and of his connection to the past. Throughout, Alexander remains a rather allusive protagonist, his encounters with others continually hampered by an inability to communicate successfully. In addition to the obvious problems of language, much of the dialogue in the film is oblique and evasive, adding to the general sense of confusion which surrounds Alexander as he tries to negotiate this foreign city and culture to which he claims a bond. As his quest becomes increasingly frustrated, so Sellar subtly switches focus towards a consideration of the ways in which Alexander uses the past to evade confronting his feelings for Elena, who has announced that she is pregnant with his child, and embracing his opportunity to be a father. But as in the case of Alec Dundas in *Debatable Land*, Alexander Novak's problem is the fear of taking responsibility for his own future and those of others that constitutes the dilemma he is finally forced to confront. And in order to face the future he must renounce his fixation with the past.

## THE LURE OF AMERICA IN FILM AND TELEVISION

While some Scottish fictions send their protagonists out into the outside world, in other cases that world is inhabited imaginatively, transforming the local cultural experience in the process. A key example of this is the lure of the United States that has influenced many Scottish writers and film-makers. This is partly a consequence of population movement, with America being a major destination for Scottish emigrants from the eighteenth century onwards. But there are also certain ideological connections between Scotland and the USA that may also help to explain the affinity. Christopher Harvie cites Frederick Jackson Turner's famous thesis that the values of American society were essentially shaped on the frontier and suggests that eighteenth-century Scotland had also been essentially a 'frontier society' in which 'intellectuals and practical men, with their stress on "improvement" had created values and techniques for overseas settlement, together with reserves of technical competence, skilled labour and professional (notably medical) training'.[34] And while the 'emigration ideology' may have lacked the kind of official sanction which was to make the Turner thesis such an article of faith, the motivations of Scottish emigrants to America did predispose them to build their new country in particular ways. This in turn helps to explain the affinity between the Scottish egalitarian myth of social mobility and the 'American dream', as David McCrone notes:

> the Scottish myth that talent and hard work will out retains a direct
> parallel in the better-known American Dream of the potential from
> rags to riches. It is perhaps significant that there is no English
> equivalent of such force.[35]

Indeed, the enthusiastic response to American culture on the part of many Scots can be seen in terms of the idea of the USA as a land of freedom of opportunity in opposition to the rigid class-bound social organisation that was often (falsely) regarded as an English import. In the twentieth century the major forms of American popular culture that were to have a major impact on Scotland were music – particularly rock 'n' roll and country & western – and the movies. While as we have already seen, the rugged individualism of the Wild West hero or the urban American gangster has influenced the Clydesideism of Peter McDougall and Bill Bryden.

Another key creative figure who has tackled the penetration of American popular culture into Scottish working-class life is John Byrne. His *Slab Boys* trilogy of plays engages explicitly with the impact of American rock 'n' roll music and fashion on the working-class Paisley of his youth in the late 1950s, an influence that can also be discerned in his subsequent television series *Tutti Frutti*, which begins with the return to Glasgow of musician Danny McGlone who has conspicuously failed to achieve the American dream during his exile in New York. But it is in the subsequent six-part television drama series, *Your Cheatin' Heart*, broadcast in 1990, that provides Byrne's most striking inter-face of Clydeside and American culture. Set among the city's vibrant country and western scene, this drama features the attempts of a young woman, Cissy Crouch (Tilda Swinton) to find out the truth behind her husband Dorwood's imprisonment on a major drugs charge. Convinced that the C&W singer has been set up, she persuades Frank McClusky (John Gordon Sinclair), a self-styled gumshoe in a greasy burberry raincoat who writes a food column for the local evening paper, to do some digging on her behalf. The primary suspect is Dorwood's former bass player, the psychotic Fraser Boyle (Ken Stott). But as the narrative unwinds Boyle is revealed as a small player in larger turf war between rival drugs gangs involving, among others, a ruthless Scottish businessman, the Mafia and American Country star Jim Bob O'May, cur-rently touring Scotland in his long horn winnebago. This convoluted *film-noir* plot, the bulk of which takes place at night, is played out within the milieu of the Scottish country and western scene, where every other character seems to play in a band and the clubs and pubs are filled with Glasgow punters sporting ten gallon hats and cowboy boots.

Byrne's greatest achievement in *Your Cheatin' Heart*, however, is the way in which he conveys the essential hybridity of this cultural scene. The trappings might be American but the accent, and the quick draw dialogue are unmistakably Glaswegian. An illustrative example of this is provided by the piano bar situated in the Gorbals run by a smooth African-American who turns out to be a key player in the local drug scene. The establishment, which serves genuine soul food, is called the Bar L – which is also the local nickname for Glasgow's notorious Barlinne prison and consequently the waitresses are decked out in striped US prisoner's uniforms, complete with inmate numbers. The surreal Scottish-American interface is also embodied in the depiction of the music scene itself, which seems to draw in almost everyone in the drama. This runs the gamut from the C&W duo Billie McPhail (Katy Murphy) and her partner Joleen (Eddie Reader) who run a taxi service by day and play venues such as the OK Korral in Kilwinning to the Ponderosa Club in Wishaw by night; the various shady marginal characters including tattoo artist 'Cherokee' George Tierney and his cowboy brother 'Timberwolf'; to the chapter of leather-clad bikers who provide Jim Bob O'May (played by real-life American C&W star Guy Mitchell) with a guard of honour into Aberdeen and who later are seen dancing the slosh to a rendition of 'Let Your Love Flow'. *Your Cheatin' Heart* is also saturated with a particular kind of generic iconography – boots, guitars, radios, telephones and cars – that reinforces the American dimension. Yet at every point Byrne undercuts the glossy veneer by a scattergun use of Glasgwegian vernacular dialogue, which in its refusal to make concessions puts it on a par with the work of James Kelman. Indeed, within the domain of television drama Byrne's use of the Glasgow (and Paisley) idiom has only one equal in the comic creation *Rab C. Nesbitt*.

Another major Scottish writer with a similarly definitive relationship to American popular culture is Alan Sharp. Initially a novelist who made his breakthrough in the 1960s with *A Green Tree in Gedde* and *The Wind Shifts*, Sharp became a screenwriter in the early 1970s. His subsequent credits include a number of Hollywood productions, most notably Westerns like *The Hired Hand* (Peter Fonda, 1971), *Ulzana's Raid* (Robert Aldrich, 1972) and *Billy Two Hats* (Ted Kotcheff, 1973) and the thrillers *Night Moves* (Arthur Penn, 1975) and *The Osterman Weekend* (Sam Peckinpah, 1983). The formative significance of Hollywood Westerns in Sharp's boyhood in Greenock is conveyed in an early passage of *A Green Tree in Gedde*, when the main protagonist fondly recalls his visits to the local cinema nicknamed 'the Ranch because all the Hopalong Cassidys used to come there'.[36] Sharp's affinity with the Western proved to be particularly important when he was commissioned by producer Peter Broughan to write a screenplay based on the life of Rob Roy McGregor. The resulting production, *Rob Roy* (Michael Caton-Jones, 1995), starring Liam Neeson and Jessica Lange, consequently owes a great deal to the Western genre in its formal construction and thematic preoccupations. Set two years before the 1715 Jacobite rebellion, the film recounts the familiar story of the former cattle thief who falls foul of the devious Duke of Montrose (John Hurt) and is forced to take to the hills as a fugitive. At the centre of this version, however, is the villainous presence of a foppish young Englishman, Archibald Cunningham (Tim Roth), who is also a deadly swordsman. With the connivance of Montrose's factor Killearn (Brian Cox), Cunningham steals the £1,000 loan provided to Rob by Montrose and then sets about pursuing the debt, culminating in the brutal rape of Mary and the destruction of the

MacGregor homestead. After various stirring escapades, Rob finally avenges his (and his wife's) honour in a climactic duel with Cunningham.

The plot of *Rob Roy* borrows heavily from the revenge western with the hero pitted against the equivalent of the ruthless cattle baron (Montrose) and his hired gun (Cunningham). The narrative features the equivalent of saloon brawls and gunfights, including the final shootout in the fight between Rob and Cunningham. The structure of the film also has much in common with Sharp's earlier western's *Ulzana's Raid* and *Billy Two Hats* which are also about questions of revenge and feature the hunter and the hunted. But *Rob Roy* also invokes the kind of re-visionary western which was in vogue when Sharp went to Hollywood, in which the Indians are portrayed in a more sympathetic and understanding light. Consequently, Rob figures as a version of the noble Native American, struggling to hold on to his land, his tribe and traditional way of life under threat by the forces of 'progress'. In this way the film acknowledges the impending obsolescence of men like Rob Roy MacGregor and what he represents, yet at the same time he is presented cinematically as bona fide hero who in his defeat of Cunningham validates his code of honour while avenging his wife's rape. Rob and his kinsmen are also presented as part of the magnificent highland landscape in much the same way that Indians are in the prairies and rocky outcrops that form the typography of many Westerns. The MacGregors both negotiate and read the landscape in their pursuit of Tam Sibbald's tinkers who have robbed them at the start of the film, while Rob then subsequently melts into his environment when he is forced to hide from Montrose and his men. In this ways the political insights and ambiguities in Sharp's script are in tension with Michael Caton Jones's direction, which mounts the film as a tale of romantic individualism. Indeed, as Brian Woolland suggests, the film is ultimately caught in a compromise, hovering 'between a reworked western that uses the genre to examine resistance to colonialism and a good romantic fantasy that is given a historical setting'.[37] Despite his generally insightful analysis of the film, Woolland misinterprets the colonial relationships in *Rob Roy* by referring to Montrose as a 'calculating, cunning, predatory Englishman'[38] rather than the pro-Hanovarian Scottish nobleman he clearly is. And while Archibald Cunningham is presented as an Englishman, his Scottish name and the final hint that he may actually be Montrose's bastard son ultimately bring him rather more close to the fold. In this way, Sharp is demonstrating that the central tensions and conflict are contained within this representation of Scotland after the Act of Union, rather than positing them in more simplistic and reductive Scotland/England terms.

## EUROPEAN CONNECTIONS IN SCOTTISH CINEMA

*Rob Roy* provides a striking contrast with the kind of production that has come to epitomise Scottish film-making in the 1990s which bears a strong affinity with the tradition of European Art cinema.[39] This case can be made on aesthetic and institutional grounds in that most Scottish films of the past twenty-five years have tended to small-scale, highly personal works conveying the stylistic and thematic preoccupations of distinctive directors like Bill Douglas, Bill Fosyth, Gillies Mackinnon, Ken Loach, Peter Mullan and Lynne Ramsay. Such productions have also been funded by a combination of public sources such as the National Lottery in conjunction with broadcasters like Channel Four and the BBC and foreign pre-sales, primarily from Europe. The recent move towards closer collaboration between Scottish film producers and their counterparts in Ireland and Denmark have led to the production of co-productions like *The Magdalene Sisters* (Peter Mullan, 2002), *Blind Flight* (John Furse, 2003), *Wilbur Wants to Kill Himself* (Leone Scherfig, 2003) and *Skageraak* (Soren Kragh Jacobsen, 2004) that have reinforced Scottish cinema's European credentials. This argument must be qualified however in that certain high-profile Scottish films like *Shallow Grave* (Danny Boyle, 1995), *Trainspotting* (Danny Boyle, 1996) and *Late Night Shopping* (Saul Metzstein, 2001) are clearly influenced by American independent cinema. However, even here such antecedents are often cited as themselves oppositional to mainstream Hollywood and closer to traditions of the Art film tradition.

But despite the aesthetic affinities with the Continent, when it comes to Scottish cinema's engagement with European influences on Scotland in terms of subject matter, the terrain proves to be rather less rich. Very few films, for example, have dealt with the question of the immigrant experience within Scotland and the broader social consequences of inward migration. Michael Radford's 1983 adaptation of Jessie Kesson's *Another Time, Another Place* is rare in its contemplation of the impact the presence a group of Italian prisoners of war have on a lonely Scottish cottar's wife on the Black Isle in 1944. To Janie, the Italians represent mystery and excitement and fire within her the desire to know more of the world outside her own narrow and heavily circumscribed existence. While this culminates in an ill-fated sexual liaison with one of the prisoners, *Another Time, Another Place* is ultimately concerned with its heroine's craving for wider horizons, geographical, social and imaginative. Yet despite the powerful presence of the foreigner, brought to Scotland as a prisoner – and echoed in Bill Douglas's *My Childhood* – the Italians leave as soon as the war is over. And while Bill Forsyth's *Comfort and Joy* features warring Scots-Italian ice cream families as a kind of comic backdrop, no Scottish feature film to date has attempted to explore the Italian presence in a serious and sustained way.[40] This is true for most of the other major immigrant groups in Scotland, although exceptions include David Solomons' television drama *The Fabulous Bagel Boys* (2001), that engages with the Jewish community in Glasgow and a small number of short films featuring Scottish Asian and Chinese protagonists.

One ethnic group that has made its presence felt in Scottish film and television drama is the Irish. The Ulster Protestant presence in Scotland has been explored effectively by Peter McDougall in his 1970s' dramas *Just Your Luck* and *Just Another Saturday* and in literature by Alan Spence, most notably in *The Magic Flute*. The legacy of Irish Catholic culture on Scotland has been central to the work of John Byrne – in *Your Cheatin' Heart*, for example, Frank McClusky makes numerous references to his experiences at St Saviours RC school where his classmates included Fraser Boyle and the Scots-Italian gangster Lupo Ragazzo. Catholicism is also a fundamental component of the films of Peter Mullan, including all three of his short films – *Close*, *A Good Day for the Bad Guys* and *Fridge* – and his two features to date, which are all structured around ideas of redemption. In *Orphans* the stubborn and dim-witted older sibling Thomas holds a vigil over his mother's coffin in the local Catholic church during the course of which the statue of the virgin is smashed twice, the second time by the storm that also rips the roof off the church. The film also explores various issues relating to faith and religious iconography, including youngest brother's John's descent into hell with the psychotic Tanza as, having acquired a gun and bullets, he goes off in search of the man who stabbed his brother Michael, while the religious symbolism of brother Michael's re-baptism in the River Clyde is discussed in the previous chapter of this book.

But while *Orphans* retains an ambivalent engagement with questions of faith, Mullan's subsequent feature, *The Magdalene Sisters*, constitutes a much more vicious attack on the legacy of the Catholic Church. A Scottish-Irish co-production filmed entirely in Dumfries, the film is set in rural Ireland during the 1960s and follows the fortunes of three teenage girls who are incarcerated in one of the notorious Magdalene asylums for wayward females. Their alleged crimes speak volumes of a backward, fearful and patriarchal society governed in accordance of the archaic laws of the church. Margaret is punished after she is raped by a cousin at a family wedding, orphan Bernadette is incarcerated for being a temptation to the local boys, while Rose has had an illegitimate child which is whisked away to be adopted immediately after it is born. The Magdalene asylum is run by the sadistic Sister Brigit and the girls are subject to a harsh regime that also involves ritual humiliations and in the case of the mentally retarded Crispina, sexual abuse by a priest. What is particularly chilling about is the way in which Mullan depicts the hatred, disgust and fear shown towards the girls by their male relatives, Margaret's father in particular. This is further underlined by Mullan's cameo appearance as the father of a girl who has run away from the asylum, dragging her back and beating her in front of the other girls whom he berates as whores.

## CONCLUSION: INTERNATIONAL CROSS-CURRENTS AND CULTURAL TRANSFORMATION

The meaningful connection with influences and inspirations drawn from the wider sphere of international culture has played an important part in helping Scotland to find its own independent voice, with Scottish writers and film-makers drawing upon this international dimension in a variety of ways. On the one hand, the traditional figure of the wandering Scot continued to loom large, but re-imagined in relation to the new ways in which an increasingly self-confident Scotland was rethinking its own relationship to the rest of the world. This also reflected the fact that the idea of mobility itself had been transformed by the end of the twentieth century by the needs and demands of an increasingly globalised economic system. Not only did this create a new impetus for trans-national dialogue and exchange, it also opened the door to a new kind of cosmopolitanism as opportunities for international travel became more accessible. While Tom Nairn may have bemoaned the detrimental 'exodus' of the Scottish intelligentsia in the nineteenth century, geographical location no longer determines cultural engagement in the same restrictive manner. Consequently, some of the key individuals discussed in this book may primarily live in Scotland, others do not, yet they continue to contribute in vital ways to the on-going re-invigoration of the Scottish cultural imagination.

Within the broader nexus of political, economic and cultural change that has transformed Scotland's sense of itself, the appropriation of external cultural influences has clearly been highly significant. The very idea of outside influence has changed from being regarded as primarily negative – at best, a dilution of indigenous traditions, at worst, a process of colonisation – to being celebrated as not only positive but necessary. In an analysis consistent with his insightful elaboration of the significance of peripheral cultures considered at the beginning of this chapter, Cairns Craig explores the ways in which Byrne's *Your Cheatin' Heart* can be seen as central to the problems of national identity confronting Scotland. Craig regards Byrne's characters as like ghosts, haunting a world in which any meaningful sense of an authentic indigenous culture has been lost, while the comedy of misunderstandings that informs the verbal exchanges between them is underpinned by 'the terror of individual identities that have been constructed from nothing more than film and pop music clichés, identities that are pure fiction'.[41] Yet Byrne's achievement is to indicate the ways in which this creative appropriation of fictional elements actually provides his drama and its characters with a new and meaningful sense of identity. In this way, Scotland, in common with its fellow European nations in the aftermath of the changes wrought by the collapse of Communism and the expansion of the European Union, is groping towards a new sense of itself as a viable nation. But this new identity is irrefutably locked into and dependent upon international influence and dialogue. For Craig, this is

> necessarily a dialogue between layers of imposed or remembered or adopted cultural meanings, between the universal languages of popular commercialism and the local meaning of other forms of expression. It is out of that dialogue that the 'identities' of the reborn nations emerge.[42]

A similar kind of analysis of a cultural text as an interaction between old and new, imposed and indigenous discourses is applied by Jonathan Murray to *The Magdalene Sisters*. Beyond the obvious relationship between Irish and Scottish culture posed by the production, Murray tackles the thorny issue of the film's relationship to traditions of European and American cinema, countering in the process the ways in which some critics have regarded *The Magdalene Sisters* as evidence of the ways in which art cinema provides a corrective to the banal or even pernicious influence of Hollywood. But, as Murray points out, the film 'is notable for its judicious use, not ostentatious rejection, of a number of American cinematic influences are reference points'.[43] In addition to a consideration of the prison movie genre, Murray also probes the meanings behind the inclusion of the 1945 Hollywood production *The Bells of St. Mary's* in the film, which he considers in relation to the traditional Irish ballad 'The Well Below the Valley' which features in the opening sequence. Murray suggest that Mullan incorporates these intertexts in order to demonstrate the complex interplay between internal and external cultural traditions and meanings in relation to the central thematic concerns of *The Magdalene Sisters*. He concludes his analysis by arguing that:

> Scottish and Irish cinemas are national cultural phenomena that in their increasing maturity cannot, as *The Magdalene Sisters* illustrates, be necessarily, entirely or ideally reduced to a set of self-consciously corrective local responses against traditional and/or contemporary transatlantic cinematic influences active in the domestic sphere.[44]

It is certainly the case that as an indisputably core culture, the United States of America has exerted a major influence on Scotland. However, this must be seen in the context of a wider and diverse set of influences and connections that also includes continental existentialism, the *nouveau roman* and the European art film. But whatever the mix of influences, the range of contemporary Scottish fictions explored here demonstrates the crucial dialectical interplay of the indigenous and the international, the specific and the general, the local and the global. This fundamental relationship has not only ensured the emergence of cultural expressions that are complex, multifaceted and appropriate to contemporary experience. The resulting novels, television dramas and feature films have also helped to articulate a new sense of national identity precisely through their engagement and re-engagement with Scotland's relationship not only to its self but also, crucially, to the world outside.

## NOTES

1. See Cairns Craig, 'Peripheries', *Cencrastus*, No. 9, Summer 1982.
2. Cairns Craig, *Out of History: Narrative Paradigms in Scottish and British Culture* (Edinburgh: Polygon, 1996), p. 28.
3. Ibid. p. 29.
4. Ibid. p. 30.
5. See David McCrone, *Understanding Scotland: The Sociology of a Stateless Nation* (London: Routledge, 1992). A revised edition was published in 2001 with the new subtitle 'The Sociology of a Nation' in recognition of the restoration of the Scottish parliament.
6. Linda Colley, *Britons: Forging the Nation 1707–1837* (London: Vintage, 1996), p. 136.
7. Ibid. p. 139.
8. Angus Calder, 'Imperialism and Scottish Culture', in *Scotlands of the Mind* (Edinburgh: Luath, 2002), p. 179.
9. Between the 1820s and the 1910s some two million Scots emigrated, a greater percentage of the national population than any other European country apart from Ireland. See T. M. Devine, *The Scottish Nation 1700–2000* (London: Penguin, 1999), p. 468.
10. Other notable immigrant groups include Lithuanians, many of whom became miners in the Lanarkshire coal fields in the latter half of the nineteenth century. Polish and Russian Jews arrived around the same time as the Lithuanians settled mainly in the Gorbals area of Glasgow; followed by the Poles, many of whom had been based in Scotland during the Second World War and who elected to remain after Poland became Communist. The English have also formed a sizeable minority group in Scotland, making an important if sometimes under-acknowledged contribution to all aspects of Scottish life and culture.
11. Tom Nairn, *The Break-Up of Britain*, second Edition (London: Verso, 1981), pp. 123–5.
12. Christopher Harvie, *Scotland and Nationalism*, third edition (London: Routledge, 1998), p. 240.
13. Carol Craig, *The Scots' Crisis of Confidence* (Edinburgh: Big Thinking, 2003).
14. Ibid. see Chapter 3 and pp. 230–1.
15. David McCrone, *Understanding Scotland: The Sociology of a Nation*, second edition (London: Routledge, 2001). See pp. 161–3.
16. Murray Smith, *Trainspotting* (London: BFI, 2002), p. 25.
17. *The Fall of Kelvin Walker* was initially written and produced as a television play in 1968.

18. Alasdair Gray, *McGroty and Ludmilla* (Glasgow: Dog & Bone, 1990).
19. Stephen Bernstein, 'Scottish Enough: The London Novels of Alasdair Gray', *The Review of Contemporary Fiction*, Vol. 15, No. 2, Summer 1995, p. 171.
20. Alasdair Gray, *The Fall of Kelvin Walker* (Edinburgh: Canongate, 1985), p. 143.
21. Alasdair Gray, *Something Leather* (London: Jonathan Cape, 1990), pp. 172–3.
22. Chrisopher Harvie, 'Grasping the Thistle', in *Travelling Scot* (Glenarduel: Argyll Publishing, 1999), p. 201.
23. Alasdair Gray, *Poor Things* (London: Bloomsbury, 1992).
24. Stephen Bernstein, *Alasdair Gray* (Lewisburg: Bucknell University Press, 1999), p. 119.
25. William Boyd, *The New Confessions* (London: Penguin, 1988), p. 11.
26. Douglas Dunn, 'Divergent Scottishness: William Boyd, Allan Massie, Ronald Frame', in Gavin Wallace and Randall Stevenson (eds), *The Scottish Novel* (Edinburgh: Edinburgh University Press, 1993), p. 156.
27. William Boyd, *The New Confessions*, p. 291.
28. Candia McWilliam, *Debatable Land* (London: Bloomsbury, 1994), p. 1.
29. Ibid. p. 215.
30. Ibid. pp. 124–5.
31. Ibid. p. 136.
32. Aileen Christianson, 'Muriel Spark and Candia McWilliam: Continuities', in Aileen Christianson and Alison Lumsden (eds), *Contemporary Scottish Women Writers* (Edinburgh: Edinburgh University Press, 2000), p. 107.
33. Candia McWilliam, *Debatable Land*, p. 130.
34. Christopher Harvie, *Scotland and Nationalism*, p. 60.
35. David McCrone, *Understanding Scotland: The Sociology of a Nation*, p. 79.
36. Alan Sharp, *A Green Tree in Gedde* (London: Four Square, 1966), p. 14.
37. Brian Woolland, 'Rob Roy: Man in the Middle', *Jump Cut*, No. 43, July 2000, p. 31.
38. Ibid. p. 36.
39. See Duncan Petrie, 'Devolving British Cinema: The New Scottish Cinema and the European Art Film', *Cineaste*, Vol. xxvi, No. 4, Fall 2001.
40. At the time of writing a new film called *American Cousins* (2003), written by Scots Italian Sergio Casci and directed by Don Couts deals with both the Italian diaspora and the American influence on Scotland.
41. Cairns Craig, 'The Haunted Heart', *New Statesman and Society*, 5 October 1990, p. 27.
42. Ibid. p. 28.
43. See Jonathan Murray, 'Convents or Cowboys? Millennial Scottish and Irish Film Industries Imaginaries in *The Magdalene Sisters*', in John Hill and Kevin Rockett (eds), *National Cinema and Beyond: Studies in Irish Film 1* (Dublin: Four Courts Press, 2004).
44. Ibid.

# Afterword

*Devolution and Beyond*

The preceding chapters have explored what I consider to be the most interesting and significant developments within the interlinked spheres of Scottish cinema, television drama and the novel. Such a study is inevitably selective and consequently there are various individuals and numerous works that I have either been forced to omit or consign to the footnotes. The sheer output of Scottish writing during the past twenty-five years has been staggering, as surveys such as the recently published *Scottish Literature* attest.[1] However, reliable maps of this rich and increasingly diverse terrain at least exist in addition to a limited but significant body of critical analysis. As a relatively new phenomenon, indigenous Scottish cinema has as yet failed to generate the same degree of serious debate. Ironically, there was conspicuously greater engagement during creatively more fallow periods that tended to either bemoan those images of Scotland that did exist or to ponder hypothetical questions of the 'what kind of cinema do we want?' variety. With 2004 marking a quarter century since the modest watershed of Bill Forsyth's *That Sinking Feeling*, a more appropriate sustained critical engagement with this particular sector may be engendered. More problematic is the field of Scottish television drama. Of the three distinct media examined in this book this remains by far the most critically neglected with little more than a handful of broadsheet review articles and the odd essay on individual series such as *Tutti Frutti* or *Taggart*. The nature of the present study also precludes the inclusive survey that is so conspicuously lacking. Moreover, my focus on the overtly 'auteurist' works of John Byrne, Peter McDougall and Donna Franceschild is guided primarily by a sense of the quality of such dramas. For this I make no apology, indeed, my selection also reflects the growing conviction that within the increasingly conservative and rating-obsessed world of television such challenging work would now be impossible to commission. However, had this been a larger project I would certainly have considered some of the most popular Scottish television dramas such as prime-time BBC series *Hamish*

*MacBeth* and *Monarch of the Glen*, indigenous national soaps like *Take the High Road* and the ill-fated *River City*, or even youth-oriented dramas such as *The Young Person's Guide to Becoming a Rock Star* and *Tinseltown*.

Another significant absence in this book is any serious consideration of the continuity of the Kailyard and tartanry traditions of cultural representation. Such images have become particularly allied to the kind of touristic national promotion – memorably dubbed 'Scotland the Brand' by David McCrone[2] – consistent with the shift from an era of industrial capitalism to a service-based, leisure economy. A high-profile popular television series like *Monarch of the Glen* fits the bill perfectly, the breathtaking images of picturesque highland scenery, the baronial splendour of the fictional estate of Glenbogle, and the cast of largely sympathetic quirky characters demonstrating the tenacity of various tropes central to Kailyard/tartanry. Other key represen-tations here would include Bill Forsyth's 1983 feature film, *Local Hero* and the Oscar-winning Hollywood feature *Braveheart*, which was co-opted by both the Scottish Tourist Board and the SNP in the mid-1990s as the centre piece of marketing campaigns.[3] My main reason for omitting an analysis of such fictions is the sheer familiarity of a critical analysis that is much more effectively elaborated elsewhere, coupled with a desire to move beyond the apparent obsession with these regressive tropes that has blinded many to the more productive achievements and traditions within Scottish cultural ex-pression. It is also the case that most other nations with a significant tourist industry continue to reproduce and project similarly reductive 'brand images' – from the Irish Leprechaun to the New Zealand Kiwi (or Hobbit!). What is more important is that alternative cultural expressions and representations are identified, discussed and analysed in order to counter such market-driven distortions.

This book is primarily interested in some of the cultural developments that helped to transform Scotland's sense of itself over the past twenty-five years, paving the way for enhanced political self-expression manifested in the restoration of a devolved Scottish Parliament in 1999. As I write, a mere four years and one parliamentary term on from that momentous return, the jury remains out on the impact and benefits self-government has brought. While certain small gains have been made – which often emphasise divergent values between Scotland and the British New Labour project, ironically a political phenomenon that is also Scottish-dominated – the bright optimism of 1999 has significantly dimmed. In the field of culture, the new Scottish executive launched a Cultural Strategy in August 2000 which, three years on, seems to suggests a real commitment to the promotion of cultural activities, albeit in tandem with Sport and Tourism and bound up with the UK-wide New Labour emphasis on cultural *industries* and economic activity. One notable intellectual development since devolution, however, has been a renewed and reinvigorated sense of Scotland's role in history. This process has been on-going for some time and, indeed, is central to the post-1979 developments examined in this book. But the past couple of years have seen an apparent intensification through the publication of various books about the Scottish Enlightenment that emphasise the crucial role played by Scottish intellectuals in the development of Western thought,[4] and the role of Scotland in the Empire.[5] The latter in particular has once again foregrounded the significant Scottish contribution to the forging of Britishness, helping to demolish the debilitating perception that Scotland had been previously colonised by its larger partner in the Union. If we also include the numerous single volume histories of Scotland that now adorn the shelves of the nation's bookshops, this constitutes a forceful rhetorical challenge to Cairns Craig's insightful and eloquent examination of Scottish narratives as forming a kind of 'counter-history'. With a renewed sense of self-confidence and appreciation of tradition the Scots would appear to be writing themselves back into history, at least rhetorically. It is my hope that *Contemporary Scottish Fictions* will make its own contribution to that process of debate.

## NOTES

1. Douglas Gifford, Sarah Dunnigan and Alan MacGillivray (eds), *Scottish Literature* (Edinburgh: Edinburgh University Press, 2002).
2. David McCrone, Angela Morris and Richard Kiely, *Scotland the Brand: The Making of Scottish Heritage* (Edinburgh: Edinburgh University Press, 1995).
3. See Cairns Craig, 'Visitors from the Stars: Scottish Film Culture', *Cencrastus*, No. 11, New Year 1983, John Caughie, 'Whose Local Hero?', *Cencrastus*, No. 14, Autumn 1983, and Colin McArthur, *Brigadoon, Braveheart and the Scots: Distortions of Scotland in Hollywood Cinema* (London: I. B. Tauris, 2003).
4. For example, Arthur Herman's polemic *The Scottish Enlightenment: The Scots Invention of the Modern World* (London: Fourth Estate, 2003) and Alexander Broadie, *The Cambridge Companion to the Scottish Enlightenment* (Cambridge: Cambridge University Press, 2003). A similar argument had been elaborated previously by Robert Crawford in relation to the Scottish 'invention' of English literature. See Robert Crawford, *Devolving English Literature* (Oxford: Clarendon Press, 1992) and Robert Crawford (ed.), *The Scottish Invention of English Literature* (Cambridge: Cambridge University Press, 1998).
5. See, for example, T. M. Devine, *Scotland's Empire 1600–1815* (London: Allen Lane, 2003), and Michael Fry, *The Scottish Empire* (East Linton: Tuckwell Press, 2003).

# Select Bibliography and Filmography

## CRITICAL WORKS

### Books

Anderson, C. and Christianson, A. (eds) (2000), *Scottish Women's Fiction 1920s to 1960s: Journeys Into Being*, East Linton: Tuckwell Press.

Bell, I. A. (ed.) (1995), *Peripheral Visions: Images of Nationhood in Contemporary British Fiction*, Cardiff: University of Wales Press.

Bernstein, M. (1999), *Alasdair Gray*, Lewisburg: Bucknell University Press.

Beveridge, C. and Turnbull, R. (1989), *The Eclipse of Scottish Culture*, Edinburgh: Polygon.

Bohnke, D. (1999), *Kelman Writes Back: Literary Politics in the Work of a Scottish Writer*, Berlin: Galda + Wilch Verlag.

Bruce, D. (1996), *Scotland the Movie*, Edinburgh: Polygon/SFC.

Burgess, M. (1998), *Imagine a City: Glasgow in Fiction*, Glendaruel: Argyll Publishing.

Calder, A. (1993), *Revolving Culture: Notes from the Scottish Republic*, London: I. B. Tauris.

Calder, A. (2002), *Scotlands of the Mind*, Edinburgh: Luath Press.

Christianson, A. and Lumsden, A. (eds) (2000), *Contemporary Scottish Women Writers*, Edinburgh: Edinburgh University Press.

Craig, C. (1996), *Out of History: Narrative Paradigms in Scottish and British Culture*, Edinburgh: Polygon.

Craig, C. (1999), *The Modern Scottish Novel*, Edinburgh: Edinburgh University Press.

Craig, C. (2002), *Iain Banks's Complicity*, New York: Continuum.

Craig, Carol. (2003), *The Scots' Crisis of Confidence*, Edinburgh: Big Thinking.

Crawford, R. and Nairn, T. (eds) (1991), *The Arts of Alasdair Gray*, Edinburgh: Edinburgh University Press.

Dale, S. (2002), *Alan Warner's Morvern Callar*, New York: Continuum.

Devine, T. M. (2000), *The Scottish Nation*, London: Penguin.

Devine, T. M. and Finlay, R. J. (eds) (1996), *Scotland in the 20th Century*, Edinburgh: Edinburgh University Press.

Dick, E. (ed.) (1990), *From Limelight to Satellite: A Scottish Film Book*, London: BFI/SFC.

Dick, E., Noble, A. and Petrie, D. (eds) (1993), *Bill Douglas: A Lanternist's Account*, London: BFI.

Gifford, D., Dunnigan, S. and MacGillivray, A. (eds) (2002), *Scottish Literature*, Edinburgh: Edinburgh University Press.

Hagemann, S. (ed.) (1996), *Studies in Scottish Fiction: 1945 to the Present*, Frankfurt: Lang.

Harvie, C. (1998), *Scotland and Nationalism: Scottish Society and Politics 1707 to the Present*, third edition, London: Routledge.

Harvie, C. (1999), *Travelling Scot*, Glenarduel: Argyll Publishing.

Herdman, J. (1990), *The Double in Nineteenth-Century Fiction*, Houndmills: Macmillan.

Hill, J. (1999), *British Cinema in the 1980s*, London: BFI.

Hjort, M. and Mackenzie, S. (eds) (2000), *Cinema and Nation*, London: Routledge.

Kelman, J. (1992), *Some Recent Attacks: Essays Cultural and Political*, Stirling: AK Press.

McArthur, C. (ed.) (1982), *Scotch Reels: Scotland in Cinema and Television*, London: BFI.

McArthur, C. (2003a), *Whisky Galore and The Maggie*, London: I. B. Tauris.

McArthur, C. (2003b), *Brigadoon, Braveheart and the Scots: Distortions of Scotland in Hollywood Cinema*, London: I. B. Tauris.

McCrone, D. (2001), *Understanding Scotland: The Sociology of a Nation*, second edition, London: Routledge.

McCrone, D., Morris, A. and Kiely, R. (1995), *Scotland the Brand: The Making of Scottish Heritage*, Edinburgh: Edinburgh University Press.

MacDonald M. (ed.) (1995), *Nothing Is Altogether Trivial: An Anthology of Writing From Edinburgh Review*, Edinburgh: Edinburgh University Press.

McGrath, J. (1990), *The Bone Won't Break: On Theatre and Hope in Hard Times*, London: Methuen.

McIlvanney, W. (1991), *Surviving the Shipwreck*, Edinburgh: Mainstream.

McLukie, C. W. (1999), *Researching McIlvanney: A Critical and Bibliographic Introduction*, Frankfurt: Peter Lang.

McManus, M. and Chandler, G. (1989), *Taggart's Glasgow*, Oxford: Lennard Publishing.

March, C. L. (2002), *Rewriting Scotland: Welsh, McLean, Warner, Banks, Galloway and Kennedy*, Manchester: Manchester University Press.

Miller, K. (1985), *Doubles: Studies in Literary History*, Oxford: Oxford University Press.

Moores, P. (ed.) (2002), *Alasdair Gray: Critical Appreciations and a Bibliography*, Boston Spa: British Library.

Morace, R. (2001), *Irvine Welsh's Trainspotting*, New York: Continuum.

Murray, I. (ed.) (1996), *Scottish Writers Talking*, East Linton: Tuckwell Press.

Murray, I. (2000), *Jessie Kesson: Writing Her Life*, Edinburgh: Cannongate.

Murray, I. (ed.) (2002), *Scottish Writers Talking 2*, East Linton: Tuckwell Press.

Nairn, T. (1981), *The Break-Up of Britain*, second edition, London: Verso.

Nairn, T. (1997), *Faces of Nationalism*, London: Verso.

Nairn, T. (2000), *After Britain*, London: Granta.

Neubauer, J. (1999), *Literature as Intervention: Struggles over Cultural Identity in Contemporary Scottish Fiction*, Marburg: Tectum Verlag.

Petrie, D. (2000), *Screening Scotland*, London: BFI.

Pittock, M. (2001), *Scottish Nationality*, Basingstoke: Palgrave.

Plain, G. (2002), *Ian Rankin's Black and Blue*, New York: Continuum.

Redhead, S. (2000), *Repetitive Beat Generation*, Edinburgh: Rebel Inc.

Ryan, R. (2002), *Ireland and Scotland: Literature and Culture, State and Nation, 1966–2000*, Oxford: Oxford University Press.

Schoene-Harwood, B. (2000), *Writing Men: Literary Masculinities from Frankenstein to the New Man*, Edinburgh: Edinburgh University Press.

Smith, M. (2002), *Trainspotting*, BFI Modern Classics, London: BFI.

Spring, I. (1990), *Phantom Village: The Myth of the New Glasgow*, Edinburgh: Polygon.

Stevenson, R. and Wallace, G. (eds) (1996), *Scottish Theatre Since the Seventies*, Edinburgh:

Edinburgh University Press.

Tibballs, G. (1994), *Taggart Casebook*, London: Boxtree.

Wallace, G. and Stevenson, R. (eds) (1993), *The Scottish Novel Since the Seventies*, Edinburgh: Edinburgh University Press.

Whyte, C. (ed.) (1995), *Gendering the Nation: Studies in Modern Scottish Literature*, Edinburgh: Edinburgh University Press.

Wilson, E. (2003), *Cinema's Missing Children*, London: Wallflower.

## Articles

Anderson, C. and Norquay, G. (1984), 'Superiorism', *Cencrastus*, No. 15, New Year.

Balides, C. (1984), 'Another Time Another Place: Another Male View?', *Cencrastus*, No. 16, Spring.

Bell, E. (1998a), 'Who Sings for Scotland?: Reflections from Inside a Predicament', *Cencrastus*, No. 63.

Bell, E. (1998b), 'Scotland and Ethics in the Work of A. L. Kennedy', *Scotlands*, 5.1.

Bernstein, S. (1995), 'Scottish Enough: The London Novels of Alasdair Gray', *The Review of Contemporary Fiction*, Vol. 15, No. 2, Summer.

Boyd, S. J. (1994), 'A Man's a Man: Reflections on Scottish Masculinity', *Scotlands*, No. 2.

Breitenbach, E. (1993), 'Out of Sight, Out of Mind? The History of Women in Scottish Politics', *Scottish Affairs*, No. 2, Winter.

Brown, J. (1983/4), 'Land Beyond Brigadoon', *Sight and Sound*, Winter.

Cardullo, B. (1997), 'Fiction into Film, or Bringing Welsh to a Boyle', *Literature Film Quarterly*, Vol. 25, No. 3.

Caughie, J. (1983), 'Support Whose Local Hero?', *Cencrastus*, No. 14.

Craig, C. (1983), 'Visitors from the Stars', *Cencrastus*, No. 11, New Year.

Craig, C. (1990), 'The Haunted Heart', *New Statesman and Society*, 5 October.

Craig, Carol (1986), 'On Men and Women in McIlvanney's Fiction', *Edinburgh Review*, No. 73.

Dale, S. (2000), 'An Interview with Alan Warner', *Edinburgh Review*, No. 103.

Dentith, S. (1990), 'This Shitty Urban Machine Humanised: The Urban Crime Novel and the Novels of William McIlvanney', in I. Bell and G. Daldry (eds), *Watching the Detectives: Essays on Crime Fiction*, Basingstoke: Macmillan.

Donaldson, G. and Lee, A. (1995), 'Is Eating People Really Wrong? Dining with Alasdair Gray', in *The Review of Contemporary Fiction*, Vol. 15, No. 2, Summer.

Freeman, A. (1996), 'Ourselves as Others: *Marabou Stork Nightmares*', *Edinburgh Review*, No. 95.

Freeman, A. (1997), 'Realism Fucking Realism: The Word on the Street – Kelman, Kennedy and Welsh', *Cencrastus*, No. 57, Summer.

Galloway, J. (1995), 'Different Oracles: Me and Alasdair Gray', in *The Review of Contemporary Fiction*, Vol. 15, No. 2, Summer.

Gifford, D. (1989), 'Interview with William McIlvanney', *Books in Scotland*, No. 30, Spring.

Hart, M. (2002), 'Solvent Abuse: Irvine Welsh and Scotland', *Postmodern Culture*, Vol. 12, No. 2.

Hawley, J. C. (1995), 'Bell, Book and Candle: Poor Things and the Exorcism of Victorian Sentiment', *The Review of Contemporary Fiction*, Vol. 15, No. 2.

Hendry, J, (1983), 'Editorial', *Chapman*, Nos 35/36, July.

Herbert, H. (1993), 'Tutti Frutti', in G. Brandt (ed.), *British Television Drama in the 1980s*, Cambridge: Cambridge University Press.

Hobsbaum, P. (1995), 'Alasdair Gray: The Voice of His Prose', *The Review of Contemporary Fiction*, Vol. 15, No. 2, Summer.

Humm, P. and Stigant, P. (1989), 'The Masculine Fiction of William McIlvanney', in D. Longhurst (ed.), *Gender, Genre and Narrative Pleasure*, London: Unwin Hyman.

Idle, J. (1993), 'McIlvanney, Masculinity and Scottish Literature', *Scottish Affairs*, No. 2, Winter.

Kaczvinsky, D. P. (2001), '"Making Up for Lost Time": Scotland, Stories and the Self in Alasdair Gray's *Poor Things*', *Contemporary Literature*, Vol. 42, No. 4, Winter.

Kelly, D. (2002), 'Trainspotting: Papish Punk – Proddie Rock', *Cencrastus*, No. 66.

Kirk, J. (1999), 'Figuring the Dispossessed: Images of the Urban Working Class in the Writing of James Kelman', *English*, Vol. 48, No. 191, Summer.

McGlynn, M. (2001), 'Janice Galloway', *The Review of Quarterly Fiction*, Vol. xxi, No. 2, Summer.

MacInnes, J. (1998), 'The Myth of the Macho Scotsman: Attitudes to Gender, Work and Family in the UK, Ireland and Europe', *Scottish Affairs*, No. 23, Spring.

McKibbin, T. (2000a), 'Restless Natives: Scottish Cinema at the Crossroads', *Cencrastus*, No. 64.

McKibbin, T. (2000b), 'Retouching the Real: Lynne Ramsay's Ratcatcher', *Cencrastus*, No. 65.

McKibbin, T. (2001), 'One Life Stand', *Cencrastus*, No. 69.

McKibbin, T. (2002), 'Scottish Cinema: A Victim Culture?', *Cencrastus*, No. 73.

McKibbin, T. (2003) 'Singular Ethics: Lynne Ramsay's Morvern Callar', *Cencrastus*, No. 74.

McLoone, M. (2001), 'Internal Decolonisation? British Cinema in the Celtic Fringe', in R. Murphy (ed.), *The British Cinema Book*, second edition, London: BFI.

McNeil, K. (1989), 'Interview with James Kelman', *Chapman*, No. 57, Summer.

Malcomson, S. L. (1985), 'Modernism Comes to the Cabbage Patch: Bill Forsyth and the "Scottish Cinema"', *Film Quarterly*, Vol. 38, No. 3, Spring.

March, C. L. (1999a), 'Interview with Janice Galloway', *Edinburgh Review*, No. 101, Summer.

March, C. L. (1999b), 'Interview with A. L. Kennedy', *Edinburgh Review*, No. 101, Summer.

Mathieson, K. (1987/88), 'Peter McDougall: A Boy's Game', *Cencrastus*, No. 28, Winter.

Mathieson, K. (1988), 'Bill Forsyth: Innocent or Eccentric', *Cencrastus*, No. 29, Spring.

Middleton, T. (1995), 'Constructing the Contemporary Self: the Works of Iain Banks', in T. Hill and W. Hughes (eds), *Contemporary Writing and National Identity*, Bath: Sulis Press.

Murray, J. (2001), 'Contemporary Scottish Film', *Irish Review*, No. 28, Winter.

Murray, J. (2004), 'Convents or Cowboys? Millennial Scottish and Irish Film Industries and Imaginaries in *The Magdalene Sisters*', in J. Hill and K. Rockett (eds), *National Cinema and Beyond: Studies in Irish Film 1*, Dublin: Four Courts Press.

Paget, D. (1999), 'Speaking Out: The Transformations of Trainspotting', in D. Cartmell and I. Whelan (eds), *Adaptations: From Text to Screen, Screen to Text*, London: Routledge.

Plain, G. (1998), 'An Interview with Ian Rankin', *Scotlands*, 5.2.

Porter, D. (1991), 'Imagining a City', *Chapman*, No. 63, Spring.

Rankin, I. (1999), 'Why Crime Fiction Is Good for You', *Edinburgh Review*, No. 102.

Sage, V. (1996), 'The Politics of Petrifaction: Culture, Religion, History in the Fiction of Iain Banks and John Banville', in V. Sage and A. Lloyd Smith (eds), *Modern Gothic*, Manchester: Manchester University Press.

Stenhouse, D. (1996), 'A Wholly Healthy Scotland: A Reichian Reading of *1982 Janine*', *Edinburgh Review*, No. 95, Spring.

Squires, C. (1999), 'Trainspotting and Publishing, or Converting the Smack into Hard Cash', *Edinburgh Review*, No. 101.

Sussex, E. (1982/83), 'This Other Eden', *Sight and Sound*, Winter.

Turner, J. (1993), 'Sick Boys', *London Review of Books*, 2 December.

Warner, M. (1993), 'Through a Child's Eyes', in D. Petrie (ed.), *Cinema and the Realms of Enchantment*, London: BFI.

Watson, R. (1996), 'The Rage of Caliban: The "Unacceptable" Face and the "Unspeakable" Voice in Contemporary Scotish Writing', in H. W. Drescher and S. Hagemann (eds), *Scotland to Slovenia*, Frankfurt: Peter Lang.

Whiteford, E. (1994), 'Engendered Subjects: Subjectivity and National Identity in Alasdair Gray's *1982 Janine*', *Scotlands*, 2.

Whyte, C. (1998), 'Masculinities in Contemporary Scottish Fiction', *Forum for Modern Language Studies*, Vol. XXXIV, No. 3, July.

Williams, L. R. (2002), 'Escape Artist', *Sight and Sound*, October.

Williams, N. W. (1999), 'The Dialect of Authenticity: The Case of Irvine Welsh's *Trainspotting*', in T. Hoenselaars and M. Buning (eds), *English and Other Languages*, Amsterdam: Rodopi.

Woolland, B. (2000), 'Rob Roy: Man in the Middle', *Jump Cut*, No. 43, July.

Zagratzki, U. (2000), '"Blues Fell This Morning": James Kelman's Scottish Literature and Afro-American Music', *Scottish Literary Journal*, Vol. 27, No. 1, Spring.

## FICTIONAL WRITINGS

Banks, I. (1984), *The Wasp Factory*, London: Macmillan.

Banks, I. (1986), *The Bridge*, London: Macmillan.

Banks, I. (1992), *The Crow Road*, London: Scribners.

Banks, I. (1993), *Complicity*, London: Little, Brown.

Barker, E. (1991), *O Caledonia*, London: Hamish Hamilton.

Bissett, A. (ed.) (2001), *Damage Land: New Scottish Gothic Fiction*, Edinburgh: Polygon.

Boyd, W. (1988), *The New Confessions*, London: Penguin.

Galloway, J. (1989), *The Trick Is to Keep Breathing*, Edinburgh: Polygon.

Galloway, J. (1994), *Foreign Parts*, London: Jonathan Cape.

Gray, A. (1981), *Lanark: A Life in Four Books*, Edinburgh: Canongate.

Gray, A. (1984), *1982 Janine*, London: Jonathan Cape.

Gray, A. (1985), *The Fall of Kelvin Walker*, Edinburgh: Canongate.

Gray, A. (1990a), *Something Leather*, London: Jonathan Cape.

Gray, A. (1990b), *McGrotty and Ludmilla*, Glasgow: Dog & Bone.

Gray, A. (1992), *Poor Things*, London: Bloomsbury.

Kay, J. (1998), *Trumpet*, London: Picador.

Kelman, J. (1984), *The Busconductor Hines*, Edinburgh: Polygon.

Kelman, J. (1985), *A Chancer*, Edinburgh: Polygon.

Kelman, J. (1989), *A Disaffection*, London: Secker & Warburg.

Kelman, J. (1994), *How Late It Was, How Late*, London: Secker & Warburg.

Kennedy, A. L. (1993), *Looking for the Possible Dance*, London: Secker & Warburg.

Kennedy, A. L. (1994), *Now That You're Back*, London: Jonathan Cape.

Kennedy, A. L. (1995), *So I am Glad*, London: Jonathan Cape.

Kesson, J. (1983), *Another Time, Another Place*, London: Chatto & Windus.

McIlvanney, W. (1977), *Laidlaw*, London: Hodder & Stoughton.

McIlvanney, W. (1983), *The Papers of Tony Veitch*, London: Hodder & Stoughton.
McIlvanney, W. (1985), *The Big Man*, London: Hodder & Stoughton
McIlvanney, W. (1989), *Walking Wounded*, London: Hodder & Stoughton.
McIlvanney, W. (1991), *Strange Loyalties*, London: Hodder & Stoughton.
McIlvanney, W. (1996), *The Kiln*, London: Hodder & Stoughton.
McLean, D. (1992), *Bucket of Tongues*, London: Secker & Warburg.
McLean, D. (1995), *Bunker Man*, London: Jonathan Cape.
McLean, D. (ed.), (1997), *Ahead of Its Time: A Clocktower Press Anthology*, Jonathan Cape.
McWilliam, C. (1994), *Debatable Land*, London: Bloomsbury.
O'Hagan, A. (1999), *Our Fathers*, London: Faber & Faber.
Rankin, I. (1987), *Knots & Crosses*, London: The Bodley Head.
Rankin, I. (1990), *Hide & Seek*, London: Barrie & Jenkins.
Rankin, I. (1992), *Tooth & Nail*, London: Century.
Rankin, I. (1992), *Strip Jack*, London: Orion.
Rankin, I. (1993), *The Black Book*, London: Orion.
Rankin, I. (1994), *Mortal Causes*, London: Orion.
Rankin, I. (1995), *Let It Bleed*, London: Orion.
Rankin, I. (1997), *Black & Blue*, London: Orion.
Rankin, I. (1998a), *The Hanging Garden*, London: Orion.
Rankin, I. (1998b), *Death is Not the End*, London: Orion.
Rankin, I. (1999), *Dead Souls*, London: Orion.
Rankin, I. (2000), *Set in Darkness*, London: Orion.
Rankin, I. (2001), *The Falls*, London: Orion.
Rankin, I. (2002), *Resurrection Men*, London: Orion.
Ritchie, H. (ed.) (1996), *New Scottish Writing*, London: Bloomsbury.
Rush, C. (1985), *A Twelvemonth and a Day*, Aberdeen: Aberdeen University Press.
Spence, A. (1990), *The Magic Flute*, Edinburgh: Canongate.
Warner, A. (1995), *Morvern Callar*, London: Jonathan Cape.
Warner, A. (1997), *These Demented Lands*, London: Jonathan Cape.
Warner, A. (1998), *The Sopranos*, London: Jonathan Cape.
Warner, A. (2002), *The Man Who Walks*, London: Jonathan Cape.
Welsh, I. (1993), *Trainspotting*, London: Secker & Warburg.
Welsh, I. (1994), *The Acid House*, London: Jonathan Cape.
Welsh, I. (1995), *Marabou Stork Nightmares*, London: Jonathan Cape.
Welsh, I. (2001), *Glue*, London: Jonathan Cape.
Welsh, I. (2002), *Porno*, London: Jonathan Cape.

## FEATURE FILMS

*Another Time, Another Place* (Director and Writer: Michael Radford, Producer: Simon Perry, 1983).
*The Bill Douglas Trilogy: My Childhood* (Director and Writer: Bill Douglas, Producer: Geoffrey Evans, 1972), *My Ain Folk* (Director and Writer: Bill Douglas, Producer: Nick Nascht, 1973), *My Way Home* (Director and Writer: Bill Douglas, Producer: Richard Craven, Judy Cottam, 1978).
*Breaking the Waves* (Director and Writer: Lars von Trier, Producer: Vibeke Windelov, Peter Aalbaek Jensen, 1996).

*Comfort and Joy* (Director and Writer: Bill Forsyth, Producer: Davina Belling, Clive Parsons, 1984).

*Gregory's Girl* (Director and Writer: Bill Forsyth, Producer: Davina Belling, Clive Parsons, 1981).

*Ill Fares the Land* (Director and Writer: Bill Bryden, Producer: Robert Love, 1983).

*The Magdalene Sisters* (Director and Writer: Peter Mullan, Producer: Frances Higson, 2002).

*Morvern Callar* (Director: Lynne Ramsay, Writer: Ramsay, Liana Dognini, Producer: Robyn Slovo, Charles Pattison, George Faber, 2002).

*My Name Is Joe* (Director: Ken Loach, Writer: Paul Laverty, Producer: Rebecca O'Brien, 1998).

*One Life Stand* (Director and Writer: May Miles Thomas, Producer: Owen Thomas, 2000).

*Orphans* (Director and Writer: Peter Mullan, Producer: Frances Higson, 1999).

*Prague* (Director and Writer: Ian Sellar, Producer: Christopher Young, 1992).

*Ratcatcher* (Director and Writer: Lynne Ramsay, Producer: Gavin Emerson, 1999).

*Rob Roy* (Director: Michael Caton-Jones, Writer: Alan Sharp, Producer: Peter Broughan, Richard Jackson, 1995).

*Shallow Grave* (Director: Danny Boyle, Writer: John Hodge, Producer: Andrew MacDonald, 1995).

*Small Faces* (Director: Gillies MacKinnon, Writer: Billy MacKinnon, Gillies MacKinnon, Producer: Billy MacKinnon, Steve Clark Hall, 1996).

*Stella Does Tricks* (Director: Coky Giedrocyk, Writer: A. L. Kennedy, Producer: Adam Barker, 1998).

*Sweet Sixteen* (Director: Ken Loach, Writer: Paul Laverty, Producer: Rebecca O'Brien, 2002).

*That Sinking Feeling* (Director, Writer and Producer: Bill Forsyth, Producer: 1979).

*This Year's Love* (Director and Writer: David Kane, Producer: Michele Camarda, 1999).

*Trainspotting* (Director: Danny Boyle, Writer: John Hodge, Producer: Andrew MacDonald, 1996).

*Venus Peter* (Director and Writer: Ian Sellar, Producer: Chris Young, 1989).

*The Winter Guest* (Director: Alan Rickman, Writer: Sharman MacDonald, Alan Rickman, Producer: Ken Lipper, Edward R. Pressman, 1997).

## TELEVISION DRAMAS

### Single Dramas

*And the Cow Jumped Over the Moon* (Writer: Donna Franceschild, Director: Penny Cherns, Producer: Aileen Forsyth) txd: 15/8/91.

*Down Where the Buffalo Go* (Writer: Peter McDougall, Director: Ian Knox, Producer: Andy Park) txd: 19/1/88.

*Dream Baby* (Writer: David Kane, Director: Angela Pope, Producer: David M. Thompson) txd: 29/5/89.

*The Holy City* (Writer and Director: Bill Bryden, Producer: Norman McCandlish) txd: 28/3/86.

*Ruffian Hearts* (Writer and Director: David Kane, Producer: Ian Madden) txd: 30/9/95.

*Shadow on the Earth* (Writer: David Kane, Director: Chris Bernard, Producer: David M. Thompson) txd: 13/3/88.

*Shoot for the Sun* (Writer: Peter McDougall, Director: Ian Knox, Producer: Andree Molyneaux) txd: 16/3/87.

*The White Bird Passes* (Writer and Director: Michael Radford, Producer: James Hunter) txd: 20/4/80.

## Series

*Blood Red Roses* (Writer and Director: John McGrath, Producer: Steve Clark Hall) Three parts, txd: 4/12–18/12/86.

*A Mug's Game* (Writer: Donna Franceschild, Director: David Blair, Producer: Catherine Wearing) Four parts, txd: 28/1–18/2/96.

*Taggart* Thirty-one stories featuring Mark McManus from *Killer* (Writer: Glenn Chandler, Director: Lawrence Moody, Producer: Robert Love) Three parts, txd: 6–20/9/83 to *Prayer for the Dead* (Writer: Barry Appleton, Director: Richard Holthouse, Producer: John G. Temple) Three parts, txd: 11–25/1/95. (For full list, see Tibballs, G. (1994), *Taggart Casebook*, London: Boxtree.)

*Takin' Over the Asylum* (Writer: Donna Franceschild, Director: David Blair, Producer: Chris Parr) Six parts, txd: 27/9–1/11/94.

*Tutti Frutti* (Writer: John Byrne, Director: Tony Smith, Producer: Andy Park) Six parts, txd: 3/3–7/4/87.

*Your Cheatin' Heart* (Writer: John Byrne, Director: Michael Whyte, Producer: Peter Broughan) Six parts, 11/10–18/11/90.

# Index